THE COMMUNITY ORGANIZATION METHOD
IN SOCIAL WORK EDUCATION

The Community Organization Method in Social Work Education

HARRY L. LURIE

VOLUME IV

A Project Report of the Curriculum Study
Werner W. Boehm, Director and Coordinator

COUNCIL ON SOCIAL WORK EDUCATION
345 EAST 46TH STREET, NEW YORK 17, N. Y.

Printed in the United States of America
by H. Wolff Book Manufacturing Co., Inc.

PANEL PARTICIPANTS

The affiliations listed are those of the participants at the time of panel membership.

Frankie V. Adams
School of Social Work
Atlanta University
Atlanta, Georgia

*Mildred Barry
Welfare Federation of Cleveland
Cleveland, Ohio

Margaret Berry
National Federation of Settlements
and Neighborhood Centers
New York, New York

Martha Branscombe
United Nations
New York, New York

Bradley Buell
Community Research Associates
New York, New York

Kay Phyllis Burns
Canadian Welfare Council
Ottawa, Ontario, Canada

*Genevieve W. Carter
Welfare Planning Council
Los Angeles, California

Nathan E. Cohen
New York School of Social Work
Columbia University
New York, New York

*Martin M. Cohn
Jewish Welfare Fund
Cincinnati, Ohio

Rudolf T. Danstedt
National Association of Social
Workers
Washington, D.C.

Owen Davidson
Community Chest of Montclair
Montclair, New Jersey

Sidney Dillick
Rhode Island Council of
Community Services, Inc.
Providence, Rhode Island

*Arthur Dunham
School of Social Work
University of Michigan
Ann Arbor, Michigan

Frederick J. Ferris
School of Social Work
Boston College
Boston, Massachusetts

Thompson R. Fulton
Department of Social Work
West Virginia University
Morgantown, West Virginia

* Participants whose names are preceded by an asterisk contributed position papers which appear in Appendix.

*Arnold Gurin
Council of Jewish Federations &
Welfare Funds, Inc.
New York, New York

Adriana de Guzman
School of Social Work
University of Puerto Rico
Rio Piedras, Puerto Rico

Ernest B. Harper
School of Social Work
Michigan State University
East Lansing, Michigan

Jane Hoey
National Tuberculosis Association
New York, New York

Donald S. Howard
School of Social Welfare
University of California
Los Angeles, California

Nelson Jackson
National Urban League
New York, New York

Harold A. Jambor
School of Social Work
University of Hawaii
Honolulu, Hawaii

*Arlien Johnson
School of Social Work
University of Southern California
Los Angeles, California

George T. Kalif
School of Social Work
Richmond Professional Institute
College of William and Mary
Richmond, Virginia

John C. Kidneigh
School of Social Work
University of Minnesota
Minneapolis, Minnesota

*Hertha Kraus
Department of Social Work and
Social Research
Bryn Mawr College
Bryn Mawr, Pennsylvania

Merrill Krughoff
United Community Funds and
Councils of America, Inc.
New York, New York

Very Rev. Monsignor John J.
Lennon
National Catholic School of Social
Service
Catholic University of America
Washington, D.C.

*Robert MacRae
Welfare Council of Metropolitan
Chicago
Chicago, Illinois

*John McDowell
National Federation of Settlements
and Neighborhood Centers
New York, New York

*Wayne McMillen
School of Social Service
Administration
University of Chicago
Chicago, Illinois

*C. F. McNeil
Health & Welfare Council of
Philadelphia
Philadelphia, Pennsylvania

Campbell G. Murphy
Community Welfare Council of
  Dayton & Montgomery County
Dayton, Ohio

*Wilber I. Newstetter
School of Social Work
University of Pittsburgh
Pittsburgh, Pennsylvania

Beatrix Park
School of Social Work
Boston University
Boston, Massachusetts

George Rabinoff
National Social Welfare Assembly
New York, New York

Katharine Radke
School of Social Service
St. Louis University
St. Louis, Missouri

Maysie Roger
University of Manitoba
Winnipeg, Manitoba, Canada

Louise Root
Community Welfare Council
Milwaukee, Wisconsin

Murray Ross
School of Social Work
University of Toronto
Toronto, Ontario, Canada

Philip Ryan
National Health Council
New York, New York

Omar Schmidt
Hennepin County Welfare Council
Minneapolis, Minnesota

*Everett C. Shimp
School of Social Administration
Ohio State University
Columbus, Ohio

*Violet M. Sieder
New York School of Social Work
Columbia University
New York, New York

Rex A. Skidmore
School of Social Work
University of Utah
Salt Lake City, Utah

Sue Spencer
School of Social Work
University of Tennessee
Nashville, Tennessee

Bessie Touzel
Ontario Welfare Council
Toronto, Ontario, Canada

Wayne Vasey
Graduate School of Social Work
Rutgers University
New Brunswick, New Jersey

Ernest F. Witte
Council on Social Work Education
New York, New York

Benjamin Youngdahl
George Warren Brown School of
  Social Work
Washington University
St. Louis, Missouri

Henry L. Zucker
Jewish Community Federation of
  Cleveland
Cleveland, Ohio

Project Consultant

Harry L. Lurie, M.A.
Consultant to
Council of Jewish Federations
  and Welfare Funds, Inc.
New York, New York

PUBLISHER'S NOTE

Board Policy

This project report of the Curriculum Study is published in accordance with the policy adopted by the Board of Directors of the Council at its meeting on October 9–11, 1958. The policy adopted provides that:

The content of Curriculum Study reports are the responsibility of the Curriculum Study staff;

These reports will be published by the Council as submitted to it by the Study staff and given the widest possible distribution;

The Council, through all possible channels, shall encourage thorough consideration and discussion of the findings and recommendations and their implications for social work education and practice.

The Board decided further that:

Publication and distribution of the Curriculum Study reports does not imply Council acceptance of the findings or recommendations;

Implementation of any of the recommendations of the Study can come only after the field has had full opportunity to consider the reports, the appropriate bodies of the Council have considered and recommended action which would modify or change existing policies and standards.

The Board sincerely hopes that the many challenging questions which the Study presents will be given the mature, deliberate and objective consideration they merit and which characterize the true profession.

The Board wishes to register on behalf of the Council its sincere appreciation to the Study staff whose dedicated service brought the Curriculum Study to a successful conclusion.

The thirteen volumes of the Curriculum Study have been numbered to facilitate reference and identification. The comprehensive report has been numbered Volume I, the report on undergraduate education because of its comprehensive nature has been numbered Volume II. The other volumes have been numbered in alphabetical order by title as follows:

VOL.
I   OBJECTIVES FOR THE SOCIAL WORK CURRICULUM OF THE FUTURE
II THE PLACE OF THE UNDERGRADUATE CURRICULUM IN SOCIAL WORK
    EDUCATION
III THE ADMINISTRATION METHOD IN SOCIAL WORK EDUCATION
IV THE COMMUNITY ORGANIZATION METHOD IN SOCIAL WORK EDUCATION
V   EDUCATION FOR SOCIAL WORKERS IN THE CORRECTIONAL FIELD
VI AN ORIENTATION TO KNOWLEDGE OF HUMAN GROWTH AND
    BEHAVIOR IN SOCIAL WORK EDUCATION
VII EDUCATION FOR SOCIAL WORKERS IN THE PUBLIC SOCIAL SERVICES
VIII EDUCATION FOR SOCIAL WORKERS IN THE REHABILITATION OF THE
    HANDICAPPED
IX THE RESEARCH METHOD IN SOCIAL WORK EDUCATION
X   THE SOCIAL CASEWORK METHOD IN SOCIAL WORK EDUCATION
XI THE SOCIAL GROUP WORK METHOD IN SOCIAL WORK EDUCATION
XII SOCIAL WELFARE POLICY AND SERVICES IN SOCIAL WORK EDUCATION
XIII THE TEACHING OF VALUES AND ETHICS IN SOCIAL WORK EDUCATION

Acknowledgments

The Board is pleased to make public acknowledgment of its appreciation to the following foundations and organizations whose grants made possible the financing of this Curriculum Study:

FIELD FOUNDATION
ITTLESON FAMILY FOUNDATION
NATIONAL INSTITUTE OF MENTAL HEALTH, DEPARTMENT OF
    HEALTH, EDUCATION, AND WELFARE
NATIONAL TUBERCULOSIS ASSOCIATION
NEW YORK FUND FOR CHILDREN
OFFICE OF VOCATIONAL REHABILITATION, DEPARTMENT OF HEALTH,
    EDUCATION, AND WELFARE
ROCKEFELLER BROTHERS FUND

Although all projects of the Curriculum Study were interdependent and each contributed to the others and to the comprehensive report—and the staff worked as a team under one director—certain grants were more particularly earmarked for designated projects. Accordingly, acknowledgment is made of this circumstance in the appropriate volumes.

In addition to grants from these organizations, the Council on Social Work Education made substantial contributions from its own funds.

                              —Ernest F. Witte
New York, New York   *Executive Director*
May, 1959   *Council on Social Work Education*

Preface

This comprehensive three-year study of curriculum in the education of social workers has been completed under the auspices of the Council on Social Work Education. It has comprised twelve separate projects, one of which is reported in the following pages.

The twelve individual project reports are published separately by the Council to meet the needs of social work educators and practitioners whose interest is especially concentrated in the subject matter of one or more of the projects. No single report, however, can be understood in its proper relation to the whole study without reference to the comprehensive report, *Objectives for the Social Work Curriculum of the Future,* in which the findings and recommendations of the total study are presented. The various project directors worked together as a staff under the over-all guidance of Dr. Werner W. Boehm, Director and Coordinator of the Curriculum Study. Their goal was not only to develop desirable educational objectives for each project's particular area of the curriculum or suggested by particular considerations of practice, but, in addition, to do so in a way that would merge them all into a total educational experience.

Each project was designed to fit into a master plan for the study of the total curriculum. The findings and recommendations of each are relevant to those of the whole Study and have in turn been influenced by all other projects. To be understood, each report must therefore be considered in relation to the comprehensive report, which it supplements by supplying details for the particular area of the social work curriculum.

WHY THE STUDY WAS UNDERTAKEN

Many issues facing social work education were identified in the Hollis-Taylor Report of 1951.[1] It confirmed that the great preponderance of persons engaged in social work activities were still without professional education. It raised such questions as:

Does social work have a well-defined and identified function?

Does it possess a systematic body of knowledge, skills and attitudes in the various areas of social work practice?

Is the content of social work education sufficiently well developed so that it can be transmitted, and is it of such caliber that it can be included properly as a professional discipline within a university?

Progress toward answering these questions was made by the adoption of the Council's Curriculum Policy Statement in 1952, but further study was indicated. Social work education had also to face other issues:

How could it meet the greatly increased need for social work personnel?

How best could it train for a professional practice still in the process of rapid change and development? Can it be broad enough in scope to enable social workers to function in fields just emerging as well as those already established? Will breadth of education to encompass all fields of professional practice result in dilution of competence for specific fields?

How could it inculcate qualities of leadership and statesmanship while at the same time training for competence in specific practice?

Should undergraduate education serve primarily as a basis for graduate training or also prepare personnel for certain social work positions?

The Study considered that materials from which answers to all these questions might emerge would be obtained by focusing upon

1 Ernest V. Hollis and Alice L. Taylor, *Social Work Education in the United States* (New York: Columbia University Press, 1951).

fundamental questions of curriculum planning and not by piece-meal consideration of the specific questions posed. In education for social work as for other professions, the fundamental considerations in curriculum planning apply, as presented succinctly by Dr. Ralph W. Tyler.[2] Paraphrased for purposes of this study they are:

What are the desirable educational objectives for professional education?

What learning experiences should be selected and devised and how organized, to realize these objectives?

What are the effective means of evaluating whether the objectives have been attained?

Without a clear formulation of the objectives of social work education, that is, the knowledge, skills and attitudes students are expected to acquire, it becomes impossible to plan the learning experiences needed or to evaluate their success. Consequently, the Curriculum Study singled out as its major task identification of the desirable objectives of social work education.

Also, in accordance with Dr. Tyler's definition, each project framed its educational objectives in terms of both the *content* to be covered and the kind and quality of *behavior* to be expected from the student in relation to the content. For example, "familiarity" with a certain area of content becomes distinguishable from behaviors involving more complex manipulations or deeper "understanding" of content at other levels of student learning.

HOW THE STUDY WAS CARRIED ON

The individual projects of the study fell into the following major areas:

1. Specific curriculum areas—projects devised to examine the curriculum in the areas identified by the Curriculum Policy Statement of 1952: Human Growth and Behavior, the Social

[2] Ralph W. Tyler, *Basic Principles of Curriculum and Instruction* (Chicago: The University of Chicago Press, 1950).

Services, Social Work Methods (casework, group work, community organization, research, administration).

2. Selected fields of practice—projects devised to study elements of practice in rehabilitation, public social services, and corrections.
3. Undergraduate education for social work.
4. Content on social work values and ethics found throughout the curriculum.

Each project was planned to identify educational objectives in existing curricula; to formulate a series of desirable objectives, the desirability of which was determined by judging their importance, consistency and compatibility with a statement of the nature and function of social work; and to review the objectives in the light of educational theory as to the possibility of their being learned in the time and conditions available. Project directors had consultation and assistance from specially selected panels of educators and practitioners in social work and related disciplines.

WHAT THE STUDY HOPES TO ACCOMPLISH

Responsibility for planning and constructing curriculum belongs basically to the social work schools and departments. As a group they have already come far toward definition of common educational goals for the profession and of content all curricula must have to reach such goals. The Curriculum Study is expected to provide guides for the resolution of the major issues and common questions that it is anticipated will arise in the curriculum planning of all member schools and departments of the Council on Social Work Education.

Foreword

The basic method used in this project was to obtain expressions of opinion from a number of teachers and practitioners concerning what had seemed at the outset of the study to be the important aspects of the subject that needed to be explored. An outline of topics was prepared on the basis of the consultant's experience in social work and through reading of recent papers, reports of committee discussions, a review of the bulletins of the schools of social work, and other sources. The preliminary outline was sent to more than forty teachers and practitioners for their reactions and comments and for the listing of other important topics and questions. On the basis of the reactions, a revised list of important questions and topics was prepared. Practically all of the persons to whom the preliminary statement had been sent responded to this request.

The next step was to obtain from selected individuals a statement of their views on a specific subject. Again, there was an almost complete acceptance of these requests for cooperation, and fourteen statements were received which are referred to as "position papers." They cover all of the major topics and questions that were listed for study.

A first draft of this report was circulated among the contributors for comments and criticisms, and their generous response was of great help in revising the report. Some of the comments are quoted. I wish to thank all of those who commented and especially Arthur Dunham, George W. Rabinoff, Meyer Schwartz, Frederick J. Ferris, Harold A. Jambor, Bessie Touzel, Mildred Barry, George T. Kalif, Violet Sieder and the members of the Curriculum Study staff for their extensive criticisms.

The summary of findings and conclusions embodied in this report represents the reactions of the consultant to the source material—the position papers, the literature reviewed, working papers and preliminary reports from other projects of the Curriculum Study, especially *The Nature of Social Work* by Werner W. Boehm, and the discussion in the workshop on Community Organization held at the Annual Program Meeting of the Council on Social Work Education in January, 1958. The views expressed and the conclusions reached are those of the writer, who has, however, felt free to use excerpts or paraphrased sentences from the position papers with or without attribution to the source when they formulated a particularly clear statement of a point. Such excerpts can give only a partial view, not the comprehensive thinking, of those who are quoted, and the position papers themselves should be read for the full opinions of the contributors.

I want to acknowledge with deep appreciation all of the material presented to this study by the various contributors and most of all by the authors of the position papers. These latter represent the experience of outstanding teachers and practitioners of community organization in the field of social work. They have given me valuable insights into the subject of this section of the Curriculum Study.

Contents

PANEL PARTICIPANTS V

PUBLISHER'S NOTE ix

PREFACE xi

FOREWORD xv

I THE TEACHING AND PRACTICE OF
COMMUNITY ORGANIZATION 3

II TOWARD A DEFINITION OF COMMUNITY
ORGANIZATION AS SOCIAL WORK 17

III BASIC CONCEPTS IN EDUCATIONAL
OBJECTIVES FOR COMMUNITY ORGANIZATION
PRACTICE 26

IV ELEMENTS OF COMMUNITY ORGANIZATION
METHOD IN SOCIAL WORK PRACTICE 37

V SOME ASPECTS OF COURSE CONTENT AND
FIELD INSTRUCTION 48

IV GENERAL COMMENTS 54

APPENDIX — Position Papers

FIELD WORK TRAINING IN COMMUNITY
ORGANIZATION by Mildred C. Barry 67

PRACTICE THEORY IN COMMUNITY
ORGANIZATION by Genevieve W. Carter 85

TRAINING FOR COMMUNITY ORGANIZATION
IN SOCIAL WORK by Martin M. Cohn 111

QUALIFICATIONS FOR COMMUNITY
ORGANIZATION WORKERS by Arthur Dunham 121

COMMUNITY ORGANIZATION METHODS AND
SKILLS IN THE PROGRAMS OF NATIONAL
AGENCIES by Arnold Gurin 133

COMMUNITY ORGANIZATION METHOD AND
SKILL IN SOCIAL CASEWORK PRACTICE
by Arlien Johnson 148

CONTENT IN COMMUNITY ORGANIZATION
COURSE (BASIC) by Hertha Kraus 162

COMMUNITY ORGANIZATION
by Robert H. MacRae 169

COMMUNITY ORGANIZATION METHODS AND
SKILLS REQUIRED FOR EFFECTIVE PRACTICE
OF SOCIAL GROUP WORK by John McDowell 175

THE TEACHING OF COMMUNITY
ORGANIZATION by Wayne McMillen 185

A POINT OF VIEW ABOUT COMMUNITY
ORGANIZATION FOR SOCIAL WELFARE
by C. F. McNeil and Robert B. Lefferts 197

BASIC COURSE IN COMMUNITY ORGANIZATION
FOR SOCIAL WELFARE FOR ALL STUDENTS
by Wilbur I. Newstetter and Meyer Schwartz 209

THE CASE FOR A CURRICULUM IN COMMUNITY
ORGANIZATION FOR SOCIAL WELFARE
by Everett C. Shimp 231

THE TASKS OF THE COMMUNITY
ORGANIZATION WORKER by Violet M. Sieder 246

BIBLIOGRAPHY 261

THE COMMUNITY ORGANIZATION METHOD
IN SOCIAL WORK EDUCATION

The Teaching and Practice
of Community Organization

An effective relationship between teaching and practice determines the development of professional standards; advances in the theoretical and conceptual basis for practice are best achieved through mutual efforts toward such a goal. Together the schools and the field shape the character of service available from the graduates of the professional schools and stimulate their contribution to the growth of theory and practice. If there is too wide a discrepancy between the nature of practice and the content of preparation of the student the disharmony will be reflected in dissatisfactions on the part of the agencies, the schools and the students.

THE CURRENT STAGE OF DEVELOPMENT

Some writers on the subject of community organization assume that there is a fairly close agreement between teaching and practice and that the concepts taught in the schools are accepted by practitioners and implicit in their practice. On the other hand, some practitioners believe that their actual aims and procedures are not realistically described by the concepts offered in the classroom. Similarly, teachers are frequently aware of the inability or unwillingness of many practitioners to explain their work in terms of general concepts rather than empirical details. It is not important, nor necessarily desirable for teaching to reflect current practice; the function of the university is not to produce facsimiles of the practitioners of yesterday or of today, but rather to select the most promising students available, develop their knowledge and skills, imbue them with the ideals of service and thus prepare

them to become the practitioners of tomorrow. Any wide divergence between teaching and practice may, however, be a reflection of an undesirable rather than a desirable difference of goals.

While there may be a disagreement among teachers and practitioners on how closely practice in the field approximates the concepts of the courses on community organization in the schools, there seems to be a widespread assumption that neither in teaching nor in practice has community organization approached the degree of conceptualization or the coordination of theory and practice considered generally as having been achieved in casework and (with less certainty) in group work. As stated in one position paper:

> There are no generally accepted criteria for student admission to this specialization; there is no clearly defined content for course sequence commonly accepted; there is little conceptual communication between the school faculties and the community organization practitioners . . . (and) agencies have slowed the process by their employment practices and reliance upon apprenticeship training. (Barry)

The stage reached in the progress of any profession is usually a reflection of the conditions which exist in the nature of practice and it is desirable that we explore these conditions as a background for determining the objectives and content desirable for programs seeking to prepare for practice in community organization.

THE NATURE AND EXTENT OF COMMUNITY ORGANIZATION PRACTICE IN SOCIAL WORK

While there may not be full agreement on the meaning of "community organization" in social work, and the extent to which it can appropriately be applied to the activities of social workers, the term is widely used for a category of positions held by professional social workers in the social welfare field. This category includes executive, sub-executive and staff workers in community welfare councils and financial federations in national, state and local wel-

fare conferences, and in national and state programs for service to local welfare agencies; in neighborhood, area and regional service and planning agencies; in sectarian and ethnic group associations and federations; in intergroup relations and planning bodies; and in a number of other fields. Social workers engaged primarily in "community organization" are also to be found occupying a special staff role in medical and psychiatric agencies which give direct service.[1] The distinguishing feature of all these positions is that they are primarily concerned with maintaining and developing the programs and standards of welfare agencies and services rather than directly helping individuals and groups. "Efforts to develop, extend, integrate the welfare community and its programs can be called *community organization for social welfare.*" (Johnson)

The number of "community organization" positions is small and seems to include a varied group of key roles and positions of prestige in the welfare field. It comprises less than five percent of the entire body of social workers and it appears at the present time to furnish an even smaller proportion of beginning positions open upon graduation from a school of social work. A report of employment status [2] as of October 1957, recent graduates of schools of social work who had been enrolled as students in the spring of 1957, revealed that less than two percent had majored in community organization.

THE EXTENT OF THE PREPARATION OF STUDENTS FOR PRACTICE IN THE FIELD OF COMMUNITY ORGANIZATION

The fact that less than two percent of the 1957 graduates of schools of social work enrolled in the spring quarter were community or-

[1] Rabinoff suggests that the executives of all social agencies as administrators are engaged in the development of specific welfare programs and should properly be classified as "community organization workers." The overlap between the content of administration and of community organization in the work of any agency administrator is acknowledged both here and in the report of the project on administration of the Curriculum Study.

[2] David C. French, Survey of Employment Statistics (January, 1958).

ganization majors is of great significance and needs to be evaluated. It cannot be ascribed to a desire on the part of the schools to prepare "generic" social workers. The survey to which we refer found that the balance of the graduates had majored in other specific sequences, the overwhelming majority in casework.

The low percentage of community organization majors reflects only to a small degree the availability of a major sequence of community organization courses in the schools. In a summary of the 1956–1957 Bulletins of 19 graduate schools of social work [3] which included a number of the largest and the oldest schools, nine were found to be offering a sequence of courses for majors in community organization. Five additional schools did not list such a sequence but stated that they were equipped to plan arrangements for such a major for qualified students. (All the schools were offering at least one full course aiming to provide an introduction to the concepts and/or practice of community organization.) The small percentage may reflect to some extent the relatively fewer openings for beginning practice in community organization agencies as compared with openings for casework and group work practice. It is reported, however, that there are more openings for beginners than the number of available graduate students who have majored in community organization.

Graduates of schools of social work are considered by many agencies and teachers as being more desirable candidates for community organization positions after social work experience. Many job openings are believed to require a level of competence beyond what could reasonably be expected from graduates without previous professional experience. It has been stated, however, that there are an increasing number of openings for students upon graduation which do not require previous social work experience. In addition, new positions created by the spread of agencies in the older established field of community financial federations and

3 Faye Portner, *Training for Community Organization* (New York: Association for the Study of Community Organization, 1952). This was a study based on responses to a questionnaire returned by 34 member schools of the American Association of Schools of Social Work for the academic year 1946–1947.

planning bodies and in such newer programs as community development, housing, urban and regional redevelopment, welfare projects of labor groups, and others are currently enlarging opportunities for employment of social workers in the field of community organization practice.

It is also difficult to explain the small proportion of students majoring in community organization in view of the fact that the majority of community organization positions are on the executive and sub-executive level, with higher than average salaries and with a much higher ratio of men than in other categories of social work practice. The knowledge that the achievement of a substantial role in the field of community organization is likely to be deferred for a considerable length of time after graduation may act as a deterrent and predispose students to select a major that promises an easier entry into professional careers. Students who may think of community organization practice as a goal may assume that such an opportunity may come later, perhaps after a number of years of experience in casework or in group work practice, with or without additional academic preparation.

Some observers, however, are inclined to believe that other factors may account for the small number of students who follow a major community organization sequence including (1) a lack of scholarships and fellowships, (2) the prestige status of casework among the faculty and in the field, especially of psychiatric casework and (3) the attitude of some faculty advisors who depreciate the community organization sequence and tend to divert some qualified students who want to prepare for community organization practice to other sequences.

A knowledge of the method of community organization would seem to be of increasing importance for social workers in the field of public assistance. There is a growing acceptance on the part of public welfare organizations of their responsibility for meeting the social welfare needs of the community and of the need of public welfare personnel "for cooperative effort with various groups and organizations for . . . community organization and social

planning." [4] This aim would seem to reinforce the need for more attention by schools of social work to preparing personnel for the field of public welfare with training in the method of community organization.

It is not within the scope of this report to attempt an exploration of the conditions and practices of the social welfare agencies that may account for the lack of development in schools of social work of educational programs for the practice of community organization. It is perhaps more important in this study to consider what may be the internal factors that have retarded the development of the teaching of the methods of community organization in some schools of social work.

While the extent and number of opportunities for the practice of community organization is on the increase, most schools of social work offer only a single course on that subject (a required course in all but a few schools). In most schools the subject of community organization is considered important primarily as an area of additional knowledge which is desirable for students who are preparing for casework or group work practice. The emphasis of such a course may vary from material on the social welfare structure to that of presenting community organization as a method of social work parallel with casework and group work.

In most of the schools, field placements of students are primarily in agencies giving direct services. Relatively few schools have developed field instruction programs devoted specifically to preparing students for the practice of community organization nor have they developed effective relationships for field training with agencies engaged in community organization.

4 "Public Welfare in Community Organization and Social Planning," A Statement approved by Board of Directors of the American Public Welfare Association (December 1, 1953).

FACTORS THAT INFLUENCE
CURRICULUM OBJECTIVES

The basic criterion which determines the scope and content of community organization courses in the curriculum is whether the school aims to prepare students for this among other specializations. (The concept of a "generic" social worker is to be found more in theory than in practice, due largely to the development of specialized sequences in schools of social work.) Under the existing limitations of the two-year graduate course of study the term "generic" in actuality would mean the preparation of students for beginning practice only in agencies which were equipped to offer a considerable period of in-service training and were willing to employ workers on an apprenticeship basis. Current training and employment practices indicate, however, that even a non-specialized preparation for social work would provide personnel considered more desirable by some agencies faced with the necessity of filling staff positions with individuals who have had little or no formal training for social work.

The following comments on the above paragraph were received from Frederick J. Ferris formerly the director of the community organization program at the Boston College School of Social Work and help to clarify the position of the writer of this report:

The stress in the 1940s upon special requirements marked a phase in the development of these specializations. Concern today is with making the curriculum more generic so as to avoid the dangers that overspecialization produced. The concept of generic social work is much emphasized, for example, the courses in basic concepts and processes in many schools. Effective in June, 1959, the CSWE will accredit schools for their basic curriculum and "there shall be no accrediting of any specialization by any definition." This, of course, does not mean that specializations will not be offered by the schools.

The Changed Policy on Specializations in Social Work Education and Plans for Its Implementation in June, 1959, on March 19, 1957 (mimeo, *Accreditation Committee on Specializations, Prepared for*

NASW by Council on Social Work Education), states that "Specialization in social work is conceived as process. The primary processes in direct service are social casework, and social group work. Other processes are: community organization . . ." The Committee on Specializations did not at that time include community organization as a primary direct process. "This decision has been questioned and will come before the Committee for reexamination." "Schools of social work would need to continue to take responsibility for preparing students with a skill in some one process and to think of possible enrichment of curriculum for a variety of fields of practice . . ." It would seem to me that a basic criterion for determining the scope and content of community organization courses is whether the school is preparing students for casework, and/or group work, and/or community organization practice. It does not seem that the question is one of preparing for generic or specialized practice. Schools are interested in providing a basic generic foundation for all students, and in addition a beginning competence in one process.

Some aspects of practice, as in other professions, can be acquired more easily and more effectively in the field than in the classroom, and these need to be differentiated from those that are better acquired in the class. When these are defined such aspects of practice can then be developed in the agency setting during the period of field instruction, during internships or in beginning professional practice. Field placement training without the accompaniment or the background of conceptual training is not conducive to the development of the highest type of professional service, but conceptual training without the values to be found in the best type of field practice also has its limitations. A combination of opportunities to practice explored for its meanings with expert guidance on the job or in the classroom—that is, clinical practice in a setting organized for teaching purposes—begun at an appropriate time and continuing through the period of classroom instruction, reading, observation and group discussions—undoubtedly offers the best type of preparation and might be considered as a desirable goal for beginning professional practice in community organization work. The shortcomings of preparation for community organization

workers today may be due to a considerable degree to the limitations of the field work instruction. A number of schools are aware of these defects and are trying to set up special training facilities comparable to the clinical facilities available for medical students in university sponsored medical schools.

It is apparent that the current use of personnel without social work education is due to a large extent to the shortage of graduate students. Some agencies engaged in the practice of casework or of group work and recognized as setting standards for the field have placed limits on their programs instead of adding staff members who lack a reasonable degree of preparation. The community organization agencies with advanced standards similarly prefer qualified students with experience in social work and with special preparation for the field of community organization, but are usually less able to restrict their functions and programs and therefore have had to adjust their employment policies accordingly.

Since the largest number of openings for social workers occurs currently in the casework agencies with a much smaller number in the group work field and only a very small fraction in community organization agencies, it would seem logical that the curricula offered by the schools of social work would reflect this distribution of job opportunities. However, this numerical distribution distorts to some extent the vocational requirements of the field of social work. A substantial number of graduates spend only a brief period of time in direct practice with individuals and small groups, many soon changing to supervisor and executive positions requiring a considerable amount of administrative or community organization responsibilities. In view of this tendency it would seem essential for all students planning to enter casework or group work practice to be given sufficient acquaintance with the nature of administrative and community organization processes to enable them to undertake such tasks relatively early in their careers. It is questionable, however, whether the required single two hour credit course that is available in the large majority of the schools of social work for casework and group work majors can be considered adequate

for such a purpose. (The area of overlap between administratives and community organization referred to in footnote 1, page 5, should be noted again in this connection.)

A THEORY ABOUT RETARDED DEVELOPMENT OF CONCEPTUAL THINKING IN COMMUNITY ORGANIZATIONS

We may speculate on the reasons for the current stage of development in defining the conceptual aspects of community organization practice. Compared with the progress in casework and of group work is the retardation due to the lack of a gifted theoretician in this field, and if so, why this lack? Is community organization practice completely an art and therefore not subject to the development of specific theories of procedure? Neither reason seems plausible. Similarly, retardation cannot be ascribed to the relatively late development of practice. Community organization practice is not a new development; it is indeed the earliest stage in the history of modern social work. The creation of "Charity Organization Societies" and "Settlement Houses" were the result of community organization effort; they predated the definitions of casework and group work practice by several decades. The lack of development of theory to describe community organization practice cannot be attributed to lack of time.

The progressive movements of the late 19th and early years of the 20th century saw the rise of the complex of social welfare agencies in which the majority of professional social workers are now practicing the methods of social casework and of social group work. These community welfare services created through the processes of communal growth and development now constitute a vast network of agencies which depend upon the continuing processes of community organization and administration for their maintenance and vitality.

Although the techniques used for the creation of the modern social welfare structure may have been largely intuitive, represent-

ing the special talents of able pioneers, the procedures were frequently subjected to reactions, criticisms and evaluations from the participants and from other critics. Some underlying social work "principles," vaguely defined though they may have been, began to emerge. The writings and speeches of Jane Addams, Florence Kelley, Thomas Devine, Homer Folks and many other social work organizers and reformers began to illuminate the "how" as well as the "what" and the "why" of the new profession.

With such auspicious origins, why was there not a more rapid development and refinement of goals and methods in community organization? Perhaps the explanation is to be found in such factors as the complex character of our social organization, the resistance to social change, the controversial attitudes about the processes responsible for social change that were encountered by these social work pioneers, and about the social theories that seek to explain the nature of social organization. The means used to accomplish the desired goals seemed to be obvious—mobilization of social forces through exposure of evils, exhortation and persuasion. In a crusade, dynamic leadership is more important than any other factor. Some crusades succeeded but more were failures. And group organization began to replace individual enterprise in social work movements. The dynamic leader retained an important role but he began to function more as a member of a team. Agencies for community organization began to emerge which operated as group entities, not as individual enterprises.

Theory was looked upon as fanciful; practice was the hard reality. The concept of social planning and of community development was for a long time regarded with ill-concealed contempt by practical men of affairs. Designs for social change were thought radical and subversive; a society which worshipped individualism was not receptive to the institutionalization of social reform and social action as an established pattern of community living.

Under such conditions it was perhaps impossible for a school that would attempt to teach how the social order could be improved through systematic changes in social organization to arise

under auspices that would be acceptable to the "power structure" of the community. Without such an underlying concept of social change, all teaching of community organization under "respectable" auspices would necessarily be lacking in a general foundation of theory and would emphasize descriptions of agencies and programs and knowledge about formal and mostly superficial details of techniques.

With the growing prosperity of the nation in the 1920's and the use of government for the organization of community welfare programs in the 1930's, we seemed to have arrived in social work at the point where definition and conceptualization could begin to develop. The earliest and most significant development has been in the theory of casework. The social welfare agencies attempting to serve individuals and families were able to change their direction from emphasis on procedural to broader conceptual bases developing through the cooperation and interaction of leaders in the teaching and the practice of casework. The process was helped by the fact that social work in this field could begin to draw on the psychological theories of behavior, a somewhat less controversial field of social theory than those of government and economics with which the organization of community programs is largely involved. Similarly with the easing of tensions, community organization is now facing less controversial goals and objectives. The new facets of welfare organization such as the systems for social security; public health, housing and urban redevelopment programs; the community planning councils and welfare federations based on more systematic and orderly processes of establishment begin to evidence the possibilities of a more clearly defined methodology.

Casework began to make progress toward conceptualization when it could project method in relation to a theory of the nature of the individual. Conceptualization in community organization in this country, I believe, will also begin to progress since there is now a greater receptivity toward social planning in the community in general and greater interest on the part of social workers in questions of social policy and theories of social process.

CURRENT PROGRESS
TOWARD CONCEPTUALIZATION

In spite of the apparent retardation in the development of the teaching of community organization as compared with other social work fields, it should be noted that faculty members of the few schools that do place emphasis on this field of practice have made considerable progress in exploring the problems involved in teaching this method, in defining the conceptual basis of the theory and practice of community organization and in seeking to establish effective relationships between the teaching and practice. Indications of this progress are to be found in such places as the workshop on Community Organization held in January 1958 at the meeting of the Council on Social Work Education, recent publications on this subject by the Council, the increasing clarity of concepts beginning with the Lane Report in 1939 and illustrated in the topical articles on "Community Organization in Social Welfare" for the *Social Work Year Books* beginning in 1945, publication of several recent textbooks on the subject, and other individual and group efforts. McMillen believes that courses in community organization, which were dissimilar in content from one school to another in the past, are now much more alike.

> The social work student of today will cover material a very considerable proportion of which would be much the same in any other school. The differences that persist are predominantly in organization and division of material among courses and, more especially, in the objectives and the methods of teaching.[5]

The establishment of Association for the Study of Community Organization, whose interests are being continued by the Community Organization Committee of the National Association of Social

[5] Comment by Arthur Dunham: "I wonder what evidence McMillen has for this statement . . . I doubt that anyone knows enough to generalize on this point. This is one of the holes in our knowledge about community organization in the curriculum of schools of social work."

Workers, the participation of agencies in CSWE and the increasing number of full-time members of faculties of schools of social work with previous community organization experience are contributing to current development of theory.

A number of schools of social work are responding to growing interest in the development of the teaching of community organization. Curricula are under study and course content, field instruction, student qualifications and other aspects are being analyzed. These schools are attempting to revise courses and adapt the curriculum in accord with the emerging concepts of the nature of community organization practice, and with the broadening requirements of the field of practice.

Toward a Definition of Community Organization as Social Work

Since one of our concerns in the Curriculum Study is with the relation of teaching to practice, it may be desirable as an initial step to attempt to define the area of operation in the organization of the community[1] and its programs which may be considered appropriate to social work.

THE SOCIAL COMPLEX AND THE FIELD OF SOCIAL WORK

Within the structure of American society, the collective life of the population is expressed in a complex of political, economic and cultural institutions. Among these institutions, are those that are part of the structure of government. These operate within a legal framework under the prevailing authority of the political state and are financed wholly or largely from governmental revenues. Such public provisions and institutions cover a wide range of collective needs—from the maintenance of roads and highways, police and fire protection, sanitation, health services and medical care, education, correctional and adjustment services, economic assistance and social security plans, housing, and so on—to programs for research, scientific studies, national defense and international co-

[1] "The community itself is a constantly changing social entity. Not without some stability, to be sure, a certain amount of social cooperation, and a certain degree of permanency, but with boundaries that tend to be increasingly flexible, functions that are altered in response to the demands of a super-community social system, and interests that have to compete with non-localized group interests for the allegiance of the people." Warner E. Gettys, "The Field and Problems of Community Study," in *The Fields and Methods of Sociology*, ed. by Bernard Luther Lee, New York: Roy Long & Richard R. Smith, 1934.

operation. There are few aspects of collective organization important to the life, liberty, security, and cultural growth and development of mankind that are not within the purview of the modern state and the trend seems to be toward expanding the welfare functions of government.

Alongside this complex development and expansion of governmental responsibility and governmental authority, we have large voluntary systems operating under the aegis of the state and to a greater or lesser extent subject to its regulation. Within this setting voluntary enterprise remains the dominant element of our economic life, represented both by small scale and by large scale business organization. In addition to operations for providing goods and services undertaken for the profit of the entrepreneurs—individuals, partnerships and corporations—there are some economic enterprises under voluntary auspices developed on a non-profit or cooperative basis as well as the many types of welfare services operating within the structure of private philanthropy.

Since a large part of modern social work had its origins in the system of private philanthropy, many of the agencies and programs that derive from or that continue under such auspices are usually considered as being within the field of social work. (However, not all philanthropically derived or supported institutions are classified as social work agencies. For example, many schools and colleges, art museums, libraries, and so on, are also non-profit agencies depending on philanthropic support but are not ordinarily classified as social work, though some of them may operate under the auspices of a social work agency, such as, a music school, an art class or a library as functions of a neighborhood or community center).

The operation of governmental programs for financial assistance, social security, and medical care, and the use of social workers in the courts, health and correctional institutions indicate that our definition of community organization as social work needs to be related to this complex network of public and voluntary functions. History has shown many changes and displacements in the functions and programs of social work. We must assume that such

changes are likely to continue, arising from changes in the problems that grow out of the conditions of social life. What will be considered as social work in the future obviously will be affected by changes in social values and community standards and by attitudes of professional social workers as to their role and functions.

THE VARIOUS CONNOTATIONS OF THE TERM "COMMUNITY ORGANIZATION"

There are various connotations in which the term community organization is commonly used: (1) as referring to a structure or stage of development as in the "organized" and the "unorganized" community, (2) as a field of practice such as "planning social welfare services," "federated fund raising," "national service agencies," and (3) as a method, "a way of working on an orderly conscious basis to effect defined and desired objectives and goals." (Shimp)

The fact that a term has multiple uses is no barrier to its being applied with clarity so long as the different connotations of structure, field and method are evident in the specific context in which the term is used. Neither should the fact that the term is applied both in social work and in other fields prove an obstacle, nor should we be disturbed to find that there is a broader classification of community organization workers including urban developers and public works organizers, city planners, chamber of commerce secretaries, political leaders and others, and that the community organization worker in social welfare may utilize many techniques and methods used by organizers in other fields.

> The practitioner will draw on a considerable range of methods and techniques . . . *not peculiar to the social work profession such as:* fact finding and research, consultation, negotiation, group conference, committee operation, interpretation, education, mobilization (of manpower, finances, and so on) administration, recording, design of social facilities and services. (Kraus)
> Both the politician and the PTA president are sensitive to human

relationships, make use of principles of involvement, and use successful previous experience in working with people to guide them in their actions. (Carter)

The term "community" is similarly used in different connotations —political and geographical subdivisions such as neighborhood, town or city, metropolitan region, state, nation, and so on, or on a social and psychological base as in "community of interest," "professional community," "ethnic" or "sectarian community," and so on.

THE RELATION TO
GENERAL SOCIAL WORK CONCEPTS

The definition of community organization in social work can be related to concepts suggested as appropriate for social work as a whole in the Curriculum Study document *The Nature of Social Work:* "Social work seeks to enhance the social functioning of individuals, singly and in groups, by activities focused upon the social relationships which constitute the interaction between man and his environment. These activities can be grouped into three functions: restoration of impaired capacity, provision of individual and social resources, and prevention of social dysfunction."

It is obvious that while this definition is appropriate to community organization as well as other aspects of social work, it is not a static definition. Social work is not a closed or finite aspect of social organization. What may be conceived as necessary "to prevent social dysfunction and provide individual and social resources for the enhanced living of individuals and of groups" will depend upon the social intelligence, the quality of humanitarian sentiments and interests and the spiritual qualities of any specific society. It will also depend on the capacity of that society to produce the material resources and to permit the changes in social relationships which may be required for effective achievement of social welfare goals and objectives. Such goals and objectives will vary among differ-

ent parts of the collective society and among different cultures. Under primitive conditions, the restoration of impaired capacities of individuals may depend on the development of improved standards of sanitation, control of epidemics, provision of schools and introduction of modern methods into agricultural production. An undeveloped society brings into focus the relation of the essential tasks of community organization and planning in contrast to those that would be appropriate in a community which has achieved the capacity for relatively high standards of community living and group well-being. As a method, however, community organization in both developed and undeveloped societies may have a great deal in common, especially in the psychological aspects of how people in a collective body act and interact, progress or regress in their social objectives.

The achievement of welfare objectives may require the cooperation of social and physical planners and other professional and technical personnel in the same way that some casework objectives may need to enlist the services of physicians, psychiatrists, home economists, job finding and placement personnel and other professional and technical services. Similarly, the community organization worker, as well as the caseworker may need to work in close association with other helping services, not only those of the other helping professions but of legislators, fund raisers, public relations experts, and physical planners. The specialized services of an expert from another field or of a group of experts from varied disciplines may be obtained by referring a problem from one to another potential helping agent for whatever action the latter considers appropriate to his function. This may take the form of securing advice from the experts or may proceed through a prior or ad hoc organization of teamwork in which the social worker and other team members have assigned roles with respect to solution of a given community problem or project. The welfare objective may involve activities recognized as, or similar to, the functions of agencies that are staffed by social work personnel. It is this latter type of situation that is usually recognized as community organization in social work.

Community organization workers in social work frequently bring to their tasks a basis of knowledge and of competence which is related to their preparation and/or their experience in the agencies which serve consumers, that is services for individuals, families and groups that constitute the clientele of family, child care, recreational and group services and other social welfare agencies. A considerable part of the program of the community organization agencies in social work is concerned with the planning, coordination, improvement and maintenance of such services (both under governmental and voluntary auspices). Organizers in health, education, economic improvement and urban development, similarly bring to their tasks training and experience concerning the objectives and the nature of their respective fields. Such organizers may share with social workers, at least in part, the social values and objectives that are inherent in modern social welfare undertakings, in the same way that social workers may share with the other professions and technical personnel, knowledge and skill in using the techniques that are required for the successful attainment of a definite goal.

The statements in the preceding paragraph cannot be adequately documented at this time because of the lack of material on the nature of practice in social work community organization and of the practices of community organizers in other fields. However, leading practitioners in social work are convinced that there are many common elements in their practice and in the practices of community organization workers in other fields. It is generally believed that there are differences as well, though these have not yet been clearly stated and defined. We may, however, assume that methods in community organization for social work are not likely to be of a mechanical or routine character. There is great variability in the situation, the setting, the nature of the participants in the process, and the aims and purposes that the activity seeks to further.

What is done in community organization in social work will reflect the values, the conditions and the personnel in the specific situation and, if on a professional level, should be in accord with

the philosophy and the principles which presumably underlie all social work effort. There may, therefore, be little utility at this time to try to set forth arbitrary distinctions between the methods of community organization in general and those which are distinctive to social work. The qualities of community organization, as in other fields of social work, must be judged by the values and ethics of the profession of social work, which perhaps may be instrumental in the selection of techniques and procedures employed, as well as being ingrained in their intrinsic character. In any event no such scale of measurement or differentiations of techniques is now available for analysis of community organization procedures.

A distinction between "organizing a program," such as developing a school or a family welfare service following a decision of the community to undertake such a project, and "working with the community" in the process of arriving at such decisions would be arbitrary. Both types of procedures are frequently involved in the evolution and completion of a specific project.

IMPORTANCE OF THE METHOD OF COMMUNITY ORGANIZATION IN CASEWORK AND GROUP WORK PRACTICES

What aspects of the methods of community organization practice are of greatest importance to practitioners of casework and of group work? It is apparent that the functions of the agency, size and specialization of staff, the community setting and other factors determine how much administrative and community organization responsibility needs to be assumed by the individual social worker in his role as a staff member. In some settings, for example, that of child welfare work in a rural area, or in welfare agencies or programs operating with only a single professional worker (or two or three workers), as well as in larger agencies—such as those which accept broad responsibilities for community education, the worker who helps individual clients will need to use a considerable amount of group work and community organization skills. In addi-

tion, all caseworkers should be able to identify the difficulties experienced by their clients arising from lacks and gaps in community resources and welfare provisions. In order that this knowledge of community needs and problems can be translated into effective community action, social workers will need to participate in the communal programs of their agency and in the programs that are undertaken by the aggregate of community agencies. Similarly group workers "in almost any setting in which they customarily practice will need knowledge and skill . . . in the intergroup work process and the educational and promotional process." (McDowell)

A TENTATIVE DEFINITION

On the basis of the foregoing we may suggest the following goal for a sequence in community organization in a school of social work:

> The aim of a sequence of courses in community organization should be to prepare students by giving them an understanding of and concern for, plus an ability to promote, social well-being by means of the organization, maintenance and improvement of community welfare programs and services, considered as integral parts of the overall structure of community life.[2]

The general objectives of a curriculum designed to prepare students for the practice of community organization are well expressed in the conclusions of the Curriculum Study document, *The Nature Of Social Work,* as to prepare all students of social work. This states that "as a framework for ordering educational

2 Sieder identifies community organization in social work as having two concerns:
"1) with solving problems of or involving intergroup and interorganizational relationships which affect the welfare of the community;
2) with providing a network of interrelated and integrated services for the prevention and treatment of social ills."
See page 37, quotation from Kraus for a more detailed definition of the nature of the helping process in community organization.

objectives . . . an appropriate combination of undergraduate, graduate and in-service training should provide: (1) pertinent knowledge on the interaction between man and society; (2) appropriate attitudes toward man, society and their relationships; and (3) skills for carrying out the activities required by the functions of social work."

How do such educational objectives apply to preparation for the practice of community organization?

Basic Concepts in Educational Objectives for Community Organization Practice

KNOWLEDGE

1. OF THE SOCIAL SCIENCES AND OTHER DISCIPLINES AS BACKGROUND

Basic knowledge for all types of professional practice is not acquired merely through exposure to factual information, but must involve an understanding of the nature of the data and an ability to appraise and interpret them and to develop generalizations which represent in our present state of knowledge an intelligent appraisal of the meaning of that information. For the community organization practitioner such knowledge should be focused on the relationships and interactions between the processes of the collective society and the nature of the individual as a unit in that society. Such knowledge should constitute one of the major objectives of all systems of education, and such an objective is theoretically to be found in all school programs from the elementary to the university level.

In the liberal arts colleges there are courses on history and on the nature of man and on the nature and the history of his social institutions. Such courses are given in departments of history, sociology, political science, economics, anthropology, geography, biology, physiology, psychology and social psychology. Most of these courses have been grouped under the general term of the social sciences or the social and behavioral sciences.[1]

Presumably such studies aim to provide the student with a back-

---

[1] I consider the term "social and behavioral sciences" to be tautological. If the term psychology covers both behavior which is social produced and conditioned and the physiological structure of man, the term might then be social and physiological sciences.

ground of knowledge which will help him to understand himself, other human beings and their social institutions. The courses that are offered under the classification of the "Arts" or the "Humanities" also contribute to such understanding, since the current tendency is to consider literature, philosophy and the plastic arts as the creative products of gifted individuals in specific historical and cultural settings.

Concepts and terms derived from social science courses can be seminal in the development of social work theory and are often essential ingredients toward its development. On the other hand, they can have a distorting or sterile effect. (There are instances of both in the history of social work). Rarely can they be applied directly; they should be refracted through the process of relating the situations in social work to the social science concepts for the light the latter may reflect. A social science concept at best is a point of view; it may be plausible but it needs always to be kept in mind that it is usually partial and tentative and that it can never fully describe all of the complex elements in any human situation.[2]

It certainly can not be used as an automatic guide to social diagnosis or to social planning. An excellent corrective against fragmentary social science theories is through an eclectic approach. Thus sociology and anthropology may help to broaden concepts derived from psychiatry and psychoanalysis; the history and political science may correct distortions of social understanding derived from economic theory and vice versa. The current imperfect state of our social science theories is generally acknowledged, especially by the more competent of the social scientists.

Social studies that aim to instill scientific attitudes, offered by teachers without dogmatism and with proper skepticism as to their finality as truth, will be stimulating and fruitful to the student in

2 Ernest Greenwood, "Social Science and Social Work: A Theory of Their Relationship," *The Social Science Review* (March, 1955). "While it may be desirable to familiarize social workers with the vast knowledge of the social sciences, it is highly doubtful that significant effects upon social work practice will be wrought in this fashion . . . The conversion of social science theory into practice must be an empirical one, not a mental one."

helping to understand himself, man and society. However, we must consider that the student body will have obtained an undergraduate education in hundreds of different colleges and universities. We must be aware of the consequent lack of standardization. There is likely to be too great divergence, incompleteness and particularistic biases among students to assume that, because the various college courses have the same or similar titles, the students have been exposed to the same knowledge and discipline in all of them. To assure that such undergraduate courses have given the students the basic social science background would require the development of a much closer collaboration than now exists between the schools of social work and the undergraduate colleges. In view of the diversity of theories being espoused by teachers of the social sciences, this would be a formidable undertaking.

Since the students enrolling in a school of social work will have had their undergraduate training in various universities, special attention will have to be given to the student's social science knowledge. This might take the forms of (a) a test to determine the adequacy of undergraduate preparation, or (b) the offering of refresher and orientation courses planned by the school of social work with the university of which it is a part.

The purpose of such courses would not be to correct or to revise the concepts or theories derived from the undergraduate courses but to try to relate the theories and concepts of social work to some frame of reference which the student of social work needs in order to understand the nature of man as a member of the human collective. Such a course would be a primary requirement for students with inadequate social science preparation.

All social work courses should have a relationship to and should deepen the social science knowledge of the student. It is obvious that qualified teachers of social work courses must themselves be adequately equipped with a meaningful background in social science theory and be able to apply such knowledge in the presentation of material in the history, the social structure and the methods of social work. In one school of social work the experiment is

being tried of having some courses given by a combination of a faculty member qualified to teach social work with a member of a social science department. Such collaboration may be helpful in giving the student a knowledge of social science theory and its applications to current social work concepts. It may have even greater value in helping the respective faculty members to bring social science theory and social work concepts into a closer alignment. This process might also be helpful in coordinating the undergraduate and the graduate courses with the aim of organizing an adequate social science background for careers in the profession.

2. OF SOCIAL POLICY

Since communtiy organization work involves questions of social policy and how it is formed amid the strains and stresses of society in the modern state, a background of history, sociology, economics and political science is essential for an understanding of the relation of social welfare programs to the social order in which they function. With the current gaps and inadequacies in undergraduate preparation in the social sciences (although it is believed that preparation today is considerably in advance of what was available in the past) consideration needs to be given now to supplement the student's knowledge of social science theories with an understanding of the dynamics of social organization and the nature of the social processes involved in the life of the community, state and nation. Such a course of study (which has been developed in at least one school of social work) would parallel what many schools now undertake for giving students an understanding of the individual person, under the caption "Human Growth and Development." It may be considered fundamental for the preparation of students for community organization practice and would require more or less time depending on undergraduate social science preparation and the social science aspects of other social work courses. The bringing in of an appreciable amount of such content into the courses on human growth and development would seem to be a

minimum requirement for students who are not planning to major in community organization.

A course on the graduate level for community organization majors on the history and development of social work and social welfare should be more than a repetition of factual knowledge that may be offered in undergraduate courses which deal with the history of social institutions. It should acquaint the student with the current structure of the welfare services, their history and development, emphasizing the changes in social policy that have taken place in these programs as seen against the political, economic and cultural settings in which changes have taken place.

Other social work courses such as those on the history of social work, the development of public welfare, and on the methods of casework and group work, are desirable for students planning to major in community organization as for all students.

Many of the position papers make reference to the range of knowledge that is desirable for the community organization worker. The following sections (3, 4, 5) are related to the points outlined and discussed by Cohn, Kraus, McMillen, McNeil and Lefferts, Newstetter and Schwartz, and Shimp.

3. OF THE FIELD OF COMMUNITY ORGANIZATION

A thorough knowledge is called for of the areas of service in the total field of social welfare, with particular emphasis on understanding the general principles and relationships among the various fields and the professional standards of each field. Also required is knowledge of the development of the American community and its various types of political, economic and cultural institutions. A further area of content involves knowledge of certain special processes used in community organization practice, (public relations, fund raising, adult education, intergroup relations and so forth) with particular emphasis on where to find information, how to relate to professionals in these fields, and how to adapt such information to the responsibilities of the community organization worker.

4. OF COMMUNITY STRUCTURE

Areas of consent required under this heading are:

The organization of community health, welfare and recreation services; the instrumentalities our society has created for the purpose of
advancing the community organization process in social welfare.

The social structure of community life, including the institutional
structure for governmental and voluntary institutions, the class and
caste system, ethnic and religious group divisions and separations,
the power structure as it operates in government, in the economic
life of the community and in the development and control of social
policy and social welfare institutions.

The structure of the organizations for supporting, maintaining,
planning and coordinating of the welfare services of the community,
the history of the development of this structure and the nature of the
structural variations of contemporary governmental and voluntary
programs.

Comments in positions papers state: "The really important objective is to provide the student with knowledge of the institutional structure upon which practitioners must depend in the
furthering of the community organization process."

"Instruction in the methods by which social policy is formulated
. . . an examination of the processes by which government determines social policy today. Private 'governments' in the form of the
trade union movement, organized business and industry, organized
religious forces, fraternal and patriotic societies also exercise substantial influence in determining social policy."

5. OF COMMUNITY ORGANIZATION AS METHOD

Some aspects of community organization processes and techniques
that should be included in the knowledge to be made available to
the student are indicated in the sections on fields and on structure.

Other suggestions are as follows:

A knowledge of the processes and methods used in casework and

in group work practice. The research techniques used in social work and in social sciences "sufficient to make for effective provision of administrative and interpretive services and their integration into the community organization process." "Knowledge of technical skills used in interviewing and individual consultation "with particular emphasis upon the nature of relationships in social work, use of the professional self, role of the professional worker, the place and role of the boards, the committees and other volunteer participants." "Knowledge in the use of administration, committees, conferences, interviewing, recording, community relationships, research methods, consultation, budgeting, promotion and educational methods. The worker must know how adequate and efficient financing of community services are developed."

ATTITUDES AND VALUES

Several of the papers stress the fundamental importance of a basic philosophy for putting knowledge into the proper perspective for the practice of community organization in social work. Such a philosophy must be considered as the most distinctive aspect of social work practice. As stated by MacRae, individuals in fields other than social work apparently using some of the common techniques and procedures "may be engaged in the development and promotion of social nostrums and panaceas reflective of man's stupidity or credulity rather than his intelligence or nobility . . . they may be employed in socially evil and divisive programs aimed at setting off race against race and religious group against religious group."

Shimp states that "the philosophy and attitudes of a community organization specialist encompass the same basic beliefs held in other areas of social work, with emphasis in some special areas." These beliefs are:

1. The worth and dignity of the individual and faith in democratic processes.

2. The desirability of improving relationships among individuals, groups, organizations of people, neighborhoods and communities.
3. The right of individuals, groups and communities to differ but still retain a responsibility for the well-being of others.
4. The ability of individuals, groups and communities to change.
5. The processes of interaction as an instrument to effect change.
6. The right of self-determination.
7. That the end result cannot be divorced from the means.
8. That in a democracy, participation of people from all walks of life is essential in reaching appropriate decisions.
9. That a worker's self-awareness is an integral part of his performance and accomplishment.
10. That an orderly process is essential and compatible with desirable change in value systems and social institutions.

These beliefs taken as a whole, we are convinced, extend beyond those held or practiced currently by many professional caseworkers and group workers but still embrace the basic beliefs of the two groups. We recognize the role of casework and group work, but believe it demands a larger perspective on the part of the community organization specialist.

The development in the student of professional attitudes, an acceptance of the goals and values of social work and of the relationships to people appropriate to the character of a helping profession is an objective of the entire curriculum and can find expression in many if not all of its parts. Community organization is concerned with general welfare provisions, for which the well-being of individuals is or should be the prime consideration. There are some relationships in the community organization process which condition the interaction between the social worker and those with whom he becomes involved that differ from relationships of the caseworker to his client or of the group worker to his specific group. The members of the board, the colleagues in communal projects, the legislators, and the administrators of the governmental and volunteer services, the various conflicting and cooperating groups involved are not clients in the sense that the individual

receiving casework services or the groups involved in a group work activity are clients of the social worker. These associates in the community organization process do not ask for help for their personal needs but for furthering the activity in which they are engaged. The cooperators in a community organization project are associated with the community organization worker who is attempting to make available to them the expert knowledge or the skills and techniques or the leadership qualities essential to the success of the enterprise. The individuals associated in the project similarly have their special interests, initiative and expertness and the task of organization is to enable the process to move ahead to the development and achievement of the goals which will express the aims and the spirit of social work.

A number of statements on attitudes and relationships contained in the position papers are pertinent.

The community organization worker must bring to his task . . . special personal aptitudes as . . . imagination and social vision; initiative and resourcefulness; an ability to work with all kinds of people without regard to economic, social, racial, religious or status factors; intellectual and professional integrity which permits compromise on substantive matters without compromising on basic principles. (Sieder)

Another writer suggests that the community organization worker should have

. . . ability to relate to people and to facilitate positive relationships among individuals and groups; ability to handle oneself professionally, in many different roles, with various types of people, and to handle criticism and praise; ability to understand and accept the reality of the situation and yet to see the potential for change. (Barry)

PERSONALITY FACTORS

Attitudes and values can be developed and are objectives of the educational process parallel to the development of knowledge and

the acquiring or deepening of skills and techniques. Personality factors are an element in the capacity of the student to acquire attitudes that are essential and will facilitate the process of developing professional values. It may be difficult for individuals with certain personality patterns and emotional qualities to modify or change those patterns of behavior for qualities that may be of a very different character. It should, however, be possible in the educational process to induce changes in attitudes based on the acceptance of values inherent in the profession of social work; education may help to establish the desirable qualities and not merely add a veneer of plausible but undependable qualities. However, because of the difficulties involved in establishing desirable personality patterns, several of the position papers emphasize the necessity of selecting students for community organization majors who possess at the outset the personality qualities or predispositions considered more likely to be essential for effective performance. The following statements illustrate this point of view:

> The student should be evaluated as a social worker and then, more specifically, as a community organization worker . . . some of the personality characteristics and motivations which are an asset in other social work specializations may not be particularly important in community organization . . . a person with temperament and sensitivity suitable to a treatment role may not be well suited to community organization . . . Characteristics such as social mobility, ability to relate to others quickly and to communicate easily, satisfactions in high pressure or tension situations, comfortableness in new and changing activities and roles, are assets to a community organization practitioner if his personality is sufficiently well integrated so that they are kept in control and balance. (Barry)
>
> Personality factors are of very great importance . . . the community organizer must possess a deep respect for people . . . a belief in their capacity for change and self determination . . . an abiding belief in the democratic process which will enable him to resist the temptation to manipulate people . . . a democratic rather than an authoritarian personality . . . a genuineness which elicits confidence and cooperation . . . some of the zeal of the crusader . . . disci-

plined by respect for facts, a readiness to compromise, and a clear capacity to work within the democratic process. (MacRae)

It should be noted that these opinions on the kinds of personality and temperament that facilitate the work of the community organizer represent conclusions drawn from experience in practice, teaching and observation of student careers. As such they are entitled to respect but further systematic study of personality factors, program results and agency settings would be desirable to substantiate or modify such opinions, and to show whether and how they differ from personality requirements for all social workers.

Elements of Community Organization Method in Social Work Practice

While there is a close interrelationship among knowledge, attitudes and techniques—indeed one without the other is likely to prove sterile or result in stereotyped or misdirected action—separation may be permissible for purposes of teaching, providing the inherent interrelationships are acknowledged and kept in mind in the teaching process. Techniques are employed in furtherance of consciously recognized objectives and goals. A general statement on the broad functions of the community organization worker is provided by Kraus as follows:

> The helping process in community organization is a professional service made available to communities and community groups toward the development of a more integrated, more cooperative society which will support a strong fabric of common facilities and services to meet the common needs of its members. Moving toward this goal help and technical aid may be in order in *developing and strengthening the social foundations and social objectives* of a community, or the entire society, irrespective of the immediate strengthening of specific resources related to selected needs.
>
> This may mean a focus on improving human relations, favoring cooperative interaction and mutual aid in traditional areas of tension. It may involve the development of more, and more effective, channels of communication across economic, social, cultural, sectarian and racial barriers. It may also imply the building of a wider awareness of social problems, of unmet or neglected needs, of limited or ineffective resources relating to such needs. Social development may involve the strengthening of common understanding of the strong interdependence of economic and social development, of the importance of human resources and human relationships for the stability and productivity of the economy. It may need to focus on

providing a broader and deeper understanding of the major elements of social change as they affect individuals and communities. It may deal with traditional and changing welfare goals, and the widening scope of the welfare potential. (Kraus)

The carrying out on a professional level of an objective, or of a specific project in the furtherance of that objective, is not a hit-or-miss activity; it should not proceed on a "trial and error" basis. The methods of social work involve consciously planned and directed procedures.

Four core activities can be distinguished: (1) assessing the problem; (2) planning for solution of the problem; (3) implementing the plan; and (4) evaluating the outcome. (Boehm)

A somewhat similar statement is contained in the following:

Phases of social work method which reflect a configuration of elements common to all three of our methods (casework, group work and community organization) are (1) social study and diagnosis of particular social conditions; (2) assessing and utilizing strengths in the situation; (3) modification or change. Social work method, hopefully, brings about change in a given social situation . . . directed to some defined social goal . . . social change constitutes the end product of our social work methods, and the *means* by which it is brought about must be within the value system and the sanctions of the profession; (4) evaluation of change in relation to goals. (Carter)

The teaching of process to be undertaken on a professional level requires the development of conceptual ability—not the rote learning of the details of a case situation that the instructor considers to have had a successful outcome. The conceptual analysis of process is developed in the classroom, or in class consideration of observations made during field work practice. For this purpose reports of student practice, case records of community projects, many other types of written materials available to the teacher that have community organization content and show community organization principles can be utilized.

ANALYZING THE PROBLEM

Ability to analyze the problems in a specific project as a whole or in a particular stage of the project is an ability founded on the capacity to use knowledge, to apply theory to practice in an integrated way. A large and substantial undertaking may call for more than an ability to see the potential problems and difficulties and the possibilities for solving them, deriving from what the worker already knows from his education and his experience; it may involve a systematic assembly of knowledge on the particular subject from various other sources or the acquisition of new data based on original research. The community organization worker does not need to become a specialist in social research, but he must know enough about the research process to be able to utilize research effectively, to understand its meaning and its limitations. Most important is the ability to foresee the need for bringing new data into a situation that would otherwise be decided by the group based on inadequate, obsolete or erroneous data. The community organization worker himself will probably need to undertake a considerable amount of fact gathering and fact organizing. To perform this effectively, he needs to be able to assess the validity of available information, keep an open mind and understand the implications of the data.

The capacity to formulate and develop an appropriate and meaningful generalization from the array of data is of great importance in community organization work as it is in teaching. Indeed McMillen ranks this skill as of the highest importance.

> The practitioner of community organization works with a group that is struggling with a problem . . . The ability to formulate may be the major professional contribution to the process. This ability involves two components: (1) aptitude in discerning among the relevant and irrelevant comments of members of a group a core principle or proposition to which a considerable number of the comments can be related; and (2) skill in stating the core principle or proposition clearly and, above all, succinctly. (McMillen)

As McMillen implies, the study-action method in a community organization project is most frequently a group process, developed in and through a committee structure. The assessment of the problem may also proceed informally through the reactions of individuals, singly and in groups outside the formal committee meetings, and the community organization worker must frequently channel these reactions through formal group action. Principles of group process as developed in a course on that subject may prove conceptually helpful if related to new and different aspects which are likely to arise under the conditions of group activity in a community organization project.

Knowledge of these factors has had a considerable influence in recent years in the development of the "self-study" in which help and leadership may be given by the community organization consultants and research workers. The social agencies and other groups concerned must participate in the study process if there is to be real acceptance of the problem analysis and the proposals for action based on that analysis. The group process in community organization usually involves the participation of those whose interests are likely to be involved and who will have the responsibility for carrying the proposed program into effect. Participants in the community organization process usually have the power to accept or to veto findings and recommendations in which they may or may not have participated. Important state and national decisions and actions in government may be enforced where there is a difference of only one vote, but the community organization worker in voluntary group effort knows that majority decisions against the wishes of a determined and unconvinced minority are frequently self-defeating and unenforceable. Such situations arise at the stage of problem analysis as well as in the stage of program planning and development.

PLANNING THE SOLUTION

In community organization, analysis, planning the solution and implementing the plan are interrelated processes, and do not neces-

sarily occur as successive steps in a time sequence. As in other social work methods, these three steps are likely to be a continuing process, as new situations give rise to new interactions among the individuals and the groups involved in a community project; planned solutions are modified or new plans substituted, and initiative in the implementation of a play may shift from one to another set of participants.

Like the study process, planning for the solution of a problem in community organization is likely to be a group process and involve the participation of many communal elements. So far as the community organization worker is concerned "planning the solution" involves primarily planning the process whereby the group will be able to function most effectively and expeditiously to arrive at agreement concerning what needs to be done. He is concerned with how to achieve the cooperation of the group directly involved and of related groups and forces in the community to undertake what is presumed to be the desirable solution of the problem.

The carrying through of a community organization project, therefore, means for the community organizer serving in various roles and capacities as the technician, the consultant and the active element in a communal undertaking. The requirements are (1) the ability to organize, (2) the ability to give or to provide leadership and (3) the ability to promote group action.

ORGANIZING SOCIAL WELFARE PROGRAMS AND SERVICES

Since one of the basic goals in a consciously directed process of community organization is the development of adequate services and resources to meet needs, and their continued maintenance on a progressively improving standard of service, the ability to organize is the core of the process. Programs of community service depend upon an effective structure.

Steps in the process may involve determining the key personnel required for initiative and dynamic action in a given situation; making

initial contacts with such people directly or through other influential leaders and associates; establishing the opportunities for interested or potentially interested people to become associated for the purpose of learning about the program objective and forming an organization; establishing a formal structure through by-laws, committees, officers, and so on; continuing planning so that the nucleus leadership stimulates and recruits other individuals for program involvement. (Gurin)

Every new project and all on-going programs and services must find their place in the total network of organized communal activities, and each agency needs to be constantly on the alert concerning its relationship to this network in a dynamic and changing society. Many aspects of community organization procedure therefore resemble methods in administration of agencies and programs. Continuing appraisal is needed of the relationship between the functions of a specific program and those of related agencies and developing communal projects. New developments arising from the creative efforts of professional staff, new methods promising improved service, changes in the extent or character of the problem arising from demographic, economic or cultural factors all these may require changes in the structure, support and maintenance of a project. How to keep the agency alert to changing problems, changing community conditions and changing personnel is the core of responsibility of the leadership and such responsibility is usually centered in the executive and his professional associates.

Developing and maintaining financial support is similarly a task which involves the ability to organize in both the voluntary system and the governmental systems of welfare services. This is seen more clearly in the work of chests and other financial federations where the potential contributing group is considered to be the entire population of an area or selected segments of that population. Organizing financial support may involve the instilling or the nurturing of responsibility on the part of the potential contributors, the assignment of leadership roles to develop this responsibility and to establish the machinery of campaign organization, interpretation, solicitation and reporting required for the carrying

out of the fund raising plan. In a federated fund situation the resources to be obtained must be related to the basic requirements and the legitimate functions of the agency projects and programs. Priorities must be established since available resources universally fall short of legitimate needs; the relation of campaign goals to needs as established through the processes of budgeting, and so on. Relations with contributors, agencies, professional and volunteer groups are all involved in the processes of fund raising and fund distribution, organizing and developing the most effective types of relationships among these groups is the basic task of community organization for financial support.

Methods of community organization and the ability to organize are also essential in the financing of welfare services under governmental auspices even if the structures for determining financial needs and obtaining the financial requirements seem to operate on a less complicated basis. The public interest and support for a particular category of projects and services, the attitudes of the legislative and executive branches of government, the competition for the available funds among the numerous legitimate claimants—these are constant aspects of the processes of governmental budgeting and financing.

The administrator of a specific public service, unlike the executive of a voluntary agency, is not required to participate in the organization of the tax assessments or the borrowing program of government or in the collection of the taxes.[1] But since all financing involves questions of social policy, the administration must understand and, within the legal restrictions imposed on him must participate in the development of public policy. Because of the importance of the public services to the interests of the voluntary social welfare agencies, civic groups and similar bodies, the community organization worker serving in the voluntary field frequently becomes involved in seeking to influence the provision and budgeting of public services, as well as the many administrative decisions of the governmental officials and administrative

[1] "But he is required to justify his budget and obtain support through the administration and the legislature."—George W. Rabinoff.

bodies related to the welfare field. There are local welfare planning councils, conferences of agencies on a local or state basis, and
national welfare bodies for whom this participation constitutes a
major function and responsibility.

Some of the devices used in the method of community organization are of an administrative character. McMillen describes these
as "the mechanisms and procedures that facilitate orderly development of group affairs, such as the preparation of agenda, the writing of minutes, the drafting of resolutions, memoranda and the
like." A separate course in administration will probably cover
these aspects which are important in the tasks of the community
organization worker, and effective collaboration between those
who are responsible for the teaching of community organization
methods and administrative principles and techniques will help
give requisite attention to these aspects of the process. The period
of field work instruction should provide for actual experience in
administrative techniques, such as keeping minutes of a committee
meeting, either as a part of the schedule of activities of the student
within the agency or as a supplemental task required by the student's field work instruction.

Social workers with responsibility for the administration of an
agency or project or who participate in the social policy and social
action projects of groups and associations of welfare agencies engage through such activities in the organization and allocation of
community resources. Students need to understand the organization process itself and also what special technical skills the various
parts of the process require, such as those of accounting, of ad-
vertising and publicity, the methods and the media for effective
communication and interpretation. When such professional and
technical skills are enlisted they need to be aligned with community organization process as means to some specific end, not as ends
in themselves. The goals sought in the welfare program must be
guided by accountability and responsibility to the public and by
the ethical standards which are of the essence of social work.

Particular attitudes and work habits facilitate the processes of
organization. Frequently there are work pressures, a multiplicity

of current projects and assignments, leaving little time for intro-
spection and evaluation which need to accompany the professional
approach to community organization tasks. The many details of
the job need to be organized and scheduled. Proper weighting
needs to be given to the use of time for the various tasks, priorities
established among the various tasks that need to be assumed, and
alertness maintained to new and changing elements in every situation. While much of the ability to work effectively comes from
experience and maturing on the job, an introduction to these
requirements can be obtained through classroom and field instruction.

RELATION OF COMMUNITY ORGANIZATION AND ADMINISTRATION

The writer is aware of the fact that in the above section on organizing social welfare programs and services he has not made a clear
distinction between what are called administrative as differentiated
from community organization procedures. This has been inten-
tional for the reason that the criteria for differentiation that have
been offered are found on application to be invalid in a great many
respects. For example, it has been suggested that the term "administration" should be applied to matters of internal agency
management, while the term "community organization" should
refer to external relationships involving the participation of a
number of inside and outside groups. How does this distinction
apply to personnel management? Like clerical service and office
management, personnel management would seem to be largely an
internal matter. But the maintenance of professional standards,
and in fact many other aspects of personnel relations in governmental or voluntary agencies, may become matters of public interest and bring in a whole galaxy of external relationships. Similarly,
relationships of board and staff are considered matters of internal
administration; they are also involved in program development
and community relations. It follows that, if the method of commu-

nity organization is conceived too narrowly, it may show little difference from the subject of administration similarly conceived narrowly; if the subject of administration is broadly conceived and related, as it should be to questions of social policy, it would contain many of the elements of method in community organization. Raising funds for social welfare and other social work functions is placed by some analysts outside the area of social work community organization method. For example:

We would limit social work community organization method to project-centered activities, involving a problem solving process, with recognizable "case" beginning and termination, and where the method incorporates the generic elements common to other social work methods. The activities are process-focused toward improved community integration as well as toward a self-determined social work goal. Fund raising, educational conferences, manipulation in power structure, public relations events, directed negotiation, marshalling forces for legislation, and similar activities are important and appropriate functions which are means for organizing the welfare resources of a community, but under the proposed definition these would be excluded as social work methods, per se, but not as legitimate social work practice functions. (Carter)

Presumably, the acquaintance with these procedures might be placed elsewhere in the curriculum. In administration? In the opinion of the writer, they are essentially based on the method of community organization and can be seen, on the other hand, to involve fundamental issues in intergroup relations and procedures, and use of professional methods.

We must conclude, therefore, that the curriculum in community organization should incorporate the subject matter of a broadly conceived approach to administration and management without an excessive emphasis on details of techniques, with the goal of helping the student to understand how administrative and community organization procedures are integral parts of program development and agency operation, and how they may be coordinated

in relation to social policy as the fundamental determinant of all communal endeavor.

LEADERSHIP ABILITIES AND GROUP ACTION

The community organizer is not primarily a secretary for or the recorder of the project but he is frequently expected to keep the record and report on the committee or group activity involved. Sometimes the term "enabler," generally recognized as one of the major roles assumed by the community organization worker, is mistakenly attenuated until it is little more than a secretarial function. It is the leadership role, however, that must constitute the essence of professional service. "Enabling" is not merely expediting a natural process, but should involve leadership on the part of the worker. The social worker in community organization must himself undertake the initial role on many occasions, and he frequently must help recruit, develop and assist other individuals to assume responsibility in the dynamic process that is essential for the achievement of the goals sought. The organizer frequently must also utilize his own leadership and that of other persons to vitalize and develop the leadership group and to prepare leadership replacements. Sieder describes this as "leadership qualities which are constructive in developing leadership in others . . . and the personality to attract the liking, respect and confidence of lay leaders and professional social workers."

One of the important components in leadership ability is confidence based on full acceptance of the goals and purposes of the project coupled with a proper humility. Leadership qualities of the individuals associated in a cooperative project, especially of the professional workers, are evaluated on the basis of knowledge, understanding, self-appraisal and use of self, and most important, ability to stimulate others (volunteers and staff associates) to take on initiative and responsibility.

CHAPTER V

Some Aspects of Course Content and Field Instruction

SOURCES OF COMMUNITY ORGANIZATION TECHNIQUES

Many procedures in community organization are similar to and derived from other social work methods and from procedures found in many different types of collective activity. Courses in the methods of casework have a bearing on the nature of the relationships of individuals to each other and offer concepts concerning various types of behavior. Group work theory is concerned with the nature of group interaction, and of relationships that facilitate or retard desirable group functioning. These courses planned for all students will be valuable in training for community organization. However, the concepts derived from casework and group work theory need to be related to the community organization setting. The cooperative nature of the collective undertaking, the relation of the leadership group to the wider public and other aspects need to be made explicit in developing the concepts of the motivations of individual behavior in community projects. A generic course on the various methods of social work may help to make these distinctions, and will need to be reinforced through presentation and discussion of community organization method both in the classroom and in the analysis of field observation and practice.

Comment from Bessie Touzel, Executive Director of the Ontario Welfare Council:

I wonder whether we need some extension or development of the material on sources of community organization techniques. Is it

sufficient to say "However, the concepts derived from casework and group work theory need to be related to the community organization setting?" It is my experience that something of the intergroup exists in most committee activities. Members of the committee so seldom, it seems to me, comprise a simple group; they represent that point of view and element in the community concerned to protect private agency policies, a business community suspicious of social work and its agencies in regard to philosophy, or the lay group concerned about the transfer of functions to the professional group, or a religious point of view and organized group related to the subject, and so on. It has occurred to me that the recognition that most persons serving on committees undertaking substantial tasks are there, not purely as individuals, but as persons consciously or otherwise representing group points of view, is important.

FIELD INSTRUCTION

There is general agreement that adequate field instruction is essential in preparing students for the practice of community organization. The nature and content of classroom and seminar discussions in relation to the scheduled activities of the student in the field placement will obviously depend upon the conditions of the placement, the range of activities permitted the student and the quality of supervision and instruction he receives from the persons responsible for his field experience. Thus it follows that the most desirable type of field placement for a community organization major is in an agency directly engaged in community organization of social welfare programs.[1] It is also assumed that the student will spend enough time for orientation, reading and observation of the setting in which he is placed and that he will be given a substantial opportunity to undertake at least some of the simpler processes of

[1] The focus of teaching in the field as well as in the classroom should be upon "how to practice community organization" as differentiated from such techniques as "how to staff a committee" or "how to run a campaign." The field practice period should be a testing ground where generalized knowledge can be particularized and theory put into practice and where abilities are developed and tested. (Barry)

the agency in carrying out its community organization projects. The student can, of course, learn a considerable amount from observation, especially if what he observes can be reviewed and analyzed with him by the instructor, but there is nothing that can take the place in the learning process of actual participation. This implies a need for careful selection of promising students and skill in adjusting the range of processes in the agency to their individual needs and abilities. There would seem to be no reason why the problem cannot be solved in community organization as it has been in other fields.

Barry believes that agencies engaged in doing community organization will become more willing to invest time and money in developing field practice programs, not primarily because it offers direct benefits to their own operations but as service to the profession and the development of professional personnel. Such an attitude, she states, will depend on the development of greater emphasis on community organization in schools of social work and on evidence that more and better workers are being prepared.

DOES THE COMMUNITY ORGANIZATION MAJOR REQUIRE FIELD INSTRUCTION IN CASEWORK AND/OR GROUP WORK?

Several writers of position papers believe it is desirable for the community organization student to have instruction in casework and/or group work, and that field experience in one of these methods would constitute a valuable and perhaps even an essential background for a community organization worker. The same view was expressed in a comment on this report received from Bessie Touzel as follows:

> I have some question, too, as to whether the young worker does not learn more thoroughly in using professional principles, in what I think are simpler settings in casework or group work. Maybe he proceeds more quickly in the long run by such beginning experience.

Field opportunities of the kind which your memo suggests as preferable are almost non-existent in most of the communities which I know. In addition, I have some feeling that the community organization person who serves later in a planning relationship to health and welfare services is more able to relate to these if he has had at least a minimum period in them. This is not to suggest that we want consultant level persons on admission to the field, but perhaps we do need someone with a nodding acquaintance with the basic services. Some of these factors will change very considerably in even a decade or two.

A different point of view on field instruction was expressed by several participants at the Community Organization Workshop in Detroit. (The value of prior professional experience in casework, and so on, was not discussed.) I agree with the suggestions at this Workshop that the theory and practice of community organization had been sufficiently developed and that a satisfactory field work placement in a community organization agency under competent supervision could provide the student with knowledge and experience in method and procedures equivalent to what the student preparing for casework practice and the student preparing for group work practice ordinarily derive from their respective field placements. It was stated at the Workshop that community organization work is a social work method which deals with problems in social interaction and that it is a method undertaken with professional self-discipline. Within the time available no student can be prepared for beginning practice in two or more fields, and it was therefore better to concentrate on community organization field practice for those students who are considered qualified to major in that sequence. Under competent supervision such field practice can help the student to gain insight into his professional role and functions as well as into the techniques of the method of community organization.

That field work placements for community organization majors should be undertaken on a full time basis followed by a year of paid internship was recommended in several of the position papers.

COMMENTS ON TEACHING METHODS

McMillen discusses the "how" as well as the "what" involved in teaching community organization. He has listed the objectives of classroom education under several headings: (1) to acquaint the student with the instruments which advance the community organization process in social welfare, (2) to acquaint the student with formulations that have some right to be considered *principles* of community organization, (3) the presentation of methods, and (4) sharpening the student's ability to select appropriate methods and to develop skills.

The content of courses in community organization in social work in the various schools, McMillen believes, now shows a great deal of similarity; the difference being in the division of material in various courses, in subject emphasis and in teaching methods.[2] Some teaching methods are considered wasteful of the students' time and ineffectual. There is a need for more case records of community organization for teaching aids but McMillen suggests that case records are not the only documents suitable for teaching community organization.

> In our present stage the case record is neither the most economical nor the most effective type of document for teaching . . . There are many other types of written materials available to the teacher that have community organization content and show community organization principles, such as "excerpts from reports or surveys, newspaper clippings, scholarly papers, speeches, agenda, minutes or digests of meetings, and so on. (McMillen)
> There are principles of community organization and they can be learned. Principles are informed observations. They rest upon observation and the interpretation of informed experience, not upon scientifically tested hypotheses. A principle in community organization is not invariably applicable because of the infinite variety of the combination of variables to which it may be applied. (McMillen)
> It is believed that there is now a sufficient amount of published

[2] Note, however, comment by Dunham on page 53.

material on community organization for social welfare to construct a course in community organization which should be offered to all students in all schools of social work. (Newstetter and Schwartz) [3]

I would like to see classroom preparation move away from training in methods and techniques toward a concentration on principles of social welfare organization and the development of powers of analysis and orderly thought . . . This assumes the opening of field work placements with adequate time for high grade supervision where techniques and methods can be learned by doing . . . Genuinely professional training in the long pull must emphasize principles and capacity for analysis. As long as the emphasis in training for social work is heavily on techniques, schools will be engaged largely in vocational training (as against professional). (MacRae)

Differences in methods of teaching will be with us always. Gifted teachers develop unique ways of attaining their objectives . . . Evidence suggests that some teaching methods now in use are wasteful of time and ineffective and that others may lend to the material the unwarranted caste of dogma. An earlier decade did much to establish the solid core of content. Perhaps the contribution of the present decade will consist in weeding out the ineffectual methods of teaching the subject. (McMillen)

[3] Dunham remarks on this statement that, while there is "plenty of published materials," it has been almost impossible "to get the schools to agree on what materials should be selected for such a course."

CHAPTER VI

General Comments

THE COMMUNITY ORGANIZER AND HIS ASSOCIATES

1. The individuals who are directly involved in determining the policies of a communal project and who make the major functional and administrative decisions are a selected body of people serving either through election or designation as representatives of larger constituencies. For that reason they are persons of status and prestige (whether actually members of the controlling power structure of the community or serving with the acquiescence or as the surrogates for the controlling group). Similarly the professionals and technicians of the associated agencies and groups are likely to have considerable status. (It is perhaps for this reason that the area and neighborhood councils are suggested as desirable initial placements and for field training, since sub-groups of this type are alleged to consist of persons of more modest prestige and status, and therefore presumably make an easier setting for an inexperienced and insecure worker.)

2. The personal views and reactions of the body of individuals with whom the community organization worker is associated have usually been the determining factors in his selection and the selection of other staff members. A conscious effort by the placement agency to change views that may not be conducive to the selection of the best qualified personnel may frequently be needed. The school of social work cannot compromise with the attitudes of employers which are not conducive to the best standards of practice, and the factors entering into such attitudes will need to be analyzed.

3. The place of the professional worker in the community setting and the nature of his acceptance will be determined by the

worker's ability to develop constructive relationships with his volunteer and professional associates which rest solidly on his professional qualities and attributes. (Where his acceptance and his relationships may have been conditioned initially by his personality and temperament or by other extrinsic factors rather than his professional abilities, these qualities may have only transitory effects.)

4. Genuine acceptance and respect will be determined by the qualities of the knowledge, values and skills which the worker possesses. In the long run it is the sincerity and professional dedication which the worker brings to the task, rather than his likable personality which determines the extent to which the individual is accepted by the group. Maturity is also important, but it is a maturity of judgment, not chronological age. (The latter frequently is mistaken for the former.)

5. The worker on a reciprocal basis must have the quality of being able to accept his associates for their assets of participation in the group process and to work with them as they are, recognizing that it is his responsibility to help them grow toward a community approach and point of view if these are initially lacking or undeveloped.

THE CONSULTANT'S GENERAL CONCLUSIONS

In our attempts to define the scope and limits of community organization in the field of social welfare, we must be on guard against the dangers of developing a frame of reference that is too restricted or too static as well as one too broad or too amorphous. Because of a desire to sharpen concepts perhaps the greater risk at this time is the tendency toward limitation and restriction. Social work, if it is to remain as a vital part of our developing social institutions, needs to be able to relate its functions both to the changing aspects of society and to the changing conceptions of what constitutes the essentials of individual well-being. Social work today must seek alignment with the tendencies in our collective life that are striv-

ing to achieve an ever-increasing standard of well-being for the entire population.

Some of the terms which have described the goals of social work as a problem-solving profession are becoming obsolete; they need to be revised in part and to take on expanded connotations. The terms most frequently used in the past have been "need," "disadvantaged," "underprivileged," "social dysfunction." They have applied largely to conditions growing out of poverty; the lack of minimum economic resources, the inability to secure medical care, the lack of proper educational or of normal leisure time facilities, family disorganization and breakdowns, lack of suitable parental care, physical and mental handicaps, and so on.

Today the concepts of what constitutes minimum standards of well-being extend to the total rather than only to the disadvantaged segment of the collectivity. It is based on the ability of the community to provide basic standards of service and maintain and advance those standards. What has been happening in the twentieth century is that the goals of social work, initially a philanthropic movement dealing with poverty, have become increasingly accepted as the responsibilities of the organized community rather than of exceptional idealistic and humanitarian individuals, religious denominations, or mutual aid or philanthropic groups. These initial goals of social work have become institutionalized as community functions involving practically the whole population in voluntary efforts or within a political structure inclusive of the entire population accepted as a government function. It is this latter development to which the term "welfare state" has been applied.

The major services that have been developed as accepted governmental functions are programs of education, health services, housing, medical and psychiatric care, cultural and leisure time provisions, economic assistance and economic security. The most important and fundamental change is the transfer to government of responsibility for the maintenance of a high level of material prosperity. It is no longer assumed to be the automatic result of the system of private economic enterprise. These newer functions

have been added to the older functions assigned to the state such
as enforcement of laws on social relationships, fire and police protection, maintenance of public sanitation, roads and highways and
national defense. There has been a steady growth in the standards
and in the extent of operations of both the older and the newer
state functions. The continuance of voluntary initiative on a large
scale under our business enterprise system which includes such
large areas as the production of goods and services for the market
should not obscure these enormous expansions of governmental
function.

Since many of the newer functions of government and of voluntary enterprise are undertaken with a goal of advancing social
welfare, it is not surprising that they involve procedures which
approximate social work methods and values which parallel those
of social work. Examples are programs for retirement or medical
care organized by labor unions for their members, with or without
the collaboration of industry; programs of public housing, public
health and veterans' care. These activities use organizing and administrative personnel with varied backgrounds of education and
experience. Social workers had a role in the initial promotion of
many of these programs and they may give casework or group work
services in some of them. If social workers are involved in their
administration, it is usually because of their special knowledge or
competence in casework and group work methods. Except in the
field of the public assistance, social workers as organizers and administrators are to be found only rarely in the newer governmental
and voluntary community welfare functions.

Social work, however, has an interest in these projects through
inclusion in interdisciplinary teams or exercised through such
instruments as community welfare councils, state welfare conferences and professional associations which use the processes of
stimulation and consultation. The social worker also acts as a member of a citizens group and through his professional association is
concerned with the broad field of social welfare. Councils and
conference bodies seek to develop intergroup and interagency

cooperation and planning, and in these ways participate in the process of community education.

The inference sometimes drawn from the preceding paragraphs is that the organization and administration of these varied aspects of the community welfare program call for professional and technical personnel whose preparation extends beyond the limits of what is generally defined as social work, and these must, therefore, be drawn from other disciplines. It would follow that the education of the organizers and administrators of large sections of the community welfare program can properly be undertaken by schools preparing specialists in public administration, public health, housing, and that such functions are not necessarily appropriate to a school of social work. (In a few instances some training programs have developed under the title of "School of Public Administration and Social Work." These are too recent for appraisal.)

I do not agree with the above position and believe that because of the origin, achievements, philosophy, aims and values, as well as the current interests of the profession, social work has a fundamental contribution to make to the organization, development and administration of a broad range of community welfare programs and services. I also believe that the development of the teaching of community organization in schools of social work potentially offers one of the most valuable and effective vehicles for developing basic values and standards for the broad field of the welfare services both under governmental and voluntary auspices.[1]

[1] See Donald S. Howard, "New Horizons for Social Work," in *The Compass* (November, 1947).

"The important new role for social work which I envisage involves the ability to analyze broad economic, social, physical, educational, and cultural aspects of work, national and community life; to appraise their effect upon the welfare of the men and women and children concerned; to ascertain ways in which these broad areas of life may better promote the well-being of individuals and communities; and to bring together the professions and resources needed to improve them. The whole, which would add up to a sort of social statesmanship, might be termed 'social organization' in that it would bring to the solution of broad social questions a combination of skills much as 'community organization' brings a defined group of skills to the solution of community problems.

Perhaps the best illustration of the kind of job for which I am saying social workers should have special competence is the position of Social Welfare Advisor in the

The suggestion is sometimes made that preparation of a professional staff for public administration and welfare programs under voluntary auspices be undertaken by a separate school of social work which would concentrate on the field of community organization rather than on other social work personnel.[2]

While there is some ground for this suggestion, I believe that there would be a considerable loss in the separation both to the fields of community organization and to that of casework and group work practice. However, if a school of social work wants to prepare community organization workers, a definite emphasis on this subject and development of curriculum and of teaching resources adequate to achieve the goal is necessary.

A broader perspective on the opportunities in the field as outlined by Howard is fundamental to aligning the program of a school of social work to the changing character of our communal welfare programs and services. It is not, however, necessary to attempt to encompass immediately all fields of public administra-

---

British West Indies as recommended by the West India Royal Commission of 1938–39.

Specific responsibilities of the Advisor, as outlined by the Commission, included: community and leisure-time services; land settlement and other rural services; social security services; care and protection of children and young persons; delinquency services; housing; industrial welfare services; investigation of social problems; responsibility for formulating a social welfare program; co-ordination and interlocking of public and voluntary services; stimulation of voluntary services and of voluntary assistance to public bodies; training of social workers, public and voluntary.

This is a far cry from casework or group work and, though related to community organization, goes considerably farther, approaching the social statesmanship which, in my opinion, offers social work unprecedentedly challenging opportunities."

[2] "If we were to have this sort of specialized emphasis on Community Organization, probably at least three schools would be needed, in view of the size of the United States. Probably a more feasible suggestion is that at least half a dozen schools, strategically located, should be strongly encouraged to develop adequate specializations in CO, along with their other training programs. At present, schools with definite CO specializations would include New York School, Ohio State, Boston College, and Michigan." (Dunham)

Dunham also refers to the experience of the Training Bureau for Jewish Communal Service which was an attempt at specialization for community organization and intergroup relations in the field of Jewish Welfare Services. The school was in operation for approximately five years and was discontinued in 1952. See "The Training Bureau for Jewish Communal Service," by Michael Freund— (mimeographed report available from the Office of the Council of Jewish Federations and Welfare Funds, New York. December, 1956).

tion and welfare services within one educational unit. A more *realistic and more adequate response* to the requirements of community organization *within what is currently accepted as professional social work* would be the direction that needs to be taken by curriculum planning at this time. Such an approach would be fruitful not only for the subject of community organization but for all of the other parts of the social work curriculum.

THE GOAL AND THE REALITY

The list of the knowledge, attitudes, abilities and techniques desirable for the practice of community organization in social work presented in this report would seem to be overly long and truly formidable. They are not easily attainable results, but are offered as the frame of reference and goal of the curriculum and the school program. There will be limitations of time and circumstance under the best of conditions that may make the actual results less than the aims set forth in the school prospectus. The quality of the student body, the extent to which the program is able to attract the most gifted individuals, the quality of the faculty and the support and encouragement of the university which sponsors the program will determine the extent to which the results may be able to approximate the objectives. It may be encouraging to remember that, as in any school, there will be outstanding as well as mediocre students being graduated, though all students have spent an equal amount of time and have had the same course of instruction. It is also well to remember that some teachers are more gifted and that some schools offering courses of the same length and of apparently similar content are more effective. If the frame of reference of attributes required for effective and socially useful results in community organization is generally applicable, it follows it should be applied to all the aspects of professional education—the selection of the student, the content and nature of the courses, the exposure of the student to the requirements of the field through his readings and study, observation and class discus-

sion, his field training and initial professional experience, the selection of the faculty and the kind of teaching methods.

What a school of social work needs to broaden and strengthen its program in community organization is more than the addition or substitution of one or more courses to a basic program that may have had outstanding success in preparing caseworkers and group workers. Without in any way depreciating the very important contributions to professional services that schools have made through their concentration on casework and the benefits to social work theory and practice deriving from such concentration, it must be recognized that some of the practices of the predominantly casework schools, the emphasis and content of the courses, the criteria for selection of students and other practices may be negative factors in developing the point of view, the basic philosophy and orientation, the criteria for student selection and the course content and course sequence that would provide the most promising curriculum for community organization. The following quotations illustrate this point of view.

1. SHORTCOMINGS IN THE CHARACTER OF THE GRADUATES OF SCHOOLS CONCENTRATING ON CASEWORK AND GROUP WORK AS SEEN FROM THE POINT OF VIEW OF A COMMUNITY ORGANIZER

The average social worker in casework and in group work has become separated from the whole area of involvement in social policy formation and implementation.

The average social worker in casework and in group work tends to separate himself from the distinctive community organization agencies, workers and programs . . . there is little understanding that a growing body of social welfare organization workers operate at times with the same ethical or philosophical basis that social work practitioners do, use similar methods and techniques of study diagnosis and treatment (plan of action) in a problem-solving context and call upon the same body of knowledge about human growth and development and dynamics of social process.

The average social worker in casework and group work does not recognize the responsibility for and the opportunities to bring to social welfare organization agencies and workers their identifications

of unmet community needs, whether with respect to total or partial gaps or inadequate coordination of existing services. (Newstetter and Schwartz)

2. DIFFERENCES IN ROLES

The role of the direct service worker and the community organization worker may be contradictory at times and a student who has to carry both roles simultaneously, or who is assuming a role contradictory to that of other staff, may be in a difficult position. The community organization worker, if conditioned by training in casework or group work, is faced with many temptations to "treat" a person or to do "group work" and must constantly be alert to the fact that those with whom he is working are not "clients." He must be helped to use his knowledge and understanding of individual behavior in different ways according to his role. (Barry)

3. STUDENT SELECTION

Some of the personality characteristics and motivations which are an asset in other social work specializations may not be particularly important in community organization. For example, a person with temperament and sensitivity suitable to a treatment role may not be well suited to community organization. In turn, some assets of value in a community organization worker may be frowned upon in the other specializations. Community organization jobs have an appeal to some that other fields of social work do not, and should be capitalized upon in recruitment.

I would have the schools reexamine their admission policies and select and encourage students to enter community organization who have the potentialities for acquiring these abilities and that flexible eductaional plans be arranged. (Barry)

4. ATTITUDE OF FACULTY

Some promising students who on admission expressed an interest in community organization were advised against such a choice and steered into other sequences.

Irrespective of the weight that can be placed on such observations and criticisms, they point up the need for considering the field of

community organization as a basic and important area requiring earnest attention on the part of schools of social work. I believe that sound programs of teaching can be developed in a number of schools depending on a willingness to experiment and a conviction that a measure of concentration on the need for social workers as organizers of community welfare programs would help to advance the aims and objectives of the profession of social work as a whole. It will not be an easy development; in part because of the complex of factors involved, in part because to be successful it may need to diverge to a considerable degree from some of the elements that have determined the successful development of education for case-work and group work that have been focused on the application of psychiatric and psychoanalytic concepts to social services for meeting individual and family problems. Education for community organization may need to add a plus factor of equal importance related to but not necessarily derived from these disciplines.

A FINAL NOTE

This report, considering the methods used, could not result in and is not a definitive report. It could only outline the opinions of the consultant and of the cooperators in the hope that these may serve not as guidelines but as stimulants to planning on the part of the schools and the profession of social work. Much earnest experimentation needs to be attempted if we want to make progress in the development of the profession of social work. A general observation that I should like to apply to characterize the current status of preparation for the practice of community organization both in the schools and in the field is that here, if anywhere, in social work there would appear to be little basis for complacency; there is perhaps also no reason for feelings of futility or frustration.

It would be redundant at this point to summarize the many conclusions which are to be inferred from or are stated in this report. It would also seem to be unnecessary to list the many areas of community organization practice and theory that are greatly in need

of systematic research on the part of the teachers and practitioners, or to urge the field to undertake experiments in widening the scope of training for a broader approach to the needs of community organization and of social welfare administration, or to make a plea for more fellowships, scholarships, internships and other urgently needed resources. If the current interest in the subject of community organization practice can be sustained and enlarged, the outlook is promising that many of these needs may be met within the next decade of social work history.

Appendix

Field Work Training in Community Organization

MILDRED C. BARRY

INTRODUCTION

Professional education has three essential ingredients, the student, the school and the practice setting. The quality of education is enhanced when all three are mutually compatible and competent.

Social work education has recognized the significance and inter-relatedness of each of these three parts. Progress has been made in work with students and in our programs in school and field. Admission procedures, with student selection based on carefully determined criteria, faculty advising and comprehensive evaluations of the student's progress indicate our concern about the student's potential capabilities and growth. Standardizing of curricula, increased educational requirements for faculties, application of basic socio-scientific knowledge to professional practice, emphasis on research, the growth of professional social work knowledge and improved teaching methods are evidence of the focal position and leadership taken by the schools. Careful selection of field practice agencies and field instructors, training courses for field instructors, conferences and other collaborative enterprises between school and field personnel, definition of educational goals, the place of practice experience, appropriate assignments and "working conditions," and careful evaluative procedures, are indications of the accepted educational role of the practice agency.

We have moved far in social work education toward fulfillment of this partnership. Instructors in class and field share a common body of professional knowledge and have common educational

goals for the student. The student can rely upon the mutual compatability of his two types of instructors and, if he has the capacity and will, can receive a comprehensive, integrated educational experience which will enable him to become a professional social worker.

Unhappily, the community organization specialization within social work has not made as much progress. The inadequacies occur in all three parts—the student, the school and the practice setting. In brief, there are no generally accepted criteria for student admission to this specialization; there is no clearly defined content or course sequence commonly accepted by instructors in school and field, among instructors from different schools nor by the general social work faculties. Furthermore, there is little conceptual communication between the school faculties and the community organization practitioners. The situation is perhaps aggravated because the schools, with their historical preoccupation with casework and their slow, reluctant acceptance of group work (achieved finally when group work became sufficiently "individually oriented" and "psychiatrically oriented") have not generally taken leadership in developing the theoretical content of this specialization. Nor have the agencies taken leadership, as did the old Charity Organization Society and others since, in pushing educational institutions to develop the community organization specialization. In fact, they have slowed the process by their employment practices and their reliance upon apprenticeship training. The picture is further complicated by the apparent overlapping or indistinction between community organization in social work and the organizing techniques and goals of other occupational groups.

Currently, through the Council on Social Work Education and the National Association of Social Workers, substantial efforts are underway to standardize this specialization.

This working paper deals with field practice in community organization. But, as indicated, field practice—or education in the practice setting—cannot be divorced from the total educational goal commonly shared by school, field agency and student. The fact that these goals are not yet clearly defined nor commonly accepted

(as can be readily ascertained by reviewing course outlines and field work programs submitted by various schools) presents a decided limitation to a discussion of field practice. Therefore, we must recognize this basic limitation as we attempt to develop objectives of field work training in this field. Perhaps the best we can do, at this stage, is to suggest some general objectives and present some of the obstacles which need to be overcome in order to achieve our over-all educational goal.

The following remarks are based on the assumption that community organization is equated with casework and group work as a specialization within social work, that it calls for the same generic body of knowledge and skill, that it has its own defined process or methodology which is an integration and generalization of its many parts and is transmissible to students through education. Our assumption is that emphasis is upon professional education rather than upon teaching a series of skills.

We now wish to suggest some general educational objectives, present a case example, point out some of the practical obstacles and offer some suggestions as to how our objectives can be met.

EDUCATIONAL OBJECTIVES OF FIELD PRACTICE IN COMMUNITY ORGANIZATION

We submit the following general objectives without elaboration.

1. The focus of teaching in the field as well as in the classroom should be upon "how to practice community organization" as differentiated from such specifics as "how to staff a committee," "how to run a campaign," "how to be a group work council secretary." This does not imply that these latter "hows" should not be learned but rather that they are learned in the context of the total process.

2. The field practice should be a testing ground (a) where generalized knowledge can be particularized and theory put into practice, and (b) where abilities, which are necessary or desirable attributes of the community organization worker, are developed and tested.

3. Opportunity should be provided so that the skills commonly needed by the community organization worker in a variety of settings are learned or perfected and their differential or appropriate use understood.

4. The practice setting should be appropriate and conducive to learning. The function of the agency should be compatible to this area of practice. There should be qualified supervision, careful evaluation, suitable assignments, reasonable "work" arrangements.

5. The student should be qualified or suitable to the practice agency, ready and able to profit by the field work experience and with a prognosis that he can be expected to achieve professional competence in the field.

6. The educational goal for the particular student should be clearly defined and the field work program developed to fulfill this objective.

CASE EXAMPLE

The following illustrates some of the practical problems which we must work out in order to achieve our objectives.

Student X applied for advanced work in community organization. He was a graduate of a school of social work with a group work major and had completed several years experience as a group worker in a community center doing some community extension work. He was interested in services to the aging and a plan was worked out for him to have field practice in the Department on Aging of a Community Welfare Council with the department director as his field instructor.

Certain limitations were recognized at the outset. Office facilities were inadequate, the director's work load made long, uninterrupted and frequent conferences practically impossible, the student's limited community organization experience and course content gave little clue to the level of practice.

The student was intelligent, eager to learn, verbally accepting of the limitations. His ethnic background, his lack of knowledge of the city and its locale, the worker-client nature of his social work relationships in previous practice, were recognized. His former

school and work experience was reported as creditable. Reference and interview data indicated he could relate well to people and to community groups, that he could handle a heavy load, was imaginative and enterprising. His educational goal was not clear; he thought he might want to teach or do community planning.

The field practice plan was for an initial period of orientation to the community, the council, the department and the field of aging through reading, visits, observation and staff conferences. Attendance at committee meetings was accompanied by information about the committee assignment, individuals and the committee process. Procedures for analysis of observation were developed. Then followed specific work assignments as a part of a larger project. These involved office details, personal and telephone contacts with individuals and organizations in the community, preparation of reports. In addition, preliminary work, preparatory to staffing a committee, was started.

At school the student took no community organization course although later a plan for individual instruction was arranged.

The student did not make the grade. Some of the reasons were:

a. He could not relate to the many different types of persons with whom he came in contact, including other professionals but particularly lay persons of high socio-economic status. He attributed this to lack of a defined, acceptable role. This was a factor but less significant than his personality pattern and his lack of social mobility.

b. His work accomplishment lessened as the weeks passed. He was frustrated by the lack of "real" jobs to perform, yet each successive assignment was more poorly accomplished. This was accompanied by a retreat from "doing" to contemplation of theoretical and analytical material.

c. He had difficulty focusing upon the "problem" as it was in time and place (in the particular community, with the existing groupings, structure, readiness, and so on) and upon possible approaches or solutions to it in view of all the pertinent factors. His security lay in attempting to transplant other familiar patterns to this situation.

d. There was little correlation between classroom content and field practice. He lacked the support of theoretical content and the field instructor was not in a position to teach him this basic knowledge.

e. He became increasingly demanding of the field instructor's time, genuinely wanting help but unable to accept his limitations.

This experience was detrimental to the student. It was difficult, time consuming and unproductive for both the school and the agency. However, it served to clarify the importance of evaluating the student and the agency in relation to their suitability to each other, to the readiness and goals of the student, educational objectives and the practical limitations within the agency setting.

In this case, efforts were made to work out a good plan between agency and school and to develop appropriate assignments. These proved inadequate. Not enough attention was paid to admission procedures, to correlation of class and field content, to agency limitations.

OBSTACLES

We wish to present several queries which point up some of the obstacles to providing good educational experience in field practice for community organization students. We shall also suggest a few considerations and principles which might be helpful in arriving at answers.

Query 1. Can a student be given a real job to do that will test his community organization practice?

In the case example above the student and the school were pushing for more meaningful, responsible assignments, yet the agency could not risk giving these to the student. The student appeared uncomfortable in this non-sectarian community-wide agency and expressed fearfulness of high status persons.

We suggest the following considerations.

a. The greater the importance of the agency, the status of the persons and organizations involved, the seriousness of the problems and the risk of failure, the less likelihood of delegating the task, or even a part of it, to a student. Probably no student, no matter how

well qualified, could staff a committee of top rank business executives or professional men. An older, more experienced student might staff a committee of agency executives and possibly second or third level "lay" persons on a non-controversial committee. A young, inexperienced student, no matter how potentially capable, would have difficulty staffing any committee under the aegis of a city-wide (or broader scope) agency but might be able to on a neighborhood basis.

b. Personal as well as professional characteristics of the student have a bearing on the assignment given. In general, and assuming the student's personal and professional ability to relate to people, the more socially mobile student fits into more settings than the student who is only adjusted to his own socio-economic group.

c. The ability to adjust to changing roles and relationships is significant. A student who needs a defined and well described role in order to function comfortably tends to be unsuited to the constantly changing roles and relationships and to the absence of clearly understood and defined roles in community organization.

d. Specialized knowledge and the ability to use and communicate it have a bearing because the status given by the knowledge compensates for the inexperience and "low" status of the student. For example, a student with previous experience and knowledge of group work or of a subject such as "delinquency prevention" can contribute this knowledge and gain status and acceptance thereby. But if this knowledge can only be transmitted through professional vernacular and thus communication is limited, the effectiveness is lessened.

e. The time factor is a limitation. Committee meetings, conferences and interviews often have to be called at the convenience of community persons involved. A student's limited schedule makes this flexibility difficult. The uncertain rate of progress and unanticipated complications make it likely that a job assignment may take less or more time than scheduled and may bunch in particular periods. The period of the school term may not coincide with the anticipated or actual length of the project. Transfer of job assignments to another person is difficult.

Knowledge content required, that is not merely subject matter but knowledge of community, people, structure, related problems and activities and developments, takes time to acquire and students usually do not have sufficient length of time to carry responsibility for a total, or completed project of major significance. Even a full time, experienced worker may need several months to "get going," particularly if community, agency and/or subject are unfamiliar.

The interrelatedness of any one activity to other activities in the department or agency call for staff conferences and other means of coordination. This is valuable experience but also presents a time factor.

f. An assistant role, particularly in the beginning, offers a chance for actual experience with opportunity to develop relationships and test practice, with less risk of failure for the student or jeopardy to the job. This gives the field instructor opportunity to direct and observe. Moreover, it is recognized by others as a learning role consistent with a student's educational objective. However, it does not give the student as much opportunity to do a job on his own or to test his skills.

We might conclude that

1. The student's "level" must be balanced against the agency (or subdivision) level and against the job level and, where there is not too much divergence, a realistic job assignment is possible.

2. Progression from an inactive, observant role, through an assistant role, to a role of supervised responsibility offers both learning and testing opportunity for the student while providing safeguards to the agency.

3. Time limitations may make it impossible to assign a major project to the student; however, a minor project or a part of a major project can be a meaningful learning experience if the student sees the part in relation to the whole process. This can be accomplished through observation, attendance at meetings, staff conferences, reading of reports and minutes, and interviews. It is of primary importance, however, for the field instructor to correlate these experiences and to relate them to theoretical content.

Query 2. Can a student be given a meaningful community or-

ganization field practice experience in an agency whose major function is direct service?

a. The first consideration is whether there is a clear understanding and differentiation, on the part of the agency and field instructor, between process and skills. If the agency merely offers the student an opportunity to practice some of the same skills or methods which are used in the community organization process but, without opportunity to engage in and understand that process, then the practice is questionable. If the distinction is not understood the learning may even be detrimental.

Referring to the case example, the student indicated that he had practiced community organization and he referred specifically to work with committees and to the development of an extension program of an agency. Part of this undoubtedly was community organization but working with a committee or organizing a new club is not necessarily community organization. We could as well assume that interviewing is casework.

b. The field instructor should be competent to instruct the student in community organization. The fact that the field instructor may be a participant in a community planning activity does not necessarily mean that he is knowledgeable about or competent to teach this specialization.

c. Participation in community planning is not synonymous with doing community organization. If, for example, the student represents the agency on an interagency council he is a participant in the process but not the worker engaged in community organization practice. The experience can have positive learning values but the distinction must be understood.

d. The role of the direct service worker and the community organization worker may be contradictory at times and a student who has to carry both roles simultaneously, or who is assuming a role contradictory to that of other staff, may be in a difficult position. One of the most confusing assignments in this respect is that of leader of an interclub council in a group work agency if it is assumed that the assignment is community organization practice. Presumably the goal of the agency is to help its members either

individually, through the group or through the intergroup. The interclub council leader keeps this goal uppermost in his mind. In community organization the primary goal is not service to the individual, or treatment, nor is it for the purpose of serving the particular intergroup (although one would hope that such services would occur as by-products). The individuals and groups involved have a purpose outside or beyond themselves. While admittedly the line of demarcation is not always clear in practice, the distinction is important in theory and in the learning situation. The community organization worker is faced with many temptations to "treat" a person or to do "group work" and must constantly be alert to the fact that those with whom he is working are not "clients." He must be helped to use his knowledge and understanding of individual behavior in different ways according to his role.

e. There are many experiences within a direct service agency that contribute to knowledge about community organization and its practice. These include such experiences as learning about services, experiencing different patterns of relationships, trying new roles, being exposed to community problems, and practicing various skills.

We might conclude that

1. Direct service agencies can offer experiences which are of value to the community organization student but usually the opportunities for practicing community organization are limited.

2. Where such field placements are made, the field instructor should be well enough versed in community organization practice to distinguish the direct service practice from the community organization practice, to help the student to be able to transfer common skills appropriately, and be particularly skillful in differentiating and relating the theoretical content of the various specializations involved.

Query 3. Are the requirements for admission to the community organization specialization realistic from the point of the field?

This question is pertinent to a discussion of field practice because an agency will be much more willing to expend time and

money on an interested and potentially good practitioner than on a person who is either a "reject" from another specialization or who is groping for his proper niche.

a. Many schools recognize the factor of maturity and experience in admitting persons to the community organization specialization. These are important factors but equally significant are certain personality traits, capabilities and attitudes.

b. Some of the personality characteristics and motivations which are an asset in other social work specializations may not be particularly important in community organization. For example, a person with temperament and sensitivity suitable to a treatment role may not be well suited to community organization. In turn some assets of value in a community organization worker may be frowned upon in the other specializations. This assumes, of course, that the student has the qualifications essential to generic social work practice.

c. Characteristics such as social mobility, ability to relate to others quickly and to communicate easily, satisfactions in high pressure or tension situations, comfortableness in new and changing activities and roles, pleasure in activity, are assets to a community organization practitioner if his personality is sufficiently well integrated so that they are kept in control and balance.

d. Community organization jobs have an appeal to some that other fields of social work do not, and should be capitalized upon in recruitment.

We suggest that:

1. Faculties in school and field review admission qualifications and procedures with some of these factors in mind.

2. Different practice levels be developed so that potentially good students, with different levels of previous experience, can be placed.

Query 4. How much education or experience in casework and/ or group work should a student have before entering community organization?

We might consider the following:

a. Direct service, or practicing casework or group work, helps

the worker know people and know services. Much of a community organization worker's job is in relation to direct service agencies and he must be knowledgeable about their work. But of more importance, he must learn how to work with people, and how to use himself in working with people. The raison d'etre for community organization in social work is people and the focus must be upon them and their needs. A student can best learn these things through direct service. It is important that he become a social worker first and a community organization worker second.

b. Community organization practice is, by nature, advanced practice, and it is difficult to find good beginning jobs either during the educational experience (field practice) or in the labor market. Even if the jobs are found the quality of practice is limited if the preparatory experience and training in social work has been fragmentary.

c. Shifting from casework and/or group work to community organization, either after one year of professional education or after graduation and work experience, has its limitations. One year in casework or group work is not sufficient for qualified professional practice in these fields, nor is it sufficient experience as a basis for practice in community organization. Without doubt a third year in community organization is the best answer but the problem is that many cannot afford a third year and, to date, have not needed it to get jobs.

This writer has for some time advocated a third year for community organization preparation. However, it is recognized that this has excluded many potentially good community organization practitioners from the field and that it has perpetuated or even extended the current practice of employing personnel untrained in community organization.

Perhaps more varied and flexible plans need to be developed. The following possibility is suggested which is not original nor entirely satisfactory but appears to offer the most advantages.

1. A third year community organization specialization with prerequisites being two years education in casework or group work and (a) experience either prior to or after the two-year schooling, or

(b) exceptional aptitudes, or (c) experience in related professions, or (d) content in class and field during the two-year training which gives some preparation and tests aptitudes and readiness for community organization. The third-year specialization should be in an agency engaged in doing community organization.

2. A two-year course (for carefully selected students) which would provide, during the second year, class content in both community organization and the direct service specialization) casework or group work) and field practice in the direct service agency, focused not on more intensive treatment, but upon administration, community activities, opportunities to participate in intergroup situations and so forth.

Such field placement might provide a student in casework, for example, with some "advanced cases" but also with opportunity to observe and participate in interagency meetings or other intergroup situations, contacts with lay boards or committees, limited job assignments which will develop skills. Preparation and presentation of data in correct, concise and clear form is an important skill which can be developed. Essential to such practice would be field instruction competent to differentiate, relate and develop knowledge and practice for these two specializations.

The second alternative should be designed for the exceptional student or the one, not particularly interested in casework or group work, whose interest and competence fits him for community organization. Caution should be taken, however, to insure against admitting those who are not really suited to practice social work in any form.

This may be the place to inject the thought that all social work students should be selected for the broad field rather than for a particular specialty. This is consistent with the theory that curriculum content should be broad. Upon this generic base the specializations are developed. To those specializations persons with specific interests and aptitudes are attracted. Unless the field of social work and the education for it is broad enough to attract those who wish to engage in community organization, administration social action and the like in contra-distinction to direct serv-

ice or treatment, we will discourage admission of those who look forward to practicing community organization and, furthermore, we will encourage the employment of untrained people in this field.

Query 5. Is it possible to develop recording procedures that are both meaningful and practicable?

Certainly we shall have to develop better methods of student recording in community organization. Records are invaluable supervisory aids and can be particularly beneficial in focusing upon particular content. The difficulties of recording in this field are obvious. One device is to select certain aspects or parts of the process for recording, such as "leadership," "interpersonal relations," "steps taken in determining need," and so on. However, the difficulty is to keep the total in perspective.

We suggest the following:

1. School and field should continue to work together to develop meaningful recording procedures.

2. Recording should be synchronized with classroom content so that the student can relate what he is seeing or doing to what he is studying in class.

Query 6. How can community organization workers (competent as practitioners) become qualified to teach community organization in the field (as field instructors)?

If one accepts the assumption that school and field should agree on content and should work as partners it is essential that field instructors know class content and that school personnel know practice. Some sharing of knowledge and experience appears necessary. However, the time element is a factor. Few community organization workers have time for training courses. Their daily tasks mitigate against deep conceptualized thinking. Many community organization co-workers come from other specializations and their frame of reference is *that* specialization rather than community organization. They may tend to be more comfortable when talking about specific functions or specific skills rather than community organization process.

Sometimes school faculties, well versed in professional "lingo"

tend to frighten away the practitioner. Frankly community organization workers have had to learn to "talk English" again. They
become less and less accustomed to conversing in professional social work terminology and the problem is accentuated in a specialization in which they are not trained. The chasm created by
lack of common understanding and agreement on theoretical content of the community organization process, coupled with difficulties of language, may be hard to bridge. And I suspect the
professor, in turn, may be overwhelmed by the action-motivated
community organization workers.

Perhaps both groups will have to find time and means for meeting together and bridging these gaps and from this will come a
common agreement about community organization content and
about how best to teach this content in class and field.

Query 7.   How can agencies engaged in doing community organization become more willing to invest time and money in
developing field practice programs?

Among the reasons why social agencies develop field work programs and contribute time and money to them are: (a) service to
the profession and the field, (b) source of future staff, (c) substitution for on-the-job training, (d) status or indication of achievement
of standard, (e) staff supplementation.

Currently none of these reasons stacks up as being too important
to many agencies doing community organization with the possible
exception of the first. Why?

Few students upon graduation from a two-year course are ready
for available staff positions and thus are not a source of immediate
recruitment. Education in the community organization specialization has not yet proved itself a good substitute for on-the-job training. Many of these agencies are relatively high status in the community and probably measure status in ways other than association
with schools of social work. Also the community's criteria for judging achievement may not coincide with those of the school so the
agency, working with and for the community, is likely to accept its
criteria. Generally, students take more time from staff than they
contribute as staff members.

Against this reality situation is pitted service to the profession and the field. This can weigh heavily but probably will not unless the profession emphasizes its importance and unless there is evidence that education will produce more and better workers than have been produced under former systems.

The various queries and comments suggested in this paper have bearing upon this point. Of course, in the long run the quality of the graduates themselves will determine the investment that agencies will make. Then, in turn, agencies will require training and will help provide it.

A SUGGESTED APPROACH

Obstacles should not deter us. When community organization practitioners are in such demand, we should be imaginative and enterprising enough to find solutions to our problems and act aggressively. Unfortunately this writer does not have the solutions but does wish to suggest an approach.

First, I suggest that we throw overboard the traditional lists of assignments and activities which the community organization student is expected to have in his field practice. These tend to perpetuate the emphasis on techniques and skills. I propose bringing them back later in their proper place.

Second, I would ascertain what abilities the community organization worker in any agency engaged in doing community organization should have or acquire. I submit the following ten "abilities" as a starter.

1. Ability to relate to people and to facilitate positive relationships among individuals and groups.

2. Ability to analyze a problem and see its potentials (including its difficulties, relation to scheme of things, possibilities of solution).

3. Ability to locate and utilize resources effectively (including human resources, studies, observations, and so on).

4. Ability to organize effective structure, such as a committee, and help it function.

5. Ability to understand and accept the reality of the situation and yet to see the potential for change.

6. Ability to handle oneself professionally, in many different roles, with various types of people, and to handle criticism and praise.

7. Ability to organize one's job, to work under pressures, to establish priorities in terms of time, intensiveness, and so on.

8. Ability to relate and differentiate the various situations within one's own job and, likewise, within the agency and the community.

9. Ability to fulfill and facilitate the agency's purposes and function and thus to perform skills necessary to the task (such as public relations, fact finding, budgeting, administration).

10. Ability and capacity to use knowledge, to apply theory to practice in an integrated way.

Third, I would have the schools reexamine their admissions policies and select and encourage students to enter community organization who have the potentialities for acquiring these abilities and that flexible educational plans be arranged.

Fourth, I would suggest that the schools be as careful in their selection of field practice agencies and field instructors for community organization as they are in the other specializations. In general, community organization field practice should be in agencies doing community organization.

Incidentally, it seems to me that area councils offer particularly well-suited placements if the worker is qualified as a field instructor, because they are less sophisticated, there is great diversity in program, the time factor is more manageable and more of the projects are within a student's capacities.

Fifth, it is important that the schools recognize the various time factors that beset agencies engaged in doing community organization. Perhaps a more efficient method of working with field instructors can be found; perhaps there can be greater flexibility in student schedules or assignments.

Sixth, both school and field should continue to work toward evolving meaningful and realistic records. The value of records in

supervision and teaching is recognized. Their focus can help the student integrate his learning.

Seventh, assignments should provide opportunity to develop skill in methodologies but should be constantly related to total process. Various learning methods should be used—reading, observing, recording, discussing, doing—and there should be greater and greater opportunities for participation and actual testing of theory through practice.

Eighth, the student should be evaluated as a social worker and then, more specifically, as a community organization worker rather than primarily as a technician or a specialist.

CONCLUSION

This working paper gives no answers. It has assumed a liberal definition of the term "objectives." It has treated the subject in brief, suggestive style rather than comprehensively.

Our major thesis has been that the *student* in community organization should be *taught* community organization, that the skills and methodologies which are utilized in that process are a part of his equipment and must be learned also but that he cannot practice professionally unless he knows why, when and how to utilize these skills. School and field share the responsibility for teaching; the content of their teaching and their educational goals must be compatible and developed together.

We have, throughout, made suggestions or drawn conclusions. Some of these will be concurred with, others challenged. Hopefully we could agree on the major thesis.

Practice Theory in Community Organization

GENEVIEVE W. CARTER

This paper is written with two general purposes: (1) To discuss theory building in community organization as a responsibility of the profession, and (2) to provide some examples of practice theory.

My comments are directed to practitioners, and, lest you are preparing for something which is not available on today's professional market, I hasten to advise you that I am not presenting a master theoretical scheme which will account for, or clarify, all social work community organization!

PART I

What is practice theory, and why are we concerned about it? What makes the professional social worker in community organization any different from the politician who is concerned with organizational processes in winning his election, or the PTA president who, with his constituency, stimulates and develops a community plan for a school dental clinic? *Both* the politician and the PTA president are sensitive to human relationships, make use of principles of involvement, and use successful previous experience in working with people to guide them in their actions. It is no longer sufficient to say that the community organizer has a two-year master's and the PTA president or the politician does not. We must be able to explain the difference in terms of the "doing" or the activities in the community organization process. Two other aspects are highly important—the social work profession clearly and unequivocally *must* provide the necessary sanction and at the same time develop a public image of the social work community organizer as a social worker—and second, community organization specialists

must, through their own interest and energies, work toward professionalization of community organization practice. There is false reasoning here, for we are inclined to believe that because we have had professional training, whatever we do in practice makes our activities professional. It is not enough to say that a profession must be communicable; it must have something to communicate—shared values of the profession, understandings about the phenomena with which we deal, knowledge (of different levels) which can guide one's action and account for causes and consequences, and skills which can result in effective operations. It is really the latter, *effectiveness,* which eventually determines whether or not the social worker is hired for the job, or the politician or PTA president. It is the function of the profession to extend our knowledge so that our members may increase their understandings of what they are doing and how it should be done. It is through theory development that we acquire these professional understandings.

There are some who say that theory belongs in the sciences and that really it is not important for community organization practice. They say that a practice should be concerned with "the doing," and not with theory. Actually, there is no professional practice without theory. Every time a practitioner treats and controls he is operating upon some theory of the situation. He is making use of principles and concepts which he uses with consistency in similar situations. The unusual, intuitive worker may practice with effective results, but he has no principle for dealing with a new situation that he has not faced before, and will approach it on a trial-and-error basis. Practice which is based only on experience is slow to adjust to a changing environment in this rapidly changing world. Theory, on the other hand, is lightfooted. Principles based on practice theory or research theory can be adapted to changing circumstances, can devise fresh combinations and possibilities, and can peer into the future. Theory and principles become communicable, and this is an important characteristic in distinguishing a profession from the skills of the politician and the PTA president.

In the application of professional method, the worker draws

from his storehouse of explanatory concepts and guiding principles, which he brings to bear in decision-making as he individualizes each situation. The concept he uses next depends upon the resulting reaction to the last activity. Because of this skill in discernment as to what he applies next in relation to where the situation is, the community organization worker becomes an integral part of the relationship process. The professional brings with him a wide range of practicing concepts because of the infinite variety of situations to be met. That is why the standard recipe or bag of tricks will never work as a substitute for professional method. In my way of thinking, the distinguishing difference in the practice of the professional and non-professional will be found in those elements and points of decision-making where the worker brings his theory, or his range of concepts, to bear on a particular situation in guiding his choices of action. For example, a workshop experience can provide helpful training on how to conduct a committee meeting. The participant may learn a sequence of actions which will work for the so-called typical committee meeting. He learns steps one, two, and three for a particular committee situation. The professional, hopefully, has a wide range of concepts or *kinds* of steps to take, and as the committee situation changes or differs he makes conscious choices, and adapts his next steps to the dynamics of the situation. I think the best way we can say it is something like this: Greater professional skill and practice means a broader range of theoretical concepts, or depth and clarity in conceptual understanding, and more precise discrimination in decision-making processes where choices of action take place.

We should say a word about distinguishing theory building as the essence of the scientific method and theory building which may emerge from good practice. There is a mistaken notion that theory building takes place entirely within the laboratory or through the rigorous application of scientific method, using ingenious observational devices or complex interview instruments. In a developing profession such as social work, most of the processes in theory development will necessarily take place outside of the laboratory situation, but (we know) controlled conditions are possible.

Practice contributes to theory building in two ways: One, through the ordering of experiences from practice and by conceptualization of these practices. This helps us to identify the important hypotheses to be tested through research methods. The second important function played by practice is at the point of verifying theory derived from research through pragmatic application in practice situations. Research-validated theory is never entirely validated until it is tested in practice situations and we find it actually does guide and improve our practice operations. This constitutes a reflexive or circular sequence through which practice theory flows. I think of theory development as a spiral, circular in its progress, but moving upward toward knowledge which more nearly represents truth.[1]

Perhaps the most sensible way to view knowledge about our profession is to recognize there are levels or degrees of "knowing." Ask the community organization practitioner if he knows what he is doing in preparing for his meeting of the neighborhood planning council, and he will retort with a, "Naturally, I know." And he does know—from his professional training, his years of experience, his analysis of his professional activities, and his study of relevant literature from the social science storehouse of knowledge.

Community organization knowledge, and consequently its theory base, can be considered in five levels which constitute the spiral-like process of theory-building.

THE EXPERIENCE LEVEL

Through many experiences, the community organizer generalizes from his successes and failures, and applies these notions consciously to new situations or similar situations. This builds pieces

---

1 The writer wishes to acknowledge the help received from the Gordon Hearn manuscript, *Toward Theory Building in Social Work* (now in publication by the Harry M. Cassidy Memorial Research Fund of the University of Toronto) which has contributed to advance and clarify the processes in social work theory building. The reader is also referred to: Ernest Greenwood, "Social Science and Social Work—A Theory of Their Relationship," in *Social Service Review*, Vol. 29, March, 1955; Genevieve W. Carter, "Theory Development in Social Work Research," *Social Service Review*, Vol. 29, March, 1955; and Genevieve W. Carter, "Comments," *Social Service Review*, Vol. 30, September, 1956, p. 257.

of theory as to why *this* or *that* technique works best. Practice theory is the abstraction which describes or accounts for the practice and makes it possible to communicate it to others. Community organization also draws from social science theory, particularly from sociology and social psychology. For instance, the community organizer may be interested in the concept of integration, as so well discussed in Murray Ross' new book, *Community Organization—Theory and Principles*. The community organizer will try to understand this concept in terms of his experience, testing out whether or not it helps him understand his operations. The community organizer's interest is in what works at the operational level. The experienced community organizer has had layers and layers of these experiences, and, for his own case of operations, he has extracted from these years of experience the kinds of activities that have brought satisfaction and results. He is able to say: "In this kind of a situation, these kinds of things seem to work." At this level he may not have explicated this rationale for the *why* or the *cause* of the successes. In fact, it may even be something else that goes along with the situation that makes it work rather than the particular action he has identified as the cause of the success. Our best examples of experience in existing literature are found in community organization case records or in descriptions of community organization projects.[2]

SYSTEMATIC EMPIRICAL INQUIRY

At this level we begin consciously to sort out and identify elements in the situation which bring about *this* or *that* result. Studies of professional practice, the pooling of experiences through group discussions, and the preparation of papers such as the three papers published last year under the Council on Social Work Education,[3]

[2] As one example, the writer has in a Prentice-Hall publication a section which gives an account of a community organization project resulting in service for transient men in the Los Angeles area.

[3] Violet M. Sieder, "What is Community Organization Practice in Social Work?" Mildred C. Barry, "Assessment of Progress Made by Community Organization in Identifying Basic Concepts and Methods for Utilization in Social Work Education" in *Community Organization in Social Work*. Council on Social Work Education, New York, 1956.

or the occasion which brings us together today, are the means by which we begin to bring order from our practice experiences which have prospects of leading into the development of practice theory. Sometimes we call this "wisdom-level" research, for lack of a better term. At any rate, it is spade work necessary to explicate practice theory, concepts, or theory fragments, which we can put on the "professional" table to examine further. "Descriptive level" research of committee member roles, or studies which clarify worker activities, are further examples.

CONCEPTUALIZATION

Another level of theory building activity is conceptualization, wherein one invents new concepts or schemes which, in a way, serve as a working hypothesis. None of us at this time can come out with something on the grand scale, such as Freud's revolutionary contention that much of behavior is motivated by unconscious impulses, but in our own primitive way we can begin to nibble around the edges. Conceptualizing involves the ability to see the enterprise as a whole; it includes recognizing where various functions or relationships depend upon one another; how changes in any one part affect all the others; and perceiving the significant elements in a situation. It is a unifying, coordinating, integrating kind of activity that pulls together a number of relevant but different situations in a meaningful whole.

VERIFICATION BY SCIENTIFIC METHOD

This is a fourth type of activity which may be carried on empirically, experimentally, or by logical inference, but always within the framework of scientific method. This constitutes our research-tested theory. One may point to an example in social casework in the work of Lillian Ripple of the Chicago Research Center,[4] where practice theory regarding client motivation is being tested through scientific or research methods. In turn, research findings affect practice theory in worker use of motivation. To my knowledge, we

[4] Lillian Ripple, "Motivation, Capacity, and Opportunity as Related to the Use of Casework Service," *Social Service Review*, Vol. 29, June, 1955, and follow-up.

have no comparable example in community organization in social work, but as a possibility first experiences of community top leadership in health and welfare activities would be amenable to research, since we have some theoretical notions about these first contacts.

PRACTICE TESTING

This last activity completes our cycle and leads the way for the whole process to begin again. Research-tested theory will point out implications for practice, where, in turn, practice, through demonstrations or experiments, tries out the new theory. Now we are back again at the experience level, and we develop new hypotheses as to those elements which did not work or which were not helpful in guiding practice.

PART II

EXPERIENCE LEVEL THEORY

Practice experience results in observations which at first are on a trial-and-error basis. For instance, I have noticed what happens when new groups meet around some community problem, or in more experienced groups when the problem is new. In such instances, the members insist on going through what I call a "directory of agencies phase." The newly formed neighborhood council wants a directory of agencies for their geographic locale. The downtown council group begins to tackle a new problem, or perhaps such a directory was made last year but it seems to make no difference—they still want to go through a getting-acquainted period with each other and with all the services. If the worker is process-focused and not pushed by circumstances into a direct goal objective, this initial phase is necessary in order to develop the working relationships needed for more complex problems to follow. I have found this need for the "directory level experience" especially important in small communities or in neighborhood planning groups. I have also observed my mistakes of trying to skip

this beginning phase because I assessed the group level through some of the competent individuals I had known in other experiences, rather than evaluating this particular group's functioning level.

Without going into the details of intervening experiences and steps, let us suppose I take these understandings from practice experience and, through conceptualization of these various ideas, invent a new term, a construct which I name *cumulative sequence*. Cumulative sequence then becomes a shorthand symbol for the learnings of experience that have been ordered into usable principles to guide future practice situations. I can explain cumulative sequence by the following: It is similar to readiness, for the sequence of selected past experiences prepares for the acceptance of the next. The new experience of group or committee becomes meaningful as it benefits from what has gone before. New committees want to experiment, to build trust, develop relationships with a subject area or problem *where the stakes are not too high*. Such committees like to spread out discussion over a wide range in their first meetings, with scattered and often unrelated pieces. This has to happen before they can sort out the relevant pieces. If the worker or other members shut off the range too abruptly they will regress and make attempts to go back to this stage. They may spend what seems like unnecessary time on mechanics of seating, ventilation, or meeting dates. Such matters are also good neutral subjects and can contribute to process development without premature blocking of unclear content discussion or unhappy feelings.

To use an analogue (which is a tool in theory building), the idea of cumulative sequence is similar to life phases in childhood development. The orderly progression of satisfactory experiences in one phase builds the foundations on which the experiences of the next phase can accrue. Maladjustment occurs if a growth phase is shut out or if there is no satisfying next step in the sequence. Committees also can get their growth stunted and get bogged down in the initial phase, especially those where the third or fourth meeting still finds the committee discussing the mechanics of meeting dates and, "Now, just what is our function?" (As they walk down

the hall after the meeting, they say it plainer, "What a waste of time!")

This brief illustration will serve to illustrate how we can use our observations from practice to develop concepts and constructs which serve as theory fragments to guide our practice in community organization. The notion of cumulative sequence in planning committees can represent a whole array of experiences and ideas about the worker's role in recognizing the need for committees to build a sequence of experiences before they can satisfactorily tackle other problems requiring a higher level of committee integration. (It does not always result in a "directory," for the same purpose can be served in other ways.)

SYSTEMATIC EMPIRICAL INQUIRY

Let me first confess that the examples I am using under this heading are not the result of systematic empirical inquiry but represent a problem focus which could be investigated systematically by the busy community organizer on some of his free weekends. (This is by way of pointing out that I know of no community organization practitioner who has time freed for systematic inquiries of this nature!)

Work logs, time studies, or day sheet schedules may constitute the instrument for data collection which can reflect the day by day activities of the practice of the community organizer. Our purpose is to bring order and classification to the types of operations performed by the practitioner. The writer has analyzed pilot studies of several community organizers in social work settings, in an effort to identify the kinds of activities and sort out those which may be claimed as social work and those which are common to other professions.

There is always a guiding theory which directs the investigator in his data collecting and analysis.

The guiding theoretical notions were to the effect that social community organization work is not the gamut of everything that is done by the worker who fulfills his job requirements. Like casework or group work, the community organizer is applying a social

work method which results in a process sequence. The caseworker conducts other important activities which facilitate the casework method, which further the work of the agency, or which contribute to community welfare. But he knows when he is using casework method with a client and when he engages in a different order of activities, such as making a speech for the PTA or when he staffs an agency board sub-committee.

The community organizer is prone to build a halo of professionalism around *every* activity which he performs and to wrap all of these activities into a package which is given the over-all label of community organization method in social work. There is professional security in this line of thinking: "I am a professional social worker, doing community organization; therefore, everything I do, ipso factor, is achieved through the use of social work methods." There is a dangerous fallacy in that kind of logic which retards the job we need to do in clarifying the social work elements in community organization practice. For it is not "who" does it, but "what and how" it is done that must be explained.

It is more and more evident that the three social work methods are becoming interchangeable between the so-called specializations. Psychiatric caseworkers also work with group methods; group workers, on one hand, are providing more individualized services, and, on the other, are working with communities on neighborhood improvement projects.

Other examples could be cited, but as this trend develops, we are being pressed to identify the core elements in the social work method. If social community organization method is to be included in the social work family, it should share these common or core elements.

The following is posed as phases of social work method which reflect a configuration of elements common to all three of our methods.

1. *Social study and diagnosis of particular social conditions*
   We use the term *condition* because it can imply pathology needing corrective service, or a social condition which requires support or

further development. Social work has a stake in both pathology and prevention. Social study and diagnosis are professional activities because of the knowledge, skill and techniques required in this discrimination process. Social work at present has no typology representing the kinds of social conditions to which social workers address themselves. Our scope of operations, in general, is directed to those kinds of conditions concerned with man's improved relationship to his social environment.

2. Assessing and utilizing strengths in the situation

The social worker moves from study and diagnosis into a focus which selectively utilizes strengths and resources in a problem-solving process. This is a helping, enabling process which results from a guided professional relationship between worker-client, group or community segment. Assessing resources or strengths may be a part of the diagnostic phase but is viewed separately because the voluntary participation client or group is so essential. Resources or strengths plus diagnosis plus the potential of the worker's role contribute to the setting of goals or objectives. In social work we would expect a high degree of self-determination in the goal setting.

3. Modification or change

Social work method, hopefully, brings about change in a given social situation. This change is directed to some defined social work goal. This concept of change is always relevant for the particular situation, while the tempo and degree of change will vary with the situation. Social change constitutes the end product of our social work methods, and the *means* by which it is brought about must be within the value system and the sanctions of the profession.

4. Evaluation of Change in relation to goals (accountability)

The client group or community group will evaluate the services of the social worker in terms of satisfaction or help. The community at large evaluates the results through its recognition of the role and place of the social work profession and through its support (both financial and through use) of the organized social services. Like other professions, service evaluation includes an obligation for accountability to the community as well as to the profession itself. There is responsibility beyond "worker-client" progress and welfare. The

social worker *accepts responsibility for the effect of his actions on total community welfare and interrelationship.*

Our philosophy may not clarify the profession's position on the "good life for man" or the "good life for society" which we try to achieve through professional methods and other activities, but the worker's professional equipment should include some sort of image of the "good life" which affects his use of professional methods.

Now, this set of four essential elements is posed for the purpose of identifying a core which each of the three social work methods should incorporate. If we could hold these essential elements as a screen *against our activities in community organization,* we might be able to differentiate the activities which can be clarified as the community organization method in social work. As mentioned earlier in this section of the article, this type of clarification could be done better through a systematic empirical inquiry rather than the few case records or pilot time studies from which these proposals are drawn. Within this limited source of "knowing," the following chart is presented as a tentative means of sorting out the community organization activities performed in a social work setting.

If one accepts the notions presented in the chart, he is limiting social work community organization method to project-centered activities, involving a problem-solving process, with recognizable "case" beginning and termination, and where the method incorporates the generic elements common to other social work methods. The activities are process-focused toward improved community integration as well as toward a self-determined social work goal. Fund raising, educational conferences, manipulation in power structure, public relations events, directed negotiation, marshalling forces for legislation, and similar activities are important and appropriate functions which are means for organizing the welfare resources of a community, but under the proposed definition these would be excluded as social work methods, *per se,* but not as legitimate social work practice functions.

CHART I

Community Organization Practice in Social Welfare [5]

Means	Ends
I. SOCIAL WORK COMMUNITY ORGANIZATION METHOD	**I**
Generic elements of the three social work methods $+$ Specialized elements of community organization	1. Change toward meeting health and welfare needs more adequately, and more cooperative and effective means of accomplishing these goals
II. OTHER MEANS	**II**
1. *Facilitating Processes* Administration—board development, budgeting, policymaking, and so on Supervision—formal and informal Other coordinating techniques	1. To facilitate communication, coordination, develop appropriate structure, controls, channels, intraagency, interagency, and intercommunity
2. *Educational Methods* Conferences, forums, workshops In-service training Interdisciplinary understandings and coordination Teaching, student field work Committee projects	2. Change in values, extend knowledge, gain understandings, professional improvement, informed citizen leadership, improved programs and service standards
3. *Research Methods* Research Systematic study Fact-gathering	3. To provide answers to questions posed, and to provide basis for decision-making and courses of action
4. *Social Action, Social Reform*	4. To effect changes in legislation, in social policy, and in community structure to meet social welfare needs
5. *Consultation*	5. Making knowledge, advice, experience available to others under their auspices and responsibility as they choose to use and implement
6. *Fund Raising* Recruiting and training leadership Developing campaign structure, methods, techniques Financial accounting to donor public	6. To provide money and leadership for health and welfare causes
7. *Publicity, Public Relations* Public information media, speeches, press, radio, TV	7. To develop the climate and understanding necessary for community support and interest in health and welfare programs
8. *Negotiation, Arbitration* Other strategy techniques	8. To effect strategic changes in community or agency power structure toward improved health and welfare programs

[5] Walter A. Friedlander, ed., *Concepts and Methods of Social Work* (Englewood Cliffs, N.J., Prentice-Hall, 1958), p. 226.

The total practice of a community organizer in social work may consist of a work load with a range of activities including three projects which are problem-centered and in which social work community organization method is the appropriate means for working with the community problem. The application of the method results in a process form with some observable phases as gleaned from experience and case records. The brief outline below explains this proposal:

A. *Reconnaissance Phase*

1. The intake period—exploration
2. Is problem feasible in view of community readiness and resources?
3. What is history of problem—who and why interested? What agency or community auspices are interested?

Problems appropriate for consideration

B. *Diagnostic Phase*

1. Formulation of problem focus
2. Prognosis for change to warrant investment
3. What structure is indicated? How will these relationships be initiated and developed?
4. What community segment is to be involved in the particular problem?
5. What are the sub-problems and issues within the problem focus? Priorities?
6. What facts or research are indicated?
7. Resources, strengths to be utilized

Problem is defined, ways and means are known

C. *Planning Phase*

1. Refinement in problem clarification
2. Structure is shaped to problem and committee needs
3. Change process is under way
4. New knowledge, shared experiences, interactions, new feelings and attitudes
5. Direction and goal more specified
6. Planning phase takes shape and course as situation requires
7. Change results already evidenced

Developmental period or project concluded—ready for termination

D. *Implementation Phase*

1. Implementation does not necessarily wait until completion of project
2. Agreements on change and what is to be implemented
3. Sorting out the "implementers" and vesting responsibility for change
4. If expected implementers not involved in process, how to reach
5. Continuing responsibility and priorities for recommended changes
6. Evaluation: (a) What social changes were brought about? (b) What improvement in community cooperation and relationships?

Like phases in any process form where a communicable method is applied, the detail of phases will vary according to the case situation and what is done about it, but the general outline is discernible. For instance, the scientific method of research when applied will take a process form of several recognizable, sequential steps, but these steps are not completely separate; they overlap.

Problem formulation may overlap into the second or third step, and in the last step, report writing, the problem may become most clear to the researcher.

In summary, what I am saying as this section is concluded is that orderly empirical inquiry is possible in social work community organization, but all that can be presented today is a direction for this type of inquiry, which, hopefully, will produce a level of knowing beyond the memories of the day's work experience.

CONCEPTUALIZATION

Conceptualization occurs at varying degrees in each of these proposed levels of knowledge about our social work specialization. At this point I am, however, referring to conceptualization as the primary activity in bringing order to an array of ideas, concepts, and professional experience. We can develop conceptual notions which can be illustrated through figures such as the client-worker interaction in a relationship field, or a figure which shows the flow and movement of a community problem. (Kurt Lewin was especially gifted in conceptual presentation.) There can be conceptual schemes which clarify and put into relationship a variety of relevant concepts. Ultimately, there can be the theoretical models. Because of the nature of social work data, our first attempt with models will be non-mathematical. A conceptual scheme can merge into a theoretical model when there is integrating valid theory to bind all the pieces together. Then, hopefully, the non-mathematical model could be developed and its elements quantified so that the mathematicians could make it into a mathematical model. Although we are far from the goals of mathematical models in theory building, it is not out of place to keep the ultimate in mind, for it helps to guide our methods in theory building for our profession.

I am not going to discuss a conceptual scheme for community needs. Social workers, especially community organizers, would be at a loss without the idea of need. Although community need is crucial in the practice of the community organizer, there are all shades of meaning attached to the concept.

Let us examine a few of these definitions to understand how

each meaning could lead into a very different direction of study and action. A clinical meaning can be attached to the concept of need, indicating drive or tension. Need can be interpreted to mean "desire" or "want." Need can have cultural overtones, e.g., need in an underdeveloped country is "enough food to keep alive." Need can be viewed in relation to the amount of money available for services. Need can be approached as utilization, or as those who are ineligible for service or as those who lack motivation and channels for reaching available service. This could go on to other examples, but it is sufficient to illustrate that the community organizer's understandings about community need are crucial in the quality of help which he can give to his committees.

The community organizer in social work is concerned about gaps in service. These gaps may be the result of no appropriate service for the condition or need under consideration, or an insufficient amount of service, or that it is not made available because of distance or channels of interpretation. Gaps may occur when a poor service or an inappropriate service is offered clients, such as continued board-and-care type of institutional service to children under five years of age.

No matter how we approach the problem, there are two major dimensions: *diagnosed conditions* (or problems) and *appropriate service for the condition*. The skeptic can say, "But social work has no typology of diagnosed conditions and no related classification of services." True as it may be, we do not close up shop and wait for the final refinement of diagnostic categories and our listing or services for differential treatment. Our progress will be made gradually problem by problem and service by service. These two major dimensions of the following "community need scheme" show a diagnostic condition screen at the community problem entrance, and the appropriate service screen at the approach through agency services.

These two approaches are the doors through which we enter for all of our community need studies. In most instances the service door is the simpler approach. What is the need for family service, homemaker service, or Boys' Clubs? The diagnosed problem entry

is more difficult for most community groups, but the avenue which committees of lay persons especially favor. Something must be done about our delinquency problems, about use of narcotics, or stranded newcomers who need subsistence relief—these are typical of their requests.

Before examining the proposed community need scheme, we should keep in mind that every community's approach to meeting human needs is placed *within their own peculiar value system.* Recognition of need, readiness to provide interest or support, levels of related professional services, attitudes, prejudices, and the brand of social justice will vary between cities and within cities. What constitutes luxury or fancy services in one community may be considered economical necessities in another. Therefore, the approach to study and action on a community need problem will always be considered within the value systems of the community. The community need problem facing a planning council or a community organization group usually begins with an undefined area of concern about a problem area of services or needs. A conceptual scheme of social services and individual needs or conditions can serve as a tool, or instrument, for organizing and for placing the planning problems. Placement of a problem is crucial for research on community need and equally important for planning activity.

The following chart puts into juxtaposition the two basic concerns, (a) the provision of services appropriate to the condition under consideration, and (b) the problem of individuals with a given condition in the community.[6]

The community organizer has this dual concern—(note the horizontal axis of the chart)—the potential client factors, and on the other hand (note the vertical axis)—the social service factors. The chart serves as a thinking-out or clarifying instrument to sharpen the problem and to place the problem so that it will focus on the

[6] The Research Department of the Welfare Planning Council, Los Angeles Region, has been developing and clarifying the concept of need in community organization for a number of years. Those who have contributed to the need scheme are: Dr. Elizabeth R. Frank, Dr. Sidney Zimbalist, Gloria Roman Robinson, Irving Piliavin, and numerous committees of the Welfare Planning Council, particularly of the Youth Services Division.

Universe of Clients

DIAGNOSTIC CONDITION SCREEN

Service Classification Screen

A particular type of Social Service

Eligible

Not eligible

Available

Not Available

With referral channels

Without referral channels

| | With condition but own resources | | With condition | |
| | With ability to use | | Without ability to use | |
	With motivation	Without motivation	With motivation	Without motivation
Now effective utilization	(1)	(5)	(9)	(13)
Potential for using	(2)	(6)	(10)	(14)
	(3)	(7)	(11)	(15)
	(4)	(8)	(12)	(16)

Without condition

Client seeking inappropriate service

Placed in inappropriate service by social worker

Service inappropriate for condition

Other types of service indicated

Adapted from Report of Research Department, Welfare Planning Council, Los Angeles Region, *A Conceptual Framework for the Study of Welfare Needs*, December, 1956, p. 4.

crucial issues of concern to the community planning group and
can set the direction for satisfaction in planning results. You will
notice that the vertical and horizontal lines successively cut out
segments of the community who may or may not be using existing
services for various reasons. This arrangement results in cells or
boxes, each having the two dimensions of *conditions* (or need) and
service. By using this conceptual scheme, we can place the problem
by determining where the lines fall for a given community problem at a particular time.

USING THE CONCEPTUAL SCHEME

The test of theory, or, in this case, a scheme with conceptual notions, is of little value to us unless it actually assists or guides our
practice. The use of the scheme requires the application of a variety
of theoretical notions from research and from practice, particularly at the points of clarifying or diagnosing conditions. Social
work "doing" is ahead in many instances of our systematized or
explicit theory. For instance, we are aware that delinquency as a
diagnostic label has little meaning for the caseworker, and, although we have no list of diagnostic types of delinquents, our
skilled caseworkers would probably better be able to handle their
practice in differentiating treatment than would we attempting to
list diagnostic conditions or delinquent types.

Let us take an example of the community's concern for day care
for children of working mothers. Because we are not yet clear
about the service required, we will approach the conceptual scheme
through the problem or condition—are we concerned about all
children? If not, then our universe of potential clients can be
limited to only those children whose mothers are working, e.g.,
those with condition. Then, what other limitations do we consider
as we sharpen the problem? Organized social services are generally
offered for those who are unable to find resources for their problem; therefore, we rule out—with condition, but own resources
(note chart). Later we may be interested in this spot in the need
scheme if there is evidence that children placed in commercial

resources are without proper safeguards. This is a different type of problem and it is important to identify it as such.

As we move into the scheme, we note: with ability or without ability. This distinction has less relevance for this problem than others where physical or mental handicaps prevent clients from utilizing services. The next step into the scheme is: with or without motivation or readiness. Provision of service usually begins with a client population which is already motivated to use, although the community may demand that social work begin or initiate the service without client motivation, such as in the Domestic Relations Courts, protective services, or getting clients with reportable diseases in for treatment, etc. This is a crucial sorting out point because any estimate of need of service must clarify these two population groups, motivated and not motivated, as the planning for each is different.

We then move into box (1), where we find clients with the conditions, with ability to use, with motivaton, and, as we look at the horizontal line to service, this becomes the present population group now being served. If our problem is placed in box (1) after we have considered the other aspects, then we can be confident that a utilization study is what we really want.

As we briefly examine some of the other cells in the need scheme, we note No. 2, which would focus the problem on clients with condition, with ability to use, with motivation and interest, but where they are unaware of the availability of the service waiting for their use. Cell 3, working mothers who want and would use the service, but where their community does not have the service available. Cell 4 indicates that clients want to utilize, but they are not eligible for the day care service under consideration. We can see how the need scheme provides a tool for clarification of thinking and can help a committee view related facts of the problem as they focus and select the core problem to which they will direct their energies. This sharpening of focus is urgent if research is to be used in the community organization activity.

If a community group begins with the service approved in their study of need, the first important step is clarification of the type of

service. Any given agency may offer several types of services and some of these services are offered by other agencies. We can describe similar types of service, at least initially, by saying they have similar objectives, methods, and deal with the same condition. The listing of these three distinguishing dimensions is simple but their application in clarifying social service is more complex.

Suppose we begin with a service which is grossly defined as substitute day care for children of working mothers where the condition (or need) includes children with more than average personal problems and where casework is important as a part of the service. This excludes the State day care center type of service and most proprietary services. It excludes all private day care nurseries which do not include both the child problems and the required social adjustment service. This defined child care service can be traced through the need scheme to the appropriate cell number. If our service is clarified or defined in more generalized terms, e.g., *any* service which will accept a child for day care where the primary need is to facilitate the employment of the mother, then our problem focus becomes something different.

One more explanation is required in this condensed presentation. The right section of the scheme which falls under the *without condition* is an important consideration, for this is where we identify inappropriate or outmoded services. There are clients who seek an inappropriate service and may receive such. For instance, the client's problem may be one of income maintenance and basic rudiments of money or home management. If the client is offered continued treatment with deep insight therapy instead of a referral to the public welfare agency and a visiting homemaker who can establish some norms for the family—then we may say the client is receiving inappropriate service for condition. In this section falls the situations where a different type of service is indicated, or where no organized service is indicated. For example, analysis of the client population of a working girls' residence disclosed several cases where the clients would be better off with no organized service, e.g., when the young women are 35 years of age,

have been in the residence for four years, have adequate employment and no special adjustment problems.

Institutional studies have also disclosed cases where the service is not appropriate for the child's needs—the child may not benefit from just any type of institutional experience, or may need an institution but inadequate service is offered.

Our approach to community need studies has brought us varying degrees of satisfaction. Those who pose the need problems have not clarified their thinking, and those who attempt to solve the problems have not gone through the logical, orderly processes necessary for sorting out the significant pieces and arriving at the focus which will really do the job for them.

In most community need problems there are three essential phases: (1) Analysis of the nature and extent of the need or condition; (2) assessment of the nature and extent of social service to meet the need; (3) development of the community norm or standard which becomes the tool against which the gaps in services can be measured (or estimated). The need scheme has been tested with a number of different kinds of committee groups. They are quick to grasp it in relation to their particular problem, and it definitely helps to set their problem focus. Particularly, they become aware of the elements or facets of the problem which they are agreeing to examine from study. In addition to providing a thinking tool, the need scheme serves to clarify the concept for community organization use.

VERIFICATION BY SCIENTIFIC METHOD

The discussion of this level of knowing in social work community organization will be brief. Our profession is yet overwhelmed with the job of clarification, conceptualization of the pertinent aspects of practice. Theory must be explicated from practice or transferred from relevant findings from social sciences before we can pose the theory to be tested. The social psychologists in their work with problem-solving groups and decision-making processes, or the sociologists in study of community phenomena, or the anthropologists in analysis of community values and behavior have important con-

tributions to offer. These, however, in most cases require translation into social work practice theory before research is feasible. Therefore, our discussion of verification of social work community organization theory by scientific methods can be concluded without past examples but with eager hopes for the future.

PRACTICE TESTING

Again, there appears to be a scarcity of research-tested theory applicable to social work community organization problems. Therefore, I will pose one example of concept clarification which can be tested in practice.

We will take, for instance, the example of the concept *community*, which is an overworked term in community organization practice. Nearly every textbook or course in community organization directs attention to the different meanings which can be attached to the concept. In practice, the community organizer is concerned with defining "community" for the purpose of *each problem* or *project*. This is different from defining "community" in terms of representation for a public agency commission or a welfare planning council board of directors. The social worker cannot follow a general formula for representation when determining "who should be involved" in a certain project. The expression "the client is the community" does nothing to guide professional activities; rather, it confuses the situation. For instance, a social worker may become engrossed with the improved interrelationships and process among his committee members of twelve agency executives (plus two well trained volunteers) and develop a report on how to decentralize the social services for a large urban area. He loses his perspective and conceives of this little committee as "the community," his client. Since the process results of the committee were excellent, the committee report and their community influence become overrated and unreal. In turn, everyone is disappointed because their months of work brought no effects.

If the concept of community is a functional one which changes with the dynamics of each community condition, then we are deal-

ing with an infinite variety of community segments. *The community segment is to be redefined for each problem or condition for each time and place.* There may be planning situations where "community" may be defined for the purpose of proposing a pattern of health and welfare services for several million people. On the other hand, a problem of securing a children's playground for a Mexican-American pocket of some 150 families isolated from the main stream of city life would require a limited, focused definition of community. This definition of community must include the elements necessary to reach into the offices of the Superintendent of Recreation or the County Supervisor's office. On the other hand, an adoptions project, the definition of community may include the medical profession, the legal profession, adoption agencies, the Independent Adoptive Parents Association, minority group leaders, family agencies, judges, community leaders who are opinion makers, and so on.

With this functional concept of community, it becomes necessary to diagnose the particularized community segment for each social condition under consideration. With this theoretical notion of community, the social worker approaches each condition with the idea of forecasting the social change channels necessary to effect the desired goal. The diagnostic phase of the community organization process then includes an analysis of the community involvement elements. This notion can be tested in practice, and, if it helps to clarify the operations in doing the job, the notion is validated as a useful one for community organization practice. In making this functional concept of the involvement elements more useful, it is helpful to keep in mind that all of the essential involvement elements do not need to be present in all process steps. For example, in the first illustration of securing a playground for the isolated Mexican-American pocket of families, it is not essential to involve the members of the Board of Supervisors—in the beginning phases of assessing need, in developing interest in a non-vocal and unsophisticated neighborhood committee. Community leaders on higher levels have limited time to give, and economical use of their available time is essential. It is not always necessary to involve

these people of high leadership level until the project reaches a strategic point of maturity.[7]

Again the writer emphasizes that theoretical notions, such as posed in this paper, must be tested in community organization practice. Unless the concepts or theoretical schemes actually work in practice and help in the doing of the job, they are not valid or they have *not been translated in terms* which have meaning for practice.

The paper is weighted with practice ideas which are explanatory in nature, with the recognition that community organization in social work can advance only as we are willing to expose our practice notions in a verbal form to which others can react. This reaction, to be helpful in advancing what we know about practice, must also be in a communicable form and not in a generalized emotional response. We must be prepared for a certain amount of uneasiness as the pieces of our practice are pulled out of their broad, blurred context for examination. Social work is dedicated to its concern about man and his social relations—to himself, his family, his neighborhood life, the social institutions in his society, and to the broader national and international scene. Achieving the "good life" becomes more complex with increasing professional specialization and interdependence between man and his social institutions. This makes our job of clarification more difficult, for "we must run fast to stand still" as we examine our professional practice in community organization and at the same time find our role in an ever-changing community scene.

Consider this paper as an initial attempt to stimulate interest in social work practice clarification. If we believe we have a specialization of community organization in social work, it is up to the professionals concerned to carve it out, for there are no resources we can seek to do this kind of job for us.

[7] Note to reader: In further clarification of the concept of community which defines the community in terms of relationships for a particular problem, one must keep in mind that this functional segment is always within the context of the broad community, and one segment is always in relation to its balance with the broader concern.

Training for Community Organization in Social Work

MARTIN M. COHN

What should be the objectives, class content, field instruction, content and method of course or courses, essential for the preparation of students for beginning positions in agencies whose major function is organizing community social work?

What part of the preparation can be encompassed in the two-year course of study for the Master's degree?

What part requires other or additional processes of preparation and of what do they consist?

This statement is presented under the following headings:

    I. DEFINITION
    II. SETTINGS AND RANGE OF ACTIVITIES
   III. KNOWLEDGE AND SKILLS
   IV. THE BEGINNING WORKER
    V. APPLICATION TO THE CURRICULUM—CLASS INSTRUCTION
   VI. APPLICATION TO THE CURRICULUM—FIELD INSTRUCTION
  VII. ADEQUACY OF TRAINING
 VIII. WHAT CAN BE DONE?

I. DEFINITION

Community organization in social work is the effective mobilization of the community's social welfare resources to serve individual and community needs. It is a field of practice and an area of service. It is not a basic process comparable to casework and group work.

II. SETTINGS AND RANGE OF ACTIVITIES

Community organizations services are provided in a variety of agency settings and in many different areas. These include community welfare councils and chests, public welfare agencies, race relations programs, interfaith relations programs, sectarian federations of voluntary social agencies, intercultural programs, health councils and associations, and many similar groups functioning on the local, national and international levels, as well as governmental and voluntary agencies in the health, education, and related fields.

The community organization practitioner may work in settings not solely concerned with social work. He may work with and be subordinate to workers with professional background and training whose ultimate goals in terms of human welfare may be similar, but whose more immediate professional goals and practices will not necessarily be those of social work.

The practice of community organization involves the following areas of activity:

1. Providing professional consultation and advice to individuals and groups (whether formally organized as agencies, committees, and so on, or not) as to the most effective means of mobilizing social welfare resources to meet human needs.

2. Stimulating activity which will lead to community action directed to mobilizing community resources by individuals and groups, whether formally organized as agencies, committees, etc., or not.

3. Providing various administrative services required to carry on the programs in *1 and 2 above,* for the agencies, committees, organized and informal groups and individuals concerned. Such administrative services include minutes and other records of activity, organization of educational and public relations programs, arrangements of meetings between groups and individuals, between various individuals, etc.

4. Under certain circumstances, keeping records of the techniques and processes involved in *1 and 2 above.* The possibility and probability of such record keeping is limited by the lack of

development of recording process in the field and is a goal for advancement of the field.

5. Provision of technical knowledge with regard to the field of social work and community welfare needs for the groups and individuals concerned under *1 and 2 above*.

6. Stimulating and carrying on, at least on an administrative level and to some extent on a technical level, educational, interpretative and promotional activity related to the development of understanding and the stimulation of activity with regard to the mobilization of community resources.

7. Stimulation and coordination of, provision of administrative services for, and on occasion some direct involvement in, research and survey processes related to *1 and 2 above*. Presentation of results of these research and survey processes.

A number of the activities listed above are based in areas outside social work and can be used to realize ends which may often be antagonistic to the broad goals of the development of human personality and better community life implicit in social work. They have values for social work as they are used to achieve social work ends. When the community organization practitioner uses them to make him a more effective "enabler," to help him stimulate individuals and groups to achieve the ends of social work, they are used for social work purposes. Even in social work they may be used to "manipulate" individuals and groups to work toward social work ends by means which controvert the achievement of those ends. The line between "enabling" and "manipulation" is a very fine one. Maintaining a clear distinction places a heavy responsibility on the community organization worker, particularly amid the pressures of present day society.

III. KNOWLEDGE AND SKILLS

The community organization professional therefore requires the following background:

A. A thorough knowledge of the basic goals and objectives of social work, against the background of the development of these goals and objectives in American society.

B. A thorough knowledge of the total field of social work; areas of service, processes, etc.; with particular emphasis on understanding of general principles in the various fields and processes; relations between the fields; professional standards, etc.; rather than on highly specialized skills or knowledge in any particular area or of any particular process.

C. Knowledge of the development of the American community, of current community processes of living, governmental structure, political process, economic structure and process, power structure, intergroup relationships, as they have developed within American society.

D. Knowledge of certain non-social work fields which must be used in community organization practice, e.g., public relations, adult education, intergroup relations; with particular emphasis on where to find such information, how to adapt it, and how to relate to professionals in these fields, rather than on highly specialized knowledge and skill in any one of the fields. Skill in applying these processes and relating professionals in these areas to the social work field in ways which will effectively achieve social work goals.

E. Familiarity with research techniques in social work and the social sciences sufficient to make for effective provision of administrative and interpretative service to the research and survey processes required in community planning as part of the community organization process.

F. Knowledge of administrative techniques with reference to minutes and similar record keeping, arrangement of meetings, planning work assignments, etc.

G. Skills in establishing relationships with people and groups and in providing stimulation and leadership in ways which will enable them to achieve the goals of social work by means which are in accordance with these goals.

H. Ability to see the total field of social work and the relationship of the various specialized services and processes.

I. Ability to accept responsibility for leadership and to recognize when and how leadership can best be given in the circumstances which present themselves to community organization practitioners.

IV. THE BEGINNING WORKER

Now how does all this relate to the curricula of the graduate schools of social work? What must and can they do to prepare the graduate for a beginning position in the field of community organization which requires at least some of the above outlined knowledge and skills.

What might be expected in a beginning position, in an agency whose basic purpose and program is in the area of community organization in social work; whose senior professional staff are social workers, and whose staff is sufficiently large to make possible limited and defined assignments under good supervision for a beginning period.

This is not often possible. One of the problems to be faced is that a graduate, or a practitioner with a very few years experience in a functional field, may be plunged into the second position in a two-man agency; or become the social worker-community organizer in a non-social work agency concerned with some activity in the social work field and social work relationships; and be given assignments requiring a high degree of the whole range of knowledge and skills outlined above.

Under the more favorable conditions mentioned, the following might be expected:

A thorough knowledge of *A, B, and C;* and *E* within the limits noted. Limited knowledge and some beginning skills in *D and F.* Awareness of the need for developing skills in *G* (hopefully with some natural aptitude).

A, B, and C should form a foundation for the gradual development of attitudes in *H and I.*

V. APPLICATION TO THE CURRICULUM—CLASS INSTRUCTION

Now what is required in the curricula of graduate schools of social work to enable the beginning student to be in this position?

A and B are basic in the present curricula. One reservation here is that schools which do not present adequate basic courses in both casework and group work, or which have schedules which would

not permit a student to participate in both, would not provide this background.

C. Such courses are available in some schools of social work and in many departments of social science. There are a number of issues as to whether the courses given in the general area of social science and sociology would require adaptation to specific social work courses. It would appear, however, that there are no insuperable obstacles to offering such courses within the present curriculum.

D. It would appear difficult, if not impossible, to make this subject matter adequately available at the average graduate school of social work and during the course of the two-year curriculum with any meaningfulness. Possibly, a practitioner who has a gift for teaching (and such exist in a few places) may be able to create some awareness. There is, however, serious question as to how meaningful the presentation of such information can be, in the absence of actual experience. There may be opportunities in field work and this is dealt with below.

E. Insofar as beginning research courses are included in the regular two-year course, this requirement is provided for.

F. Raises the same issues as *D.*

G. The development of these skills is obviously going to be easier for some students who happen to have developed, through the course of their lives, some aptitude for this type of relationship; but there are many who must acquire facility through special effort. While based on the application of casework and group work principles presented in the regular course, it is vital that these principles be adapted to relationships other than the familiar one of worker-client. Development of this facility is better suited to the field work situation.

H. The foundation should be laid in *A, B, and C* to the extent required in a beginning worker.

Some of this grows, of course, out of the whole life experience of the student, and is to some extent beyond the control of the school. The school, nevertheless, does have considerable responsibility, particularly as these attitudes are directed to the social work field.

It will be obvious to the educators who read this paper that attitudes grow from the atmosphere of the school, relationship with and example of the staff, and of the professionals with whom there is contact in the field work relationship, professional associations, etc., rather than from direct classroom work—except possibly those courses which present some historical analysis of the development of social work. While the school has definite responsibility within these areas, the possibilities within the school are also limited by the requirements of the field and the general tone in the field at any particular time. The above comments indicate that the continuation of this analysis leads into the entire problem of development of leadership in social work which is exercising the field at the present time, but which is beyond the limitation of this statement.

It should be noted, however, that the ability to take leadership when necessary is an essential part of the makeup of the community organization practitioner. While the beginning practitioner should have developed awareness of issues and an approach which may stimulate him to grow into positions of leadership at whatever level he may find his job, he nevertheless is not in his first job expected to take major responsibility for leadership, except in very restricted areas.

A final problem in this area is the arrangement of this content in relation to the total curriculum of a given school, and the point at which a student should properly choose a specialty and limit his training to this speciality.

VI. APPLICATION TO THE CURRICULUM—FIELD INSTRUCTION

With regard to field work, it would appear from the above that there are five major assignments for field instruction:

 a. The development of related knowledge and skills mentioned in *D.*

 b. The development of administrative techniques outlined in *F.*

 c. The development of skills in relationships outlined in *G.*

 d. Translating the theoretical knowledge of *A, B, C, and E* into real situations as they occur in agencies and communities.

e. Development of skill in process recording within the limitations noted in IV.

At least part of the field work should be in a functional agency and this is required by most schools. It is essential for reasons noted below (VIII-4). Because of this, the amount of time which can be spent in a community organization is at best going to be limited in relation to the above five objectives.

A field work experience in community organization should be based on carrying through, or giving meaningful assistance in carrying through, a specific project. Experience as an observer of the activities in a community organization agency is not adequate. In carrying through any such project, there must be a certain amount of time which cannot be directly related to activities meaningful in terms of the learning process. No one project is likely to provide for all five areas mentioned above, or even for the first four of them. There is still considerable variation in the levels of understanding of student supervision in community organization. Serious questions therefore arise as to whether the average field work experience possible in a two-year course could adequately meet even the four major objectives mentioned above.

VII. ADEQUACY OF TRAINING

This leaves the worker on graduation without adequate preparation in certain awarenesses and skills which are of considerable importance even on a beginning level.

It has been assumed that the content of classroom instruction noted above can be presented adequately in the two-year course. This would include basic courses in both casework and group work, community, introduction to research, as well as the other content implied in *A and B*. There has been an implication that the community organization specialty would be chosen almost at the time of entry to the course, which is not a sound practice.

Those now actively engaged in teaching and closer to present curricula of the schools will be in a better position to analyze how far all this is possible in the present two-year course.

If these areas cannot be covered in an adequate way, then a further question arises with regard to the preparation of beginning workers within the limits of the two-year graduate course.

VIII. WHAT CAN BE DONE?

The following possibilities and questions are presented for discussion. They are in some points contradictory and are not meant to be definitive suggestions:

1. Should beginning community organization jobs be defined in terms of the limitations of training possible in the schools? Whatever the schools may do to discourage graduates from accepting jobs beyond their capacity, this is not a solution in a field which needs more developed professional skills. Also, as defined above, the training now possible appears to be lacking in certain basic essentials which could not readily be picked up on the job.

2. "In service" training can be used for many of the related skills. While this is helpful to some extent for a person in a job, it is not a substitute for adequate professional training. To accept "in service" training as a solution is to admit that an adequate teaching program cannot be developed.

3. Is a third year required?

Certainly the additional time would provide additional classroom and field instruction in those areas which cannot be dealt with adequately in the two-year course.

There is implied in this statement, however, a serious question as to whether some of the related knowledge and skills in which the present course is most inadequate could effectively be taught at all in a classroom situation, even in a third year. Is this due to the nature of material, or to lack of ability at present to organize this material into teachable form?

4. Community organization is concerned with the analysis, coordination, reorganization, evaluation, of the basic social work services. It is not directly concerned with individuals and their needs, but is a "second line" service. It has been suggested that practitioners can more effectively carry through the processes of community organization as they affect agency programs and peo-

ples' needs if they have themselves had functional experience in at least one of the basic services.

This would imply that the third year should follow some period of practice in a functional agency.

From this, the concept of "internship," or "residency," of post-graduate training through practice in carefully regulated assignments, naturally develops.

The position of the writer is that the third year should follow a period of practice and be concerned with relating this practice to community organization theory. This would be the start toward the development of an "internship" or "residency" type of program as suggested above.

There are, of course, a variety of other items for speculation here. It may be that the so-called third year could be covered in a series of shorter courses related to practice and job assignment.

There is, however, considerable question as to whether such a program is practical at the present time. In view of the growing interest in the third year added to the established course, this may be a more practical immediate objective.

5. Does this mean that a three-year course should be the immediate objective? While this would still leave some inadequacies which got beyond lack of time, there would certainly be a more adequate foundation both in class and field instruction; and the additional year would provide a basis for experimentation in more effective ways of dealing with these inadequacies.

6. What recognition would be given for the extra year? Is the additional content suitable for a Ph.D.? If not (and the writer questions this), should three years be required for a Master's degree in community organization, as five instead of four years is required for a Bachelor's degree in engineering?

7. Can a three-year course in community organization stand alone, or must its development be related to a three-year course in social work? At what point does a student choose a specialty?

8. Would the prospective students and the field accept a three-year period of training? Some years ago this was asked about the two-year course and the present Master's degree.

Qualifications
for Community Organization Workers

ARTHUR DUNHAM

EDITOR'S NOTE: The opening nine pages of Mr. Dunham's position paper were published in March, 1958, by the Thomas R. Crowell Publishing Company under the title *Community Welfare Organization, Principles and Practice,* pages 288 to 295, and are, therefore, not reprinted in this volume.

PERSONAL QUALITIES

The community organization worker needs first the personal qualities of any social worker. The following list of these "personal and professional qualities" includes those given by Hollis and Taylor in *Social Work Education in the United States,* plus some additional qualities, most of them reproduced or adapted from a pamphlet sponsored by the Council on Social Work Education.

Genuine warmth, sensitivity to, and liking for, people, and a capacity to identify with a variety of persons.

A professional philosophy.

Emotional, mental, and physical health and stability.

A degree of maturity and self-security which enables a professional person to give beyond his own needs in relationship with others and to feel comfortable with authority.

Imagination, resourcefulness, and flexibility combined with personal integrity, courage, and a conviction about the value to society of the things for which social work stands.

Capacity to think conceptually.

Open-mindedness, clarity of purpose, accuracy, and ability to share.

Courtesy in all professional relationships expressed through conversation and written communications.

A belief in the broad base of citizen participation and a conviction about the right of the person, group, and community to choose alternatives and to achieve their own destiny within the framework of a stable and democratic society.[1]
Ability to work with and get along with other people.
An objective approach to problems.
An intelligent interest in social problems and issues.
Responsibility: reliability: the habit of working hard.[2]

In addition to these qualities needed by any social worker, the community organization worker needs many of the qualities of the executive. It has already been noted that the job of the average community organization worker tends to resemble the job of an executive or sub-executive more closely than that of a casework or group work practitioner.[3]

A number of formulations of qualities desirable in executives or leaders have been reviewed in this connection, but it would be burdensome and of doubtful value to compare these in detail.[4]

One of the most suggestive of these formulations is Tead's list of ten "qualities necessary in leaders." These are:

1. Physical and nervous energy.
2. A sense of purpose and direction.
3. Enthusiasm.

1 Ernest V. Hollis and Alice L. Taylor, *Social Work Education in the United States* (New York, Columbia University Press, 1951), pp. 223–224: "qualities considered important to successful practice of social work inherent in the social worker's personality endowment or developed by education and experience."
2 Compare with the "qualities of mind and heart" suggested in *Social Work as a Profession* (New York, published for Council on Social Work Education by National Committee on Social Work in Defense Mobilization, 1953), pp. 9–10.
3 These statements may be tested against the lists of community organization jobs and functional specializations presented earlier in this paper.
4 Ordway Tead, *The Art of Leadership* (New York, Whittlesey House, 1935), ch. VI. Clarence King, *Social Agency Boards and How to Make them Effective* (New York, Harper and Brothers, 1938), pp. 62–63. Pierce Atwater, *Problems of Administration in Social Work* (Minneapolis, University of Minnesota Press, 1940), pp. 11–19. Marshall Edward Dimock, *The Executive in Action* (New York, Harper and Brothers, 1945), pp. 10–12. Elwood Street, *A Handbook for Social Agency Administration* (New York, Harper and Brothers, 1947), pp. 106–110. Ray Johns, *Executive Responsibility* (New York, Association Press, 1954), pp. 42–43. Murray G. Ross and Charles E. Hendry, *New Understandings of Leadership* (New York, Association Press, 1957).

4. Friendliness and affection.
5. Integrity.
6. Technical mastery.
7. Decisiveness.
8. Intelligence.
9. Teaching skill.
10. Faith.[5]

Some attempts have been made to list qualities desirable in community organization workers.[6]

When one begins to list desirable qualities for a type of worker, there is always the danger that one will wind up, as Clarence King has said, "trying to write the specifications for an archangel." Nevertheless, it seems useful to attempt to define the qualities that are *desirable* for a community organization worker, even though it is recognized that we may never find all these qualities (at least in the desired degree) in one person.

The writer suggests, then:

1. That the community organization worker should have the qualities stated above as desirable for all social workers.

2. That, in addition, it is desirable that the community organization worker should have the following qualities:

A liking for and capacity to participate creatively in group process: capacity for working as a member of a team.

The understanding and acceptance of conflict as a normal aspect of group relations, democracy, and social growth.

[5] Ordway Tead, *Art of Leadership*, p. 83.
[6] George Rabinoff and Clarence King, "Qualifications and Training for Community Organization," memorandum to the New York City Group for the Study of Community Organization, April 4, 1940, mimeographed, 5 pp. Robert P. Lane, "Report of Groups Studying the Community Organization Process," *National Conference of Social Work, Proceedings*, 1940, pp. 467–469. Ruth O. Blakeslee, "Regional and Statewide Exchanges," *ibid.*, p. 480 (social service exchange executive). Community Chests and Councils of America, *We Want an Executive* (New York, 1947), pp. 11–12 (chest-council executives). Arthur Dunham, "What is the Job of the Community Organization Worker?" *National Conference of Social Work, Proceedings*, 1948, pp. 170–171. American Association of Schools of Social Work, *Workshop Report, Community Organization, Toronto, 1951* (memeographed), pp. 11–12. U. S. Department of Labor, Women's Bureau, *The Outlook for Women in Community Organization in Social Work* (Washington, U. S. Government Printing Office, 1951). pp. 22–23.

Self-discipline; willingness to exercise indirect rather than direct or "public" leadership; patience; perseverance.

Sensitivity in individual, group, and community relations; tact; good judgment.

Perspective; vision; the ability to distinguish "the woods from the trees."

Capacity for analysis. (Community organization is a problem-solving process.)

Imagination; inventiveness; resourcefulness; the capacity to plan creatively.

Initiative; a taste for moving forward rather than merely "staying put" or "holding the fort;" decisiveness; determination; self-confidence, united with modesty.

Capacity for clear thinking; capacity for clear, simple, and reasonably fluent communication—verbal and written.

The ability to work under pressure.

Adaptability; mental agility; the quality of being "light on one's feet."

In addition to these qualities the worker had better have a sense of humor; he will lead a grim life without it! Various additional qualities would vary with particular jobs; most community chest jobs and many others require "persuasive ability," a flair for "high-powered salesmanship," promotion, or advocacy. The chest executive needs also to be "a good organizer;" it would hardly do for him to be an artistic or philosophical isolationist, with a deep-seated distrust and abhorrence of organization and all its works. It will be well also if the chest executive deals readily with figures and has a warm, friendly, outgoing and buoyant temperament.

As a matter of fact, one could probably draw up a separate list of "desirable qualities" for each of the 23 community organization jobs listed in the foregoing pages; and it is not certain that any two lists would be exactly alike.

But this sort of thing will have to be left to job specifications for specific jobs. No school of social work is going to train students narrowly for specific jobs (at least one hopes no school will do

this); so the general list of personal qualities desirable for all community organization practitioners is about all that can be suggested as being likely to be useful for schools of social work.

A SOUND PHILOSOPHY OF COMMUNITY ORGANIZATION

A word should be added about "a sound philosophy of community organization." This is of course not in itself a personal quality, although it may be bound up with personal qualities such as fairness, self-discipline, absence of a desire to dominate, a quality of idealism, and so on.

From the standpoint of an American community organization worker, a philosophy should be rooted in democracy and oriented to its values of ultimate control by the people; the right of self-determination by the individual, the group, and the community; and cooperation and participation in the achievement of common goals.

UNDERGRADUATE COURSES

"Nothing in the curriculum of a liberal arts college is wholly foreign to social work. Art, literature, history, biology, economics, sociology, and languages are all germane." [7]

Starting from this point of departure, one faces the question: What undergraduate courses are desirable for a future community organization worker?

The question seems rather theoretical and academic: How many college students, even of those potentially interested in social work, know what community organization is, or are sufficiently interested to choose undergraduate courses with a view to a professional career in community organization? Or, to put the question

[7] *The Profession of Social Work.* (op. cit.), p. 11.

in another way—out of a hundred current community organization workers, how many of them, when they were in college, had any idea that they would "go into" community organization?

However, let us assume the validity of the inquiry, and consider the answer.

In general, the future community organization worker needs the same kinds of undergraduate courses as any other future social worker. He should certainly have at least introductory courses in sociology, political science, economics, psychology, and general and American history; and desirably in biology, social anthropology, and statistical methods. English composition, public speaking, and group discussion (if there is a course in it) are most important. Parliamentary law will be useful also. An adequate study of at least one foreign language is desirable, both for the insight into another culture and for more effective participation in foreign travel and observation of international conferences, and perhaps ultimately foreign service in social welfare.

If the college offers "informational" undergraduate courses in social work, the student will do well to take all or most of these, for orientation purposes and with the prospect of being able to enrich his later graduate study in social work.[8]

Additional courses in the social sciences which would be highly desirable would include: social psychology, group behavior, "group dynamics," social organization, community structure and community action, social legislation, social security, labor problems, American government and politics, public administration, and an elementary course in accounting.

In general, however, one would hope that the student would follow a broad and well-rounded course of studies in college, without narrow specialization, and with time and opportunity for extra-curricular activities along the lines of his choice—whether this be athletics, debating, dramatics, music, student government, religious or civic activities, or otherwise.

[8] Cf. *ibid.*

WHO SHOULD BE ADMITTED TO SPECIALIZATION IN COMMUNITY ORGANIZATION?

The two remaining questions relate to (1) field work other than in community organization and (2) experience in social welfare agencies.

Before these can be profitably discussed, it is necessary to consider the question: What students should be admitted to specialization in community organization in a school of social work?

There are at least three different points of view on this question:

1. That students without previous experience on social work jobs may be "community organization majors" in connection with their two-year Master's program in social work.

2. That only students with previous acceptable experience in social work jobs may become "community organization majors" in connection with the Master's degree program.

3. That specialization in community organization should be reserved to a post-Master's or third-year program.

The third point of view seems to the writer patently absurd, in view of the realities of supply and demand in community organization jobs. It was reported in 1951 that the accredited schools of social work graduated only about 50 students a year with specialization in community organization, whereas there was a need of at least 83 annual replacements on community organization jobs.[9] If specialization in community organization was restricted to the third year, one might expect the 50 students to drop to 15 or 20 at the outside, thus making it more than ever impossible for most community organization agencies to employ properly trained persons.

"Had we but world enough and time," (and money and manpower), it might be theoretically desirable to have the community

[9] The situation today may be worse rather than better. A recent unpublished report from United Community Funds and Councils of America regarding personnel for the chest-council field, says, "There were only 8 properly trained new graduates available this year to meet an estimated need of 25 to 35 new graduates for the field each year."

organization specialization superimposed upon the ordinary two-year Master's program; but in the present state of supply, demand, scholarships, and expense of training, such a proposal appears to be fantastically unrealistic.

The second proposal is that only students with previous social work job experience should be admitted to specialization in community organization during the Master's program. This is based on the belief that a social worker should have his first experience in a consumer-service agency: that he should enter social work at the point of helping people directly through casework or group work. Even if one accepts this idea, it does not follow that students without previous social work experience should be excluded from the community organization specialization in the Master's program. There are, in fact, two reasons against such a policy. (1) It excludes from the community organization specialization the college graduate, without experience, who has a definite bent for and interest in community organization. It is scarcely satisfactory to tell him either to specialize in casework or group work, even though his major interest is in community organization, or to go out and "get some experience" as an untrained worker. (2) Even if one wishes to insist upon consumer-service experience before service on a community organization job, it is possible for a graduate of a school to get this after his graduation and before taking a community organization job.

The writer would favor the first of the three policies stated above: That students who seem to have the desirable personal qualifications but who are without previous experience on social work jobs may become community organization majors in connection with their Master's programs.

FIELD WORK OTHER THAN IN COMMUNITY ORGANIZATION

The writer is inclined to the view that if a student enters a graduate school of social work without previous social work experience,

and if he wishes to specialize in community organization, he should normally take his first year of field work in casework and/or group work, so that he will begin his field work experience with this sort of direct service to clients or consumers.

Some representatives of schools of social work and agencies take vigorous exception to this point of view. They see in it an affront to community organization—a suggestion that casework and group work are somehow superior to or more "really social work" than is community organization. They point out, correctly of course, that community organization means "working with people;" they maintain that the community organization worker can derive the same values in establishing relationships and in working with people in community organization as in casework or group work.

The author would go as far as any one in maintaining the integrity of community organization as a social work process, on a parity with casework or group work. He would still think, however, that the future community organization worker would usually do well to have the experience of working with people within the discipline and setting of casework or group work. For one thing, such a field work experience will give him an insight into casework or group work, and what casework or group work agencies do, that he will need in his community organization practice and that he will probably never get in any other way than by working in such an agency. In the second place, it seems doubtful that most community organization field placements will actually put as much sustained emphasis on individual relationships and the understanding of human behavior as would be true of a good casework or group work placement. Indeed, it is questionable whether the community organization placement can give such primary and sustained emphasis without neglecting other important and unique "content aspects" of the placement. For these reasons the author is inclined to think that the community organization major without previous experience would do best to have his first field placement in casework and/or group work.

A word of explanation is needed regarding this phrase, "casework and/or group work." Where the student has had no con-

sumer-service experience, and is therefore to take direct-service field work, the writer believes it would be desirable, *if practicable,* for him to have *both* casework and group work field work. However, if he is to take community organization field work during two of his four semesters (which is surely a minimum for a community organization specialization), this leaves only two semesters for direct-service field work. That is, he can ordinarily have both casework and group work field work only by taking a single semester of each —an arrangement usually unacceptable to both agencies and schools, because of the shortness of the placement and of the time available for orientation, learning, and assimilation. In most cases the student will probably have to take two semesters of *either* casework or group work. It is doubtful that there is any general answer to the question, which of these is "better" for community organization majors? Each is valuable; the two types of placement have different values and different emphases. The writer inclines somewhat toward the group work placement, for most community organization majors, because there is so much group process in community organization and because in a good, modern group work placement the student is likely to obtain many of the values centering around diagnosis, development of helping relationships, and record-keeping which have sometimes been thought of as pertaining particularly to the casework process.

In many cases, even if the student has had previous social work experience, it may be desirable for him to have one or two semesters in casework or group work field work.

However, it would seem extremely unwise and arbitrary to make this an absolute rule. Suppose a student has had five years of casework experience, and seven years of community organization experience. He is now assistant executive of a council in a medium-sized city; he wishes to get his degree and prepare himself for positions of greater responsibility and opportunity in community organization. It would seem rather futile to insist that this worker spend a semester or two in casework or group work field work. Probably his time would be much better spent in taking three or four semesters of either carefully selected community organization field place-

ments or of some combination of social work placements in community organization, in administration, and/or in research.

Casework and group work agencies used for field work placements for community organization majors would presumably be the same sort of agencies used for such placements for casework or group work majors. Probably, a more "generic" agency would be better than a highly specialized one; and if there are some vestiges of community organization intertwined with the casework or group work duties, so much the better. Thus a casework placement with a rural public assistance agency or child welfare agency might be better than one with a highly specialized urban casework agency; a group work placement with a settlement might be superior to a "group work treatment" placement. But, in the main, the concern in giving the community organization major a casework or group work placement is that he shall have a first-hand, down-to-earth experience in learning casework or group work. This is valid in and of itself. His community organization field work experience will come later.

EXPERIENCE IN SOCIAL WELFARE AGENCIES

The last question for discussion is, what experience in social welfare agencies is desirable for community organization majors?

The writer's general point of view has already been expressed: (1) That it is desirable for a social worker to work on a consumer-service job before he works on a community organization job. (2) That if the student has not had previous consumer-service experience, the school of social work should make sure that he has casework or group work field work, *at least.*

If the graduate of the school has had no previous consumer-service experience (or possibly experience in working with people in a closely related vocation), some schools and national agencies would encourage or perhaps urge him to take a job in a casework or group work agency for a year or two before taking a community organization job.

The practical difficulty with this plan is that there is such a lack of qualified community organization workers in the field, that community organization agencies have a tendency to "snap up" graduates with community organization specialization, or to lure them with relatively high salaries, whether or not they have had consumer-service experience. The other difficulty is the objection expressed by one graduating community organization major: "Why should I go into a casework agency, and be a mediocre caseworker for a year or two, when I think I could go into a community organization agency and be a pretty good community organization worker?"

As to the type of consumer-service agency in which it is desirable for community organization workers to have experience, it is doubtful that this matters much, except that there might well be a preference for a more generic and perhaps a governmental agency rather than a highly-specialized, "sheltered," limited-intake voluntary agency.

Obviously, all these questions as to the qualifications of community organization workers bristle with unsolved problems, and await much more research than has been done in the past, before authoritative answers to them can be given.

Community Organization Methods and Skills in the Programs of National Agencies

ARNOLD GURIN

The objective of this paper will be analysis of the kinds of programs in which national organizations in the health and welfare field are engaged and the extent to which community organization methods and skills as we understand them in the field of social work have a place either actually or potentially in the carrying out of such programs.

To fulfill that objective completely would require more research than has gone into this statement. This is no attempt at a systematic examination of national agency programs, but the Service Directory of National Organizations, published by the National Social Welfare Assembly, was used as a source of information.

The National Social Welfare Assembly includes governmental as well as voluntary agencies. However, since the field of governmental services is being covered by a separate paper, this statement will confine itself to the voluntary agencies, although some of the observations may also be pertinent at the governmental level.

TYPES OF NATIONAL AGENCIES

The national voluntary agencies cover an extremely wide range of programs. Any classification scheme has to be arbitrary, with a great deal of overlapping among the categories. In the organization of the Assembly, its working relationships are established on the basis of areas of common interest. Two major groupings by

areas of work are represented in the Commission of Individualized Services, and in the Commission of Education and Recreational Services. Although there is some clarity in the distinction between these two major areas, a good many agencies participate in both of these Commissions.

The Assembly also has a variety of groupings based upon "problems." The Commission on Care of the Aging is one of these. Many agencies—from many fields—are represented on it. There are, in addition, groupings along certain administrative lines, such as the Committee on Field Service (which includes field service directors of national organizations) or the Committee on Personnel.

The following classification is an effort to describe some of the functional variations which may have a bearing on differentials in methods and skills:

INDIVIDUALIZED SERVICES

Family Service Association of America, Child Welfare League of America, National Travelers Aid Association, Salvation Army, American Red Cross (in part) are some of the major agencies in this group.

Most of the agencies in this category give service to local affiliates which are professionally staffed social agencies in the *casework* field.

RECREATION AND GROUP WORK

This category includes the major building-centered programs, such as YMCA, YWCA, National Federation of Settlements and Neighborhood Centers, the major youth-serving agencies, such as Boy and Girl Scouts, Campfire Girls, and Boys Clubs; the National Recreation Association and American Camping Association; the National Jewish Welfare Board and National Catholic Welfare Conference.

As in the case of Individualized Services, this group includes mostly professionally staffed local agencies, many of which have *group work* as the basic professional skill.

HEALTH AND REHABILITATION

American Foundation for the Blind, American Hearing Society, American Social Hygiene Association, Goodwill Industries of America, National Association for Mental Health, National Society for Prevention of Blindness, National Tuberculosis Association, National Health Council.

In this category, Assembly coverage is less comprehensive than in the first two groups. In addition to those agencies listed, the field includes major agencies concerned with the specific diseases of polio, cancer, heart, cerebral palsy, and so on.

Here we find greater heterogeneity as to structure, function and professionalization than in the first two categories. The local affiliates are not strictly direct service agencies, as in the casework and group work services. Some of them do give direct service of certain types to clients falling within their area of concern. Information and referral service would be a typical function. A major function of the locals, however, is public education rather than direct service.

The older and larger agencies (like TB) have well-established affiliates with paid staffs. Others may have only volunteer committees. Where there *is* paid staff, it does not necessarily include trained social work personnel. Where specialized medical or rehabilitative services are given, these professional disciplines may be represented. On the administrative side, social work personnel may or may not be used.

MULTI-FUNCTIONAL SERVICES

Lutheran Department of Social Welfare, National Catholic Community Service, National Catholic Welfare Conference, and other sectarian agencies which provide service in a number of functional fields. The National Urban League might also be considered in this category.

PUBLIC EDUCATION

Child Study Association, National Child Labor Committee, National Council on Agricultural Life and Labor, and several other

organizations operate mostly at the national level, pursuing their special objectives through educational and legislative activity. The American Jewish Committee might also be classified here, for its program of intergroup relations, although it has a more active program of local chapter work than the others.

VOLUNTEER SERVICES

The Association of Junior Leagues of America and National Council of Jewish Women specialize in recruiting volunteer women for community service projects.

FUND-RAISING, COORDINATION AND PLANNING

This is a broad category, including agencies which have primarily a community organization function. Examples are the AFL-CIO Community Service Activities, Council of Jewish Federations and Welfare Funds, National Health Council, United Community Funds and Councils of America, USO. The Council on Social Work Education might also be considered in this group.

PROFESSIONAL ORGANIZATIONS

In addition to the National Association of Social Workers, the Assembly membership includes the National League for Nursing and the National Legal Aid Association. The latter is not really concerned with advancement of a professional service, but rather with increasing the availability of such service for groups that need it and have difficulty in obtaining it. However, it is classified here because it represents a professional discipline other than social work which is involved in a community organization-type of service.

The mere listing of these many organizations points to the difficulty of generalization. Aside from the varying functions, there are, as noted, important differences in structure. Some of the agencies are organizations of organizations—others are organizations of individuals. Some have no local affiliates but operate nationally. Most of them do, however, have local affiliates which may be pro-

fessional agencies, chapters made up of individual members, or councils of like-interest groups gathered together for a special purpose (for example, local health councils).

GENERIC ELEMENTS IN WORK OF NATIONAL ORGANIZATIONS

The major characteristic of a national organization is that it represents an effort to organize on a national basis for the furtherance of a special interest. Such a special interest may be relatively small, involving limited numbers of people who have a particular problem, or it may be very broad, covering an extremely wide segment of the community, with a variety of programs and services. The best example of the latter is the American Red Cross, which is in a category of its own as a mammoth multi-purpose social agency.

Despite the great variety of programs and services involved, it does seem to me that we can define some generic elements. A more difficult problem will be to determine which of these generic elements (a) are related to the field of social work, (b) are related to community organization practice in the field of social work, and (c) can be taught successfully in a school of social work.

A review of programs and services as stated in the Service Directory of the Assembly reveals that certain types of activities are mentioned repeatedly, and are therefore characteristic of a national agency operation. These common factors can be grouped into two categories: (a) purposes or *functions* of national organizations and (b) *methods* used by national organizations in fulfilling these functions.

FUNCTIONS

Most national agencies are concerned with the following objectives:

1. *Standard Setting.* The national agency tries to establish a proper—and progressively higher—standard of work for individuals and groups who are trying to give service in its area of concern.

Frequently, meeting minimum standards represents a requirement for affiliation with the national organization.

2. *Research.* This is closely related to standard setting, since standards are improved as knowledge in a field is expanded. Thus, in the field of health, an advance in medical knowledge will bring in its wake an improved standard of treatment for the specific disease. Many national agencies sponsor and finance research activity. Many more maintain at least an informational service to collect facts about the problems in their field, service statistics, and so on.

3. *Program Content.* A major function of nationals is to suggest specific ways in which locals can work—what activities to undertake, and how to do it. This includes defining the need for staff—how many, what types of training required, and so on.

4. *Personnel.* Most national agencies are concerned with helping the local affiliate to obtain qualified personnel to carry out the service, and to train such personnel. Recruitment has become a growing concern, and scholarships and fellowship programs are undertaken to meet that need.

5. *Volunteer Leadership.* Most programs rely very heavily on the involvement of volunteers as advocates for the particular goals of the organization and as manpower to aid in the carrying out of the specific services provided by the organization. The national organization is concerned with helping its affiliates to stimulate the interest of volunteers in the program and to train them for the tasks they are asked to assume.

6. *Public Education.* One of the basic responsibilities of the national organization is to make the public aware of the needs which exist in its specialized area of concern. This relates both to general climate setting objectives, and to the specific task of recruiting interested volunteers.

7. *Legislation.* In many instances, the problems being dealt with are of such a nature that they require governmental assistance. The national organization, therefore, becomes concerned with obtaining appropriate legislation to meet the needs in which it is interested.

8. *Fund Raising.* Although last on the list, fund raising is often a major objective. One of the central purposes of a local affiliate, frequently, is to raise funds on the local level for the national program of the agency; and it is therefore a responsibility of the national to help the local organize its campaigns. National promotion, "gimmicks," professional help are tools in this process. The nature and variety of fund raising activity are so extensive that one could write a separate paper on these aspects alone. Differential factors are the size of the national budget; and the method of financing, whether through membership dues, inclusion in local chests or united funds, or independent campaigning.

METHODS

Most national organizations employ the following methods in some form, although there are, of course, great variations not only in content, but in the extent to which any specific methods are used:

1. *Publications.* These are a major educational medium to bring information to the public about the organization's area of work, to stimulate public interest, and to report on progress in the achievement of the organization's goals. Publications also include specific *program materials* of various types, which are specific guides and resources to affiliates.

2. *National Committees.* Much of the work of national organizations in such matters as standard setting, program development, legislation, and so on, is carried out through national committees. Typically, the tasks of a national organization will be subdivided among a number of committees, each of which will be made up of people having actual experience in working on the problem in different sections of the country, together with specialists in one or another aspect of the field. These committees are given specific assignments to study a particular facet of the agency's concern, and to make recommendations for future developments in the field. Frequently, such committees will be the sponsoring group for program materials and publications.

3. *Consultation.* The heart of the work of many national agencies lies in the direct consultation which it gives to individuals and

groups (most frequently affiliates) who are working directly with the problems in its field. Much of this is done through extensive *correspondence,* which gives both information and advice in response to specific requests. The largest consultative operations are, however, in *face-to-face* contacts, which take place in two general ways:

a. Through specialists in the national office who are particularly expert in a specific phase of the agency's responsibility, and

b. Through field representatives, who have a general responsibility for relating the total gamut of the national agency's work to the particular group which is rendering the service or carrying out the specific program on the local level. In the larger agencies, field services tend to be regionally based and work closely with a variety of specialized national services in providing the necessary consultation.

4. *Studies.*   This is a formalized aspect of consultation, involving systematic examination of local problems, with a combination of self-study processes on the part of the local committees, and use of specialist consultants from the national agency or from the outside.

5. *Conferences.*   Gatherings of individuals and groups working in the special area of the organization's responsibility in order to exchange experience, share information, and stimulate interest in continuing the efforts in this field.

There is great variety to the size and scope of conferences, depending on the specific purposes to be served. *Institutes* or *workshops* are usually aimed at small working groups, emphasizing specific methods and techniques. They tend to have a *training* function. Larger conferences have more of a *promotional* objective.

COMMUNITY ORGANIZATION ELEMENTS

We come now to the central question of defining the community organization elements in national agency operations.

From one point of view, it would be possible to say that the basic responsibility of a national agency is a community organization responsibility—that this is the essential nature of its task. A national agency typically is not providing a direct functional service, but it is, each in its own way, trying to organize that section of the community which it can reach in order to render that service most effectively. This would imply that community organization skill is the basic one which a national organization should seek in implementing its program.

There are, however, some difficulties in taking such a definitive position. The difficulty arises from the variations in the program content of national agencies and also from the wide divergence of professional skills which they involve. A key question is whether the essential ingredient in the professional competence of a national agency worker is knowledge of the particular program and expertness in dealing with that specific program; or whether it is skill in the processes of community organization. How this question is answered will depend not only on program content, but also will relate to the following factors:

a. Whether the work is being done directly with individuals or with organized affiliates or agencies.

b. The stage of organization which has been achieved—whether the agency is in the intial phases of promoting a program, or whether it is providing services to well-established local organizations.

c. The specific professional areas of competence which are involved in the programs—whether or not they are in the field of social work, and what particular aspect of social work they deal with.

ORGANIZATION AND PROMOTION

All national agency activities involve promotional techniques in the sense of stimulation, community education, and so on. The promotional element, however, is most pronounced in dealing with the unorganized or less organized communities. Some of the spe-

cific things which a worker must do in the initial phases of organization are the following:

a. Find ways of determining which individuals might be interested in the agency's program.

b. Make initial face-to-face contacts with such people.

c. Establish machinery for interested or potentially interested people to come together to learn about the program and to form an organization.

d. Establishment of organizational structure through by-laws, committees, officers, and so on.

e. Developing of a "fanning-out" process whereby the nucleus leadership stimulates others to become involved in the program.

The attributes necessary for performing this type of task include expert knowledge about the problem, and familiarity with the way the national organization works. However, these are not the essentials, since they can be acquired with relative ease. The major skills on this level of work are precisely the organizational skills, and that means skill in working directly with individuals, rather than working on the planning level with established organizations.

SERVICE TO ORGANIZED AFFILIATES

Once organizations have become established, the service given to them by the national organization tends to change. The emphasis shifts to a higher level of technical operation where a great deal of specific resource material and expert guidance becomes necessary. Greater prominence is given to the relationships of the organization to others in the community that are in a similar field of service and to the planning bodies. At this level, studies and surveys and technical consultation on complex problems become the most important elements. A greater degree of expertness in the specific area of the organization's concern is necessary, although generic community organization processes are still at work.

There is a great difference also depending on whether the local affiliate has professional staff or consists entirely of volunteers. In the latter case, the basic organizational skills which need to be applied to an unorganized community are still very important. At the

other extreme is the fully staffed professional agency, where con-sultation is largely to the professional in the technical areas of his work, and lay people tend to become involved through the local professional rather than by direct contact with national agency personnel.

FIELD SERVICE

Among the national agency methods listed previously, the one which has the largest element of community organization skill is *consultation,* and especially the type of consultation given through *field service.* The *field visit,* so widespread as a method of work in national organizations, can be looked upon and studied as a dis-tinctive technique in community organization, analogous to the interview or the committee process.

In this connection, it is instructive to cite the publication pre-pared by the National Social Welfare Assembly's Committee on Field Service in December, 1952, entitled "Resource Book on Field Service Administration."

The function of the field service as described in this manual is to interpret the national program to the local community and to bring back to the national agency an "understanding of the local agency's and the community's point-of-view, program and trends." The specific functions listed are similar to those which were listed earlier in this paper as functions of the national agencies. They include such matters as improving standards, interpretation, ex-change of information, and so on. However, there is a great deal of stress on the *organizing* function—stimulating a local service where it does not exist and on helping substandard agencies to qualify for membership in the national.

The importance of the field visit is brought out as follows: *"Field visiting is the major method used by field service.* How-ever, the field representative is also giving help continually through correspondence, consultation in the regional or national office, and so on."

The manual also describes the educational qualifications which

national agencies require, saying that they usually fall into one of the following categories:

A. College graduation, supplementary training provided by agency; plus tested executive experience in a local affiliate of the national agency.
B. College graduation, supplementary graduate school training; plus tested experience in the field of work of the agency or field service in a related field.
C. College graduation; degree in social work with a major in special field of agency—plus tested executive experience in a local setting.

These requirements indicate how emphasis is placed by all agencies on background in the specific field of the agency's work, either through professional training in the specialized field with which the agency is concerned, or experience at the local level within this field. There is a clear premium on experience which is directly related to the agency's function. Social work training, per se, is far from universal as a requirement.

Among other professional qualifications, "understanding of principles and practices of community organization" is one out of ten qualifications listed. Others include three involving specific knowledge of agency problems and policies, while the remaining six deal with general skills of supervision; administration; working with individuals, boards and committees; survey work; organization of local affiliates; ability to prepare and submit accurate records. Personal qualifications include such matters as good health, a warm, friendly personality, integrity, ability to work with all kinds of people, good judgment, analytical skill, flexibility, patience, speaking ability, and so on.

CAN SCHOOLS OF SOCIAL WORK TRAIN PERSONNEL FOR NATIONAL AGENCIES?

Summarizing to this point, we can say that community organization is a basic responsibility of a national agency—an inherent aspect

of its function; that this is true whether the agency operates within the professional field of social work or not; and that the generic elements are particularly important in the area of field service and in the work with less organized and less professionalized locals. The generic elements are also important in more developed situations, but there is a greater need at that level for specific skills and areas of knowledge related to the field in which the agency operates.

We have defined, in the foregoing discussion, a substantial number of common elements in community organization practice which are equally applicable both within professional social work settings and in settings which do not have this professional orientation. If we assume that community organization skills can be taught at all, then training for community organization in a school of social work should have wide applicability in many national agency settings.

Social work training should be able to produce a more effective and more skillful national agency consultant than the national agency is likely to obtain by developing its own personnel through exclusively in-service methods, or by using people without professional training, or with training in other professional fields that do not have a clear community organization function.

The additional effectiveness would come from two sources:

a. Acquisition of professional skills based on the cumulative experience of social work practitioners in community organization processes, and

b. Knowledge of needs, services and interrelationships as they affect the entire scene of health and welfare services. This would be a broader perspective than would tend to be available within a specialized field itself.

Actual experience seems to indicate a growing tendency to employ community organization personnel with past experience in social work settings—and with social work training. This is true today in many health agencies, and in other expanding programs. This seems to imply recognition of the generic organizational skills which such personnel have.

On the other hand, large, established agencies such as the Boy

Scouts, YMCA, and so on, tend to use people who have grown up in the ranks and have a background of local experience within the particular field.

This is a natural tendency in view of the fact that a national organization plays a leadership role and, therefore, requires a high level of competence in its own staff. That competence frequently has to be defined in specialized terms, since a national agency worker will be called upon to consult with experienced professionals conducting the activities locally and needs to gain their acceptance.

Aside from formal training, personal attributes are extremely important. There is an element of maturity and judgment which becomes very important in the work of national organizations, especially when one thinks of the difficulties in working with individuals in unorganized situations or in early stages of organization. Flexibility, ability to stimulate people and yet to motivate them so that they take responsibility on their own, a sense of timing, and so on—these elements of personality can be the crucial factors in a situation.

Here, as in all other aspects of community organization work, the question arises as to whether a person can be trained by the schools *directly* for community organization, without an apprenticeship in casework or group work.

Where a national organization is providing service to casework or group work agencies, there is obvious need for its staff to have competence in the underlying field as well as community organization skill. However, competence in casework or group work is not in itself sufficient to make the professional skillful in the community organization tasks which he has to perform as a member of the staff of a national organization. He, therefore, must acquire these additional skills either through formal training or experience in the field itself through executive or sub-executive responsibilities prior to joining the national agency.

For the great majority of national organizations, casework or group work is not the area of their concern. The community organization skills are the basic ones. I would, therefore, take the

position that a person can be trained for work with many national organizations directly, without a basic experience in either casework or group work. What is needed, of course, is a structure of progressive steps in training and experience, beginning with meaningful field work placements, followed by beginning positions of limited responsibilities, where there is opportunity for supervised learning of community organization skills.

Community Organization Method and Skill in Social Casework Practice

ARLIEN JOHNSON

The point of view presented in this paper is that (1) all social workers deal with individuals, groups, and community inter-groups in varying degrees depending upon the agency in which they are employed and the major service they offer there; (2) education for social work, therefore, must give students a philosophy and understanding of their total responsibility as social workers; (3) students must have comprehension of basic principles that are common in casework, group work and community organization work and the differences that characterize each; and (4) students must develop beginning skill in one method while developing appreciation of the other methods and how to work with their colleagues who are specialists in them.

Because the literature about community organization is not definitive, I have attempted to set down a systematic approach to the subject under discussion. If the statements at times seem obvious or dogmatic, it is because of this effort to put down a framework in which can be considered the caseworker's use of community organization method.

First, terminology will be considered; next, basic principles common to social work method will be presented; and finally, social community organization work in casework practice will be discussed.

TERMINOLOGY

Agreement exists that community organization as a social process goes on wherever people live together. Human groups organize for

various purposes and continuously seek to achieve balance or equilibrium as they struggle toward the same, competing, or conflicting ends. Social workers need knowledge of this social process and can find a growing body of relevant data in sociology, anthropology, and social psychology literature.

The uneven rate of social change produces "welfare problems" and needs in any society. The gaps in the usual institutional arrangements of society thus produced, as Witmer has pointed out [1] inevitably lead philanthropic individuals, organized groups, and finally government to set up programs to meet the needs of people. The common bonds among those engaged in or interested in social welfare programs are the basis for what Ross has designated as the "welfare community." [2] Efforts to develop, extend, integrate the welfare community and its programs can be called *community organization for social welfare*. Natural leaders arise to help further this social process. A social worker may or may not be a participant but is not necessarily present.

Social work has been defined as "a professional service to people for the purpose of assisting them, as individuals, or in groups, to attain satisfying relationships and standards of life in accordance with their particular wishes and capacities and in harmony with those of the community." [3] Agreement exists that the professional service may be directed primarily to an individual, to a primary group, or to a community intergroup. Social work as a professional service develops certain characteristics which might be described under three main headings, the combination of which forms *"method."*

The three parts of method are closely interrelated but for purposes of analysis, they will be described as (1) "being" (*attitudes* of the social worker toward himself and other people which are the basis of professional philosophy); (2) "knowing" (*understanding* of individual, group, and societal behavior based on knowl-

---

1 Helen Witmer, *Social Work* (New York: Farrar and Rinehart, 1942), p. 484.
2 Murray Ross, *Community Organization Theory and Principles* (New York: Harper and Brothers, 1956), p. 41.
3 Arlien Johnson, "Social Work as a Profession," *Social Work Year Book*, 1943, p. 511.

edge); and (3) "doing" (*practice* which incorporates *being* and *knowing* and applies them to specific situations). *Skill* is the way in which the practice is carried on so that maximum utilization is made of the worker's and the client's capacity for problem-solving.

The method of professional service that is directed to an individual is known as *social casework*. When directed to a primary group it is *social group work*. I propose to designate service directed to community intergroups within a defined situation, as *social community organization work*. All of these methods give direct service to specified clientele; all depend upon attitudes, understanding based on knowledge, and practice or application of what is felt and known. If we speak of these methods as providing professional service, we mean that they are used by persons who have had education and training for social work.

Social community organization work, then, might be defined as that method in social work used by a professional social worker to help people in a community (a defined situation) to find release, direction, and integration of energy into associative forms of activity that aim to develop in the participants increasingly higher levels of socialization and that usually result in progressively more satisfying balance between social welfare needs and resources.

The term *community,* as I have pointed out elsewhere,[4] is a concept to be defined as it applies to specific situations. Every social welfare agency has its own "community" or group of people actually or potentially interested in its functional program. This exists within the larger geographical community within which the agency may have cooperative or competitive relationships with other organized groups. Thus an agency may have relationships with more than one "community." The important point is that the social worker must know and define the community for the purposes for which he is to be giving professional service. Just as "person" is a concept which must be defined in order to differentiate type, size, age, and so forth, so "community" is a concept that takes form as it is defined in relation to specific situations.

[4] "Community Organization in Social Work," *Social Work Year Book,* 1945.

SOCIAL WORK METHOD

It is my contention that we are beginning to identify a philosophy and a body of knowledge, principles, and skills—which is use of these in practice—that should be recognized as common to all work with people, whether individuals, groups, or communities. This is *social work method*. In addition, special kinds of knowledge and skills are needed by the caseworker, group worker, and community organization worker which enable each to work with greater facility and depth in his specialization.

The elaboration of what is common to all method in social work is perhaps unnecessary, but a few examples may make clearer the contention that a social work method is gradually taking shape. First, with respect to *philosophy,* the profession is clarifying (1) the institutionalized settings where social work is practiced, (2) the educational and research content that makes up the organized body of knowledge that eventually will take form as theory, and (3) the interrelationships of the parts of practice, now united in one professional association. In other words, social work is developing a "culture" uniquely its own.[5] Such a culture is found in any profession and provides the norms, values, symbols by means of which the members communicate with one another and establish common bonds. Some of the ways in which the NASW is helping its members to develop a professional culture is through acceptance of a code of ethics, personnel standards and practice, and statement on public social policy. Regardless of type of service rendered or of setting, a social worker bases his practice in the philosophy or culture of his profession.

Attitudes (being) which are a part of method stem from philosophy. Take, for example, the well-known respect for others, acceptance of others, as they are and as potentially they can be;

sensitivity to persons with awareness of the worker's feelings as well as the feelings and reactions of others; respect for the individuality and integrity of the individual, group, or community. Further examples are the belief in the capacity of people to grow and change and the obligation of the social worker to "enable" this possibility; the belief that people have the right to determine their own goals within the limits of the situation. These attitudes and beliefs, rooted in understanding of behavior, are accepted by caseworkers, group workers, and community organization workers but are applied in different contexts.

Understanding (knowing) is, of course, the foundation upon which a profession rests. The kinds of knowledge that a social worker needs become increasingly broad as biological and social sciences produce findings that give new insight into behavior. For many years schools of social work gave courses in medical and psychiatric "information." But with the acceptance of the concept of the "person-as-a-whole," we have come to see that what needs to be understood is the interplay of physical, intellectual, emotional, and social factors as they affect and are affected by innate and environmental forces throughout the life span. Social work knowledge has made its own application of much material from medicine and from psychiatry particularly; it has recently begun to use material from anthropology, social psychology, and sociology to give insight into the part played by cultural differences in explaining behavior.[6] It is obvious that the community organization worker has special need of this kind of knowledge if he is to

6 As evidence, *see* this statement by a caseworker: "For valid and historical reasons, the main emphasis in casework study and diagnosis has been on the biological system of the client's body and on his personality system. While caseworkers have always paid some attention to the client's external environment, their study and diagnosis of that environment have been carried out in more or less empirical, *ad hoc* terms. It will be suggested here that study and diagnosis of the environment can be carried out in systematic terms and that such systematic study will reveal some criteria for evaluating the social health of the client's environment. Moreover, the study of the environment, as well as of the body and personality, as a set of systems provides a guide to the understanding of the 'total client in his total situation' which is the goal of diagnosis and the foundation of definitive treatment." Werner Lutz, "Testing the Social Health of the Client's Environment," *Proceedings of the Sixth Biennial Alumni-Faculty Conference,* School of Social Work, University of Pittsburgh, 1956, 39.

understand the dynamics of the organized forces within the community in which he is employed; but all social workers must have understanding of these forces as a form of behavior.

Practice (doing) is the *raison d'etre* for attitudes and understanding. Here, the art of application is dependent to a certain extent upon what the worker himself brings to education. The instrumentality through which service is given is the personality of the worker; and one aim of professional education is the disciplining of the person so that he can make maximum use of his ability within the culture of the profession. It has been well said that "knowledge without skill is ineffective, and skill without knowledge is dangerous." Skill in practice is learned by doing. And one of the problems in social work education is to give students practice in use of themselves in more than one method.

In summary, we can say that any social worker has certain attitudes, understanding, and practice in application of these, which are common to work with individuals, groups, and community configurations of people. Concepts and principles hold true generally. The kinds of knowledge which underlie these are basic to all types of practice. Having made this statement, however, we must now ask ourselves what is unique about social community organization work which caseworkers must understand in order consciously to make use of this method appropriately as part of their practice.

SOCIAL COMMUNITY ORGANIZATION WORK IN CASEWORK PRACTICE

Social casework, as the oldest and best defined aspect of social work method, had its origin, of course, in community organization for social welfare. The Charity Organization Society was at first a way of putting some order into the philanthropic giving of the community but gradually developed a method of administering such aid so that it offered "differential treatment" of individuals for "society's betterment." This two-fold purpose led the early family

service agencies to pioneer in their communities in filling in gaps such as organizing free medical service and legal aid, advocating social legislation to improve housing, working conditions, and many other remedial and protective measures.

As social work grew into a profession and social casework began to develop a body of theory, caseworkers became more and more expert in the "differential treatment" which Mary Richmond had described as the "half of social work which has to do with the social treatment of individuals, individual by individual, as distinguished from all those processes of social reform which deal with the individuals in the mass." [7] Professionalization necessarily leads to increasingly precise definition of function; and while family welfare agencies and social caseworkers still assert their belief that "in the 'good society' the welfare of the individual and society go hand in hand," [8] their preoccupation has been with deepening their skill in work with individuals, greatly enhanced by understanding gained from psychiatry.

The relatively recent interest in applying insights from the social sciences to understanding the person as a whole in his social milieu, is bringing back the caseworker's concern for the "social betterment" half of social work. But instead of his responsibility being for social reform in general and discrete activities in particular, we can now help him to see that societal process can be understood and affected by the social worker with some of the same kind of defintion of function that the caseworker has long applied in work with individuals. In other words, social community organization work is a method of helping people work together on problems and action to solve problems of community concern. The social worker must have the same kind of disciplined use of himself in relation to community leaders and groups representing organized forces, that the caseworker has in his relationship to individuals. The focus is upon enabling people to work toward goals and is not primarily upon program or legislation

[7] Mary E. Richmond, *The Long View* (New York: Russell Sage Foundation, 1915), 374.
[8] Florence Hollis, "Social Casework," *Social Work Year Book*, 1957, 525.

per se, although one of the areas of special knowledge which the community organization worker has, is of programs and social organization forms. To what extent, then, does the caseworker need to understand community organization work in order to assume his share of responsibility for social change?

Social caseworkers cannot escape observation of the causal and/ or associated factors of individual disequilibrium and social dys-functioning—often the cause behind the symptom. Indeed, Boehm has suggested that the function of social casework is to become active in such areas.[9] Caseworkers find gaps in services, the areas in which neither their agencies nor any other is operating. They are the front line detectors of how the policies of their own agency and of others are serving ostensible purposes or falling short. The channelling of such observations through the line of authority of their own agency, through committees of the community planning agency on which they may serve, or through their professional association, involves understanding and practice of the community organization method.

At the risk of over-simplifying the aspects of community organization work which caseworkers need to practice, I shall comment upon the three parts of method which I described earlier; viz., being, knowing, doing or attitudes, understanding, and practice. And I shall suggest a few learning experiences through which these may be instilled.

ATTITUDES TOWARD SELF AND OTHERS

As a caseworker is drawn into community organization work that is inherent in his job, he begins to realize that the clientele with whom he is engaged is different from the relatively well-defined group of clients served by his agency. Let us assume he has been sent by his agency to represent it on a committee of a community planning agency. The members of the committee represent power figures in the community, perhaps; and they may include social

[9] Werner Boehm, "The Terminology of Social Casework," *Social Service Review,* December 1954, 384.

workers from other agencies whose policies are in disagreement with those of the agency the caseworker represents. He discovers that feelings about authority which he thought he had worked through long ago as a student are aroused by the influential banker on the committee, by the dominant PTA president. He may feel he cannot communicate with other social workers with whom his agency's policies are in disagreement. How does he apply the principles of "acceptance?" Of starting where the group is? Of having respect for difference?

All social workers need to master what the community organization worker has to achieve; viz., acceptance and understanding of so-called laymen and of colleagues, in the same way the caseworker understands and accepts behavior of individual clients over a wide range of variation. Since so many social workers are from middle class culture, they need to have awareness of their own reactions and behavior and they need to know what to expect from upper class culture as well as from behavior of their own and other professional groups. The facts are that caseworkers too often want nothing to do with the "volunteer" and with community organization. Yet they cannot escape contact with both. Professional education, therefore, must inculcate attitudes toward self and others which will give the students ability to function in the community setting as well as in the agency office.

LEARNING EXPERIENCES

Courses in community organization, social workers report, have often been sterile and seemingly unrelated to their experience. If the course is taught as *social community organization work* with cross reference to the same principles that have been learned in casework, students begin to understand the importance of applying what they know to a different milieu. Since casework students will probably not have time in the Master's program for field instruction in a community organization agency, class assignments need 1) to relate to field work placement wherever possible, and 2) to observation of community groups in action.

Sample Assignments:

1. Analysis of the board member composition of the agency in which the student is placed for field work (or of an advisory committee to a public agency) to examine that segment of the community is represented in it and how the members differ from the clients of the agency—if they do. Determination of what is the agency's "community," or "communities."

2. Attendance at a welfare planning council committee over the period of the semester (probably three to four meetings). Take minutes which are handed in to the class instructor with an analysis of the composition of the committee and the part taken by the staff community organization worker.

UNDERSTANDING COMMUNITY PROCESS AND STRUCTURE

Most schools of social work have little in the curriculum about community process. Pittsburgh and Western Reserve have given attention to such knowledge over a long period of time—knowledge which is correlative with the human growth and behavior sequence. This kind of knowledge about conditions and forces that make for disorganization or integration of community life is indispensable for the community organization worker and should be regarded as essential for all social workers, including caseworkers. Ross, Coyle, Stein, Maas—to mention a few at random—are making useful contributions to the application of hypotheses about community life to the practice of social work.[10] Most teaching in this area is fragmentary at present; often it has to be included in the course in community organization work.

Another kind of knowledge which the caseworker needs, concerns the varieties and kinds of community structures through which cooperative effort can be undertaken. He should know that every agency has a community organization responsibility to the community which gave it being; that this responsibility is dis-

10 *See,* for example, Ross, *op. cit.,* Chapter 4 "Some Hypotheses about Community Life;" Grace Coyle, "New Insights for Social Workers from the Social Sciences," *Social Service Review,* September 1952; Henry Maas, Herman Stein *et al.,* "Sociocultural Factors in Psychiatric Clinics for Children" (Northampton: Smith College Studies in Social Work, Vol. XXV, No. 2, February 1955).

charged by every member of the staff, not just the executive—although leadership in this area rests most heavily upon this office. Social casework, Richmond said, comes in "before and after the mass movement for any given social reform;" [11] and social reform, she maintained, should be carried into the daily performance of duty of the caseworker. Without enumerating the many ways in which a social welfare agency staff promotes cooperative effort in its own field of service as well as in the social welfare field as a whole, suffice it here to point out that leadership is a phenomenon applicable to an agency quite as much as to an individual.

If the caseworker is to participate in community organization process, he must understand the coordinating and planning structures through which the process flows. This includes knowledge about the organization of voluntary and official welfare services, and how to help them develop differentially in accordance with community needs and readiness. Also the caseworker should have some background on the community chest movement which is peculiar to the United States, and of welfare council or community planning council, the neighborhood organization movement and its relationship to trends in centralization and decentralization in other aspects of community life.

Sample Assignments:
1. A notebook of clippings from small town or neighborhood newspaper to help the student learn about (a) community identification, (b) leadership, individual and from organized associations, (c) presence of sub-groups, (d) community "problems," (e) community attitudes and action with respect to social welfare services.
2. Discussion of case records that illustrate the process of community organization in upper class and/or lower class community and the difference in the activity of the community organization worker in them.
3. Attendance at a community chest campaign meeting, a welfare planning conference, or a neighborhood coordinating council. Class discussion of meaning of observations in light of theory.

[11] *Op. cit.,* 379.

PRACTICE OF SOCIAL COMMUNITY ORGANIZATION WORK

The caseworker can be helped to understand the practice of social community organization work even though he may have limited opportunity to undertake it himself while a student. A few of the principles of practice which, it would be hoped might remain with him to use when he became employed, are listed below.

1. Social community organization practice is inherent in all of social work practice. The social worker, therefore, needs to accept the concept of integrated practice. Depending upon the clientele and the agency by whom he is employed the social worker engages in the primary use of one method and in the supplementary use of other methods.

2. Principles the caseworker has learned in class and field instruction apply in social community organization work but the materials one works with are different. These include attitudes about himself and others who come from all strata of society and who may represent powerful organized forces. Other materials include understanding of process and structure of people in organized association for a purpose; that process and structure—two sides of a coin—are never ends in themselves but are always relative to a particular community for a particular purpose, with consideration for community values, norms, and so on.

3. While the caseworker's chief instrumentality is the interview, the community organization worker's chief instrumentality is the committee. From courses about group process the casework student should have developed some "feel" for committee and group process. Committee work in the student organization while a student, and in the staff after employment, give opportunity to apply learning about group dynamics, discussion leadership, minute taking, and so on.

4. Just as the caseworker becomes expert in utilizing history taking toward treatment ends, so the community organization worker has such tools as fact finding, research, interpretation, by means of which he helps people to widen social consciousness. He learns that facts must be related to the wishes and capacities of those who are "the community;" that a "fact" has reality only as people re-

spond to it (something he has learned about individual reaction).

5. The caseworker learns that the skill of the community organization worker lies in the interweaving of people, facts, and organization forms or structures in such a way that maximum consideration is given to the quality and capacity of each in relation to the goals toward which the community decides to move. He works with people at many different levels of socialization, with many different experiences, habits, memories about associative activities. He finds structures with many different degrees of vitality and usefulness but he regards organizations as a form of life and tries to enable them to grow usefully. In all this the caseworker should be aware of the process and help appropriately as he has the opportunity.

6. The caseworker should understand that the relationship which the social work expert and the layman develops is the "warp and woof" of the community organization process. The social worker is a partner with the citizen in evaluating technical knowledge, in weighing it, in relation to particular situations in the light of experience, and in acting upon it for the common welfare. But the final decision must rest with the organized association of citizens who support the professional service the social worker provides.

7. The caseworker's technical knowledge may be in a special aspect of social welfare but as he makes it available to community groups for planning purposes he realizes the contribution which his profession can make to the society of which it is a part.

How can the caseworker learn all this and practice accordingly? Too often he does not learn it and does not practice it. But as schools of social work integrate classroom teaching throughout the curriculum and widen field work experience to include understanding and observation of agency activities in community organization, students may lose their disdain of volunteers and may catch the excitement that comes from having insight into community life as a form of behavior. Unfortunately, community organization method is confused, social science materials are not yet applied so that a conceptual framework can be taught; we must rely upon experience to guide teaching. The agencies in which

casework is the major service reflect also the stage of development of community organization theory and practice. Where there is leadership of social workers with philosophy, knowledge, and experience in community organization work, young workers have a chance to develop an integrated practice of social work. But further study and effort to develop a conceptual framework for social community organization work may await a scholar who can do for this area of method what Richmond did for social casework and what Coyle has done for social group work.

Content in Community Organization Course (Basic)

HERTHA KRAUS

Our concept of social work, of which community organization is a part, obviously influences our approach to this field. As social workers in a democratic community, we are concerned with the manifold tasks of helping people to live satisfying and productive lives, to move in the direction of their own highest potential.

FACILITIES AND SERVICES

Such movement in a complex society often depends on ready access to organized facilities and services which will provide opportunities for "assisted self-help" and mutual aid. Others will anticipate dangerous intersections in the life path, or deal with common hazards of living. We are aware of the need for more effective provisions; more generally accessible, more closely related to common and repetitive needs, more productive in rendering service.

In a democratic community the strength and scope of all service resources will largely depend on the spirit of the supporting society, its understanding of basic human needs, its desire and capacity for constructive interaction, its welfare goals. As social workers, we are inevitably concerned with the strengthening of these foundations for social development, as well as with the building of its social and economic potential into meaningful units of common service.

WIDENING GOALS

As social workers we have long paid attention to neglect, injuries and wounds, to economic and health deficiencies in individual living. While we continue to help those already injured, we are increasingly eager to use our insight, knowledge and skill also for the shaping of such group measures—broad in coverage and comprehensive in reach—which may *prevent* some of these ills, or deal with them in a more satisfactory way, using our best and most recent scientific understanding.

As social workers we also hope to see a fair share of our steadily *rising economic potential,* result of our growing national productivity, applied to the development of common provisions for the common benefit. They would conserve and develop more fully our most important national resource—people.

Social work is a part of our society which, during recent decades, has rapidly grown more complex, more organized, more industrialized, more mobile. Society has also become more scientific, and perhaps a little more sensitive to human values, to the tragedy of human waste. Today's interpretation of democracy will no longer be found compatible with indifference to poisonous discrimination, to slum housing and severely blighted areas, to the ravage of destitution, of long-term unemployment, unmet sickness. The fight against disability, want and discrimination is an essential part of our present *reinterpretation of the meaning of democracy, a never-ending task,* a challenge to each generation.

It is a special challenge to social workers as a professional group. The current reinterpretation of democracy—the application of democracy's fundamental principles to dealing with common human needs—relates to the very essence of our professional function, to central social work values. We must be prepared to render active, concrete, knowledgeable assistance to this process. We must deeply understand it, be willing to share in it, and give our most skillful help.

THE HELPING PROCESS IN
COMMUNITY ORGANIZATION

Within social work, community organization practice focuses most directly on the problems faced by communities and community groups in their social development and, more specifically, on their attempts to relate social facilities and services most effectively to changing needs and opportunities.

As in other areas of social work, the helping process is applied to problem-solving. It makes use of social work values and concepts, of several areas of knowledge, of a wide range of methods and techniques, many of which are shared with other disciplines.

The helping process as a professional service is made available to communities and community groups toward the development of a more integrated, more cooperative society which will support a strong fabric of common facilities and services to meet common needs of its members. Moving toward this goal, help and technical aid may be in order in developing and strengthening the social foundations and social objectives of a community, or the entire society, irrespective of the immediate strengthening of specific resources related to selected needs. This may mean a focus on improving human relations, favoring cooperative interaction and mutual aid in traditional areas of tension. It may involve the development of more, and more effective, channels of communication across economic, social, cultural, sectarian and racial barriers. It may also imply the building of a wider awareness of social problems, of unmet or neglected needs, of limited or ineffective resources relating to such needs. Social development may involve the strengthening of common understanding of the strong interdependence of economic and social development, of the importance of human resources and human relationships for the stability and productivity of the economy. It may need to focus on providing a broader and deeper understanding of the major elements of social change as they affect individuals and communities. It may deal

with traditional and changing welfare goals, and the widening scope of the welfare potential.

Community organization practice will frequently also be concerned, beyond these foundations, with the dynamic building of more adequate resources and services in a given setting:

> These may be in the form of temporary or emergency solutions in response to a sudden need of catastrophic character. Improvised but comprehensive and meaningful action may involve many groups and individuals in effective cooperation in an area of physical disaster (hurricanes, floods, earthquakes), or in areas of severe tensions due to racial or labor conflict, sudden dislocation or in-migration of large groups, and so on.

More frequently the development of more adequate community resources, however, will aim at their continuous service, perfecting the community's permanent equipment for better living.

Communities differ widely. Each one is conditioned by its history and tradition, by its pattern of growth, by its power structure, by the composition and balance of its population groups. It is essential to understand our client, the community; and to meet and accept him on his own level if we expect to be of help.

The community's problem may be an old and neglected one, or it may be of recent origin. In any event, it is likely to be affected by the impact of change on our society, which widely influences the scope and character of needs, but also contributes to society's material and scientific potential for dealing with them effectively. Knowledge of major elements of change (at least in American society) is thus an important pre-condition for dealing wisely with the problems at hand, and may need interpretation and broad sharing.

Major professional contributions to community organization for social welfare may thus be directed toward the following areas:

1. Strengthening the foundations of social development
2. Identifying social welfare implications of a changing society
3. Identifying unmet needs

4. Standard-setting and evaluating services and facilities

5. Identifying the essentials of effective social policy and social design

6. Strengthening the problem-solving process

It would seem that the basic course in community organization would be a combination of a substance and methods course, with minor emphasis on the discussion of methods and techniques.

It is the writer's subjective opinion that such a course, covering much of the material as outlined in this statement and briefly listed in the Appendix, will be most helpful in strengthening the generic core of social work education, enabling the casework and group work specialist (and also the student of social work research and administration) to gain in perspective and general professional competence whenever and wherever he is called upon to make a contribution to broad social development, or to specific issues in social planning and the production of stronger services. It is also hoped that our profession may become qualified to contribute more consciously and continuously to the foundation area of social development considered of supreme importance.

ADDENDA

As in other areas of social work practice, the professional social worker in his helping role in the area of community organization will draw on his entire equipment of social work values, basic concepts, areas of knowledge, and also on selected methods and techniques.

VALUES

American social work values are likely to be identical with common values of American society—applied, however, with consistency and possibly greater emphasis as a foundation of the professional service. Some characteristic values reinforced in social work may be listed as follows:

Recognition of the worth and dignity of every individual
Faith in everyone's potential for growth and change
Acceptance of differences
Recognition of social as well as individual responsibility
Cooperation as a desirable way of life
Humanism

In working with community groups, social workers may assume that these values are part of the American culture, and widely accepted as valid. Jointly we are challenged to apply them in dealing with specific situations.

BASIC CONCEPTS

Underlying all social work practice are some well-known basic concepts equally meaningful to the professional contribution to community organization, such as:

The interdependence of social problems
The acceptance of the dynamics of human behavior
Culture as an important conditioning factor of individual and group behavior
The importance of working with, not for, people
The importance of the problem-centered approach

AREAS OF KNOWLEDGE

All areas of knowledge contributing to social work practice may be relevant to community organization at some point, but special mention should be made of such areas as:

Understanding of the growth patterns of urban and rural communities
Understanding of government structure and function
Understanding of major areas of social change
Understanding of individual and group behavior
Understanding of the American welfare structure and organization

In the latter area, in which social workers may be expected to

have specific competence, the community organization worker should be familiar with:

1. Patterns of organized resources
   The tradition of the "crazy quilt"
   Need for more comprehensive and more integrated patterns of services and facilities
2. Yardsticks and measurements of the adequacy of existent resources
3. Changing priorities in meeting community problems
4. Changes in social design—experimentation and new choices
5. Community-centered planning vs. agency programs and loyalties
6. Prevention, control, and rehabilitation vs. piecemeal treatment

METHODS AND TECHNIQUES

The practitioner will draw on a considerable range of methods and techniques which on the whole are not peculiar to the social work profession, such as:

Fact-finding and research
Consultation
Negotiation
Group conference
Committee operation
Interpretation
Education
Mobilization (of man-power, finances, and so on.)
Administration
Recording
Design of social facilities and services

Community Organization

ROBERT H. MACRAE

In the performance of his duties the community organizer occupies three distinct roles. On occasion, he serves as a technical and professional consultant to the community group he is serving. This implies a quality of expertness in which his judgment is sought on questions concerning which he speaks with a measure of authority. On other occasions, the community organizer occupies the role of an adult educator. In this role he is an interpreter through the use of the written or spoken word. He may also be a promoter of a "cause" such as a financial campaign or a polio vaccination effort. On still other occasions, and probably his most characteristic role, the community organizer is an "enabler." Utilizing the committee process, the community organizer helps a group diagnose a community problem, assemble the facts relevant to the problem, interpret those facts, develop a proposal for solution of the problem and, finally, assist the group to take action to secure adoption of the proposal. It is in this role that the community organizer performs his most unique and clearly identifiable task. Each of the roles suggests the methods he utilizes in performing his tasks.

Parenthetically, it should be noted that community organization is not limited to the field of social welfare. The chamber of commerce secretary, the urban renewal worker, the community development worker in Burma or Greece—each of these (and other community workers as well) is a community organizer. Furthermore, community organizers may be engaged in the development and promotion of social nostrums and panaceas reflective of man's stupidity or credulity rather than his intelligence or nobility. Community organizers may also be employed in socially evil and divisive programs aimed at setting off race against race and religious group

against religious group. The community organizer in social welfare may utilize many of the techniques and methods used by the broader classification of community organizers. The distinctive characteristics of the community organizer in social welfare are his knowledge of health and welfare problems,the services devised to deal with these problems and a thoroughgoing commitment to advance the health and welfare of the community through group action.

In order to perform his roles successfully, preparation for the community organizer is essential on both the undergraduate and graduate levels. On the undergraduate level the training of the community organizer should include the following disciplines: His formal training should be characterized by a broad and integrated liberal arts education with emphasis upon sociology, psychology, anthropology, political science and history. He should have had some training in logic so that he is able to marshal his ideas in an orderly and systematic manner. He should have had rigorous training in English composition so that he can present his ideas with lucidity and accuracy. He should have had speech training so that his oral presentations are marked by grace and effective persuasiveness.

Prior to the admission of the community organizer to graduate level instruction he should be subjected to a careful screening process which would include among other things a searching personal interview. It has been my unhappy experience to know a substantial number of young people who have been permitted to undergo the rigors of graduate training when their potential for success in community organization was negligible. Personality factors are of great importance in determining the success of a worker in the field of community organization. These factors can be determined successfully only through a penetrating personal interview of sufficient duration to determine basic personality qualities and attitudes. A successful community organizer must possess a deep respect for people coupled with the belief in their capacity for change and self-determination when choices are presented to them. The community organizer must have an abiding belief in

the democratic process which will enable him to resist the temptations to manipulate people. The community organizer will be a person who has a democratic rather than an authoritarian personality. He will possess winsomeness and a genuineness which elicits confidence and cooperation. While he will have some of the zeal of a crusader, it will be disciplined by respect for facts, a readiness to compromise, and a clear capacity to work within the framework of democratic process.

On the graduate level I speak of curriculum content with the greatest of diffidence. I have neither skill nor experience in developing a curriculum, giving its components proper weight and integrating the whole program for the development of professional competence. The comments which follow are, therefore, general observations on the part of a practitioner who would like to have community organizers associated with him who bring to the job these elements of training.

If at all possible, community organizers should have the benefit of training in either the casework or group work sequence. While it is possible to have a successful career in community organization without casework or group work training, I believe the quality of performance can be improved by such training. Such a requirement would, of course, reduce sharply the number of people entering community organization. This may be an unrealistic demand which would be self-defeating. Short of this standard, a modified curriculum should provide the community organization student with the basic principles of casework and group work process.

The curriculum should provide the community organization student with a survey course on the history and development of American social work. He needs this perspective in time. Awareness of the charity organization movement will give him a sense of participation in a historic past and, hopefully, a sense of humility. An understanding of the rise and development of public welfare services is an essential to his development. Accompanying this, I would hope for the presentation of principles on which could be developed an understanding of the appropriate division of responsibility between public and voluntary auspices. Expe-

diency, arising out of the political climate, governs too many such decisions today.

Community organizers would benefit tremendously from instruction in the methods by which social policy is formulated. In part, this suggests a historical approach. It suggests also an examination of the processes by which government determines social policy today. Private "governments" in the form of the trade union movement, organized business and industry, organized religious forces, fraternal and patriotric societies also exercise substantial influence in determining social policy. The community organizer needs to understand these processes. Not only does he need to understand these activities as social phenomena, but he also needs to know how to engage successfully in social action to advance the goals of social welfare. In too great a degree, community organizers and social workers generally have been reluctant to engage in legislative social action. The growing significance of public welfare means that the far-reaching decisions for human welfare are being made in state houses across the nation. Social work must begin to exercise a far more significant influence on these decisions. The community organizer has a responsibility for leadership in this area. Fear, inertia and ignorance restrain him today to a large measure. His training should not only give him a sense of direction, but also some of the essential skills for social policy-making.

I believe that the curriculum should provide training in the ethics of social work. This may be in formal courses or incidentally in other courses of training. However given, it is an essential component.

Without attempting to make a community organizer a social research expert, he needs training in statistical methods and basic research processes. His inadequacy in handling social data is clearly evident with all too great frequency. I would hope also that the community organization student could have a working knowledge of accounting methods, budget preparation and control, and understand how to read a balance sheet. Add to all this, instruction in the skills of interpretation and the preparation of the community organizer for his tasks will be greatly enhanced.

What I have sketched is probably unreasonable and an excessively demanding course of preparation, yet it has seemed to me out of experience that training in these skills and insights has been important to social work practice in the field of community organization. The tremendous influence community organizers exert in the growth and development of social welfare services demands a high quality of preparation. We are suggesting preparation in social statesmanship and this does not come easily or cheaply.

Now some general observations. While it is not imperative to successful community organization practice, it seems to me that direct-service agency experience is highly desirable. A man will probably be a better community organizer if he has seen the community organization job from the point of view of the direct service agency. It will give him an insight and understanding which will bring about greater acceptance of his work as a community organizer. It must be recognized, however, that there are practical problems of arranging field work in the direct service agency which will provide any substantial community organization experience. In the casework agency only the top administrative and supervisory posts are likely to possess a community organization component. In the group work agency the opportunities for community organization experience are likely to be greater but not abundant.

The provision of adequate field work experience for the community organization student must be a perplexing problem for the faculties of professional schools. Not only are opportunities limited in the direct-service agencies, but all too many community organization agencies are ill-prepared psychologically and professionally to undertake the supervision a student requires. Pressure for time is also a continuing hazard to adequate supervision. The problem of adequate field work opportunities in community organization should be the subject of concentrated and cooperative inquiry on the part of representatives of schools and agencies.

In general, I would like to see classroom preparation move away from training in methods and techniques toward a concentration on principles of social welfare organization and the development

of powers of analysis and orderly thought. This, of course, assumes the opening of field work placements with adequate time for high grade supervision where techniques and methods can be learned by doing. This is not possible to any great extent at the present time and the community organization curriculum must carry training in methods and techniques. However, genuinely professional training in the long pull must emphasize principles and capacity for analysis rather than instruction in techniques and methods. As long as the emphasis in training for social work is heavily on techniques, schools will be engaged largely in vocational training. Professional training, on the other hand, should be preparation for the intelligent application of principles, utilization of orderly thought, and powers of analysis. Community organization is a complex and demanding field of human effort. Thus far it has not been characterized by any high degree of intellectual pathbreaking. As preparation for the field moves into a new phase it must concern itself with the development of mature people, competent to give creative although indirect leadership with greater effectiveness than in the past. I hope the warmth and strong emotional content of social work will never become desiccated. This goal, however, is not in conflict with the belief that more disciplined thought and more creative analysis should characterize community organization practice in the future.

Community Organization Methods and Skills Required for Effective Practice of Social Group Work

JOHN MCDOWELL

INTRODUCTION

Social group workers, as well as all other varieties of social workers, for effective practice, require mastery of a considerable body of knowledge about the nature, structure, and organization of communities. The group worker should have a working knowledge of the political, economic and social organization of communities. He should know how each of these affect social welfare services, through their effects on family and neighborhood living conditions and through the operations of the power structure of the community in relation to social welfare administration planning, and fund-raising. The social group worker should also have a working knowledge of how social welfare services are organized, the purposes and functions of the respective operating, planning and fund-raising agencies. These are mentioned at the beginning of this paper and briefly because the body of it is written on the assumption that this generic material is being covered elsewhere in the Curriculum Study. The conviction is merely registered here that this basic knowledge about community is an essential requirement for effective social group work practice, as it is for other kinds of social work practice.

I. What knowledge and skill in community organization processes should be in the professional equipment of every social

group worker as he undertakes one of the characteristic jobs for which social group workers are employed?

For purposes of this paper, three rather different, but interrelated community organization processes are identified and dealt with from the point of view of the subject assigned. They are:

A. The intergroup work process.[1]

B. The educational and promotional process.[2]

C. Community planning for and organization of social welfare services.[3]

A. *The Intergroup Work Process:*

In order to document the need for mastery of this community organization process as a requisite to the effective practice of social group work, it is necessary to review what the process is. For this purpose, reference is made to the best-known proponent of this as the basic social work process in community organization, Wilber I. Newstetter. In his presentation to the National Conference of Social Work in San Francisco, 1947, he described this process and the function in it of the social worker. He gives as background the dual foci of the social group work process.

In the social group work process, there are two purposes to which the adjustive efforts are primarily directed:

1. The meeting of personal needs of particular individuals through voluntary group association

2. The meeting of community or societal needs.

The emphasis is directed toward mutually satisfactory interpersonal relations between members of the given

1 Cf. *Proceedings* of the National Conference of Social Work, 1947, Wilber I. Newstetter: "The Social Intergroup Work Process," pp. 205–217.

2 *Ibid.* Lester B. Granger. "Educational and Promotional Process in Community Organization," pp. 218–226.

3 Wayne McMillen. "Community Organization for Social Welfare," Chicago: University of Chicago Press, 1945, p. 38.

group through which the individuals may satisfy their need for social adjustment, development, and growth, on the one hand; and through which at the same time, certain basic community needs may be met, such as the need for people to cooperate, to learn the accepted values represented by that community, and to learn to participate in the process of modifying and creating social value in the indispensable community processes of cooperating, adjusting to division of labor, learning social responsibility, accountability, delegation of authority, and the like.[4]

The social intergroup work process likewise has two foci.

The first focus in the social intergroup work process deals with the adjustmental relations between groups and not the personal needs of the members of the intergroup who are primarily representatives of some group or groups. The need, therefore, is not primarily that of particular individuals for adjusting themselves to other individuals; it is the need of groups in a given community to maintain mutually satisfying relations with other groups. In the social group work process, one main focus is in terms of the interpersonal relations of group members. Here, this is important only as a means to an end, the end being the relations between the groups.

The second focus is again related to meeting community and societal needs, but it may be defined as specific social goals selected and accepted by the groups involved, such as, for example, child welfare service, family welfare service, recreation, housing, fair employment practices and the like. In other words, this process is directed toward the adjustmental relations between the groups in terms of some specific social goal. There is no real accomplishment in this process,

[4] *Op. cit.,* pp. 206–207.

no matter how well adjusted and related the individuals may become with respect to each other, unless and until the adjustmental relations between groups are furthered in terms of the selected goal.[5]

Social group workers in many different agency settings have frequent occasion to provide staff service to "house councils," representative agency or community committees, and other bodies which are presumed to be intergroup in character. It is, therefore, imperative that they master the knowledge and skill necessary to perform satisfactorily the functions of a social worker in intergroup work. These are outlined in considerable detail in Mr. Newstetter's presentation in San Francisco.[6] Particular attention should be given to the following in the educational preparation of the social group worker:

Understanding individuals serving as representatives of groups, especially ways in which the abilities, needs, and status of each affect his functioning as a representative of his group and as a member of the intergroup body.

Skill in helping these individuals to represent their respective groups responsibly and to perform their proper roles as a member of the intergroup body.

Skill in helping individual representatives to reconcile the values they find in these interpersonal relationships with the goals of the intergroup body.

Understanding the group processes which the intergroup body will use in establishing objectives, deciding on means and methods, assigning responsibilities and maintaining necessary controls, evaluating results, redirecting efforts, reporting to appropriate bodies, limiting activities to established objectives, and so on.

Skill in helping the intergroup body to function effec-

5 *Op. cit.*, pp. 208–209.
6 *Op. cit.*, pp. 210–213.

tively as a group within the framework and limitations implicit in its delegated responsibilities.

Understanding groups represented in the intergroup body well enough to appraise the effectiveness of their representation in that body, to recognize the relationship of their purposes and functions to that of the other groups represented, to identify differences in groups which handicap or facilitate their cooperation with other groups toward specific objectives.

Skill in helping groups potentially or actually to be represented in the intergroup body, to examine their own interest in relation to the social goals visualized, to participate in selection of social goals, to select suitable representatives to the intergroup body, and to provide for proper instruction of representatives and for adequate reporting from them. Understanding the social worker's role in the intergroup work process.

Skill in keeping one's activities and relationships within the proper framework of the social worker's role in the intergroup work process, in interpreting that role to members of the intergroup body, to the body as a whole and to groups presently or potentially represented in it.

Understanding of the scope and limitations of the intergroup body and its relationship to other groups in the agency or community.

Skill in interpreting the intergroup body to other groups or agencies and to the community.

B. *The Educational and Promotional Process:*
The agencies which employ most of the professionally educated social group workers expect them to be able to help organize and to provide staff service to groups whose purpose is to promote the service program of the agency (as in scouting) or to aid in the attainment of agency objectives in respect to a community social problem (as

in a neighborhood affairs committee related to a neighborhood center).

For successful practice of group work in assignments of this kind, knowledge and skill in relation to the following functions are required:

Understanding the relation of agency purpose and function to specific educational and promotional objectives and undertakings.

Skill in helping promotional groups to operate effectively within limitations, which may be self-imposed, agency-imposed, or required by the community situation.

Understanding the kinds of factual information required for the tackling of problems.

Skill in assembling information and in presenting it in such a way that it facilitates intelligent group decision and action. This includes ability to help groups to use reliable factual information in:

1. Capturing community attention
2. Keeping interested public accurately informed about problem being dealt with
3. Deciding on relative effectiveness of alternative action programs.

Understanding of factors affecting community attitudes, of methods of appraising attitudes, and of methods of changing attitudes.

Skill in assessing, dealing with, and changing attitudes in groups and in communities.

Understanding of the relationship of the educational process to the promotional goals and vice versa.

Skill in helping groups to plan and carry out a program of education toward specific social goals and for identifiable community audiences.

Understanding of the nature and varieties of indigenous leadeship.

Skill in identifying potential indigenous leadership, in helping to develop socially desirable qualities of leadership in individuals and groups.

Understanding of the socially useful and of the socially harmful relations between indigenous leadership and their groups and communities.

Skill in helping groups to limit as well as to support their leaders, to use leadership effectively rather than to be used by leaders.

Understanding of the role of the professional social worker in relation to the educational and promotional process within a group, an agency, and a community, his proper relationship to indigenous leadership, and to other community groups with similar or opposing objectives.

Skill in explaining the role of the social worker in the educational and promotional process to appropriate groups and in maintaining proper relationships to the group being staffed, its leadership and its subgroups, and to related community groups.

C. *Community Planning for and Organization of Social Welfare Services:*

Most social group workers, in whatever kind of agency setting they practice, sooner or later, will be called upon to represent their agency or their department in a committee of the health and welfare planning organization of their community. Many of them may be asked to pro-

vide staff service to agency or community groups engaged in fund-raising.

It is, therefore, desirable that all social group workers have a working knowledge of:

1. The functions and purposes of each type of health and welfare agency usually to be found in American communities
2. The structure and organization of health and welfare planning organizations
3. General principles in organizing efforts for fund-raising for health and welfare purposes.

Every social group worker, as does every other professional social worker, has an opportunity and an obligation to participate in the professional association of his profession. This responsibility and the role of the professional association, locally and nationally, in social welfare organization and planning should be communicated to every student in a professional school of social work.

II. What learning experiences are necessary for the effective preparation of the student planning to engage in group work practice?

A. *The Intergroup Work Process:*
In general, this subject matter should follow class and field instruction in group work process. So much of the understanding and skill used in work with groups is also used in working with intergroup bodies that the former should be mastered as a basis for the latter.

The student should be acquainted through class lectures and discussion with expositions of social work's role in working with delegate or representative groups. He should also have an opportunity to deepen and clarify his understanding, through analyzing for himself and then with others in class discussion, case records of house councils,

interagency committees, and similar groups. In field instruction, second-year students should have an opportunity to work with an intergroup council or committee under the supervision of a competent social group worker or community organization worker. Such assignments may be short-term for the duration of a specific project, but would provide the student with a basis in experience for understanding the intergroup process and the worker's role in it.

Students should also be encouraged, when appropriate, to analyze their experience with the school's student government body as an example of an intergroup organization.

B. *Educational and Promotional Process:*

Through class lectures and discussion, the social group work student should be acquainted with expositions of the nature and variety of promotional and action groups within agencies and communities. Case material based on narrative records of public affairs committees, neighborhood councils, and similar groups, frequently staffed by leisure-time agencies, should furnish valuable teaching records.

It would be highly desirable for the student preparing for social group work practice to have in his second year of field experience an assignment to a promotional or action committee, either as a representative of an agency group or as responsible for staff service to it. This should be, of course, under the supervision of a competent field instructor.

C. *Community Planning for and Organization of Social Welfare Services:*

Basic curriculum on the social services should provide most of the orientation to this area of knowledge. However, the student should be encouraged to attend meetings or conferences of the community welfare council which are open to other than voting delegates. The alert field instruction agency will make these opportunities available to student field work staff as well as regular full-time staff. It is im-

portant that the field instructor prepare the student for the meeting so that he will understand what is going on and that his questions about the experience be carefully answered afterward.

In conclusion, it should be emphasized that the three processes in community organization, which are discussed, are interrelated. Moreover, much of this work draws heavily on knowledge and skill in relation to working with groups—the practice of social group work.

Social group workers in almost any setting in which they customarily practice will need knowledge and skill in the first two processes mentioned. In the latter, the area of knowledge is valuable, but skill in practicing in it is not required of the majority of social workers in group work practice, except as it involves the other two community organization processes which are essential.

The Teaching
of Community Organization

WAYNE MCMILLEN

OBJECTIVES

The objectives of classroom education in community organization
are:

1. To acquaint the student with the instrumentalities our society has created for the purpose of advancing the community
organization process in social welfare.

2. To familiarize the student with formulations that have some
right to be considered *principles* of community organization.

3. To present the methods used in community organization and
to sharpen the student's ability to select the methods appropriate
to a specific situation.

4. To develop in the student the skills that advance the community organization process.

INSTRUMENTALITIES

The content required to achieve the first of the above-listed objectives is not included in its entirety in the classroom courses in
community organization, though some of it is more appropriate
there than elsewhere. The student needs to know the structure of
the welfare services, both governmental and voluntary, for three
reasons:

1. The coordination of the activities of the welfare agencies
(sometimes referred to as the organization of the welfare commu-

nity) is a major concern to the practitioners engaged in community organization.

2. All welfare agencies are involved to some degree in community organization (even though they may have no planned activity in the area of community organization) and are thus focal points in the process.

3. The locus from which the social worker practices community organization is almost invariably a social agency and he therefore needs an understanding of the relationship between a specific locus and the other loci within the welfare field.

It is evident that the student will be in possession of some of the content relating to instrumentalities before he enrolls in community organization. The way in which this prior knowledge is acquired will vary from one curriculum to another, and may have come in part from field work and in part from classroom courses. To cite a single illustration, a grasp of the state and local public social services may have been obtained as a result of a field work placement in a governmental agency or may have been gained in classroom courses bearing such diverse titles as, "The Field of Social Work," "The Public Social Services," "Public Assistance" and the like. It would be wasteful to repeat this material, except in brief review, in the community organization class. However, a consideration of the agencies whose primary function is community organization has added reality in a course devoted to community organization. Hence an appropriate spot for consideration of the structure, purposes, problems and methodologies of coordinating, planning, and promotional agencies is in the course in which the principles and methods utilized by such agencies are under review. The agencies considered would be those that emphasize community organization at the treatment level, such as social service exchanges, as well as those that emphasize community organization at the developmental level, such as welfare planning councils. The way in which the content relating to instrumentalities is divided among various courses, though important, is nevertheless of secondary importance. The really important objective is to provide the student with knowledge of the institutional struc-

ture upon which practitioners must depend in the furthering of the community organization process.

PRINCIPLES

The principles of community organization are informed observations. As such they are entitled to respect. They are of a different order, however, from principles in the exact sciences. For that reason there is a disposition to hold them in contempt or to declare that no principles have been established in community organization. The definition of the word "principle" is the issue here. A man suddenly confronted with responsibility for the care of three small children would probably not be interested in the advice of the first ten people he met on the street; if he is an informed individual he would be very much interested and his plan of caring for the children would be greatly influenced by the judgments of ten people with wide knowledge and experience in child welfare. The advice given him by the experts would rest on principles based on long observation and experience—and these principles constitute a valid kind of knowledge.

Principles of community organization likewise rest not upon scientifically tested hypotheses but upon observation and the interpretation of informed experience. A principle in thermodynamics may be invariably applicable; in community organization, as in child welfare, a principle is not invariably applicable because of the infinite variety of the combinations of variables to which it may be applied. Perhaps different words should be used to distinguish between these two kinds of knowledge. But in absence of any such agreed distinction, "principles" will continue to be used to refer to the generic formulations of knowledge in the area of community organization.

Accepting "principles" in this sense, we find that principles of community organization exist and that many have been formulated. Students have a right to expect to be introduced to these principles in a course in community organization. If the principles

were invariable in their applicability, presumably they could be presented as a body of truths to be integrated into the professional equipment of the learner. But there is no principle of community organization that will not require some modification in a specific situation if the attendant variables are progressively modified. Nor would there be much likelihood of success if an attempt were made to compile a complete list of the aggregations of variables in which a given principle is always applicable, partly because in any situation some of the variables are likely to remain unidentified. Hence the learning of a principle needs to be cleansed of any implication of dogma by presenting it in relation to a specific set of circumstances.

This assertion may seem to imply that principles of community organization should be taught only from the so-called community organization case records. Although principles of community organization can be abstracted from community organization case records, it is not the intent of the above assertion to imply that there is no other valid means of presenting this material. The important point is that maximum truthfulness can be achieved by presenting a principle in relation to a set of specific circumstances. The community organization case record provides only one of the means by which this objective may be attained.

Obviously the specific circumstances in terms of which a principle is presented may be outlined orally by the teacher. But we are primarily concerned here with written materials that provide the student with an opportunity for independent analysis and formulation. "Document" is a term broad enough to encompass all such written materials. It includes community organization case records, but it also includes a variety of other writings, such as statutes, ordinances, resolutions, reports or excerpts from reports or surveys, newspaper clippings, scholarly papers, speeches, agenda, minutes or digests of meetings, summaries of discussions, articles or excerpts of articles. In fact any writing in which a student, either by independent study or in group discussion, might reasonably be expected to identify a principle or a method of community organization is worthy of consideration for use as a teaching document.

There is some basis for believing that, in our present stage of development, the community organization case record is neither the most economical nor the most effective type of document for teaching purposes. These records often present a summary of the demographic, geographical, economic, and social attributes of a specific community, then proceed to outline a specific problem and to describe a group of specific personalities. Thus a considerable volume of material must be covered before the actual process of community organization is introduced. Moreover, the introductory material must always be selected from an indefinitely larger body of facts and may, therefore, reflect a bias, whereas the relative brevity of other types of documents minimizes selectivity and thus reduces the opportunity to exercise unconscious bias.

If community organization case records are ultimately to become a major teaching resource, much work will need to be done in two basic areas: (1) there is need to distinguish between the kinds of situations that lend themselves to adequate case recording and those that do not; (2) there is need to determine what is essential in case recording and what is incidental or irrelevant. Limitations must be faced and it may ultimately become clear that community organization case records must confine themselves to the operations of a specific group, such as a board or a committee, confronted by a specific problem. The attempt to record the strivings and the reactions of total communities is likely to end in some kind of unconsciously biased partialization. It seems also not unlikely that case records will increasingly emphasize the minutes of the meetings of a specific group with interspersed summaries and interpretations of the developments that occur between meetings. Such a development would require, however, a marked improvement in the quality of minutes. The bare account of actions taken, which is so often the sole content, would have to be supplemented with summaries of the discussions and with evidence bearing on the movement and the development of relationships in the group process.

Documents other than community organization case records, such as excerpts from reports, resolutions and the other types of

materials enumerated above can be selected on the basis of focus and brevity. One or more such documents can be assigned each week with assurance that the student will have time to analyze the content, to identify methods, and to try his hand at formulating principles illustrated by the material.

METHODS

Teaching that aspires to communicate a method should be accompanied by some experience in applying the method. This ideal is very difficult to achieve in community organization. Field work placements in community organization would appear to be the promising approach. But some such placements give the student little or no experience with the community organization process. Agencies are understandably reluctant to entrust to a student the management of a committee or the servicing of a board. The student all too often is assigned to routine mechanical duties and, so far as the process is concerned, becomes primarily an observer. Observation is, of course, one method of learning, but it is not the best way to learn a method. The assumption of responsibility involves emotional and intellectual demands which are not provided by passive observation. The student develops a sense of security as a result of the successful discharge of an assignment for which he is responsible. Unless a field work placement in community organization provides an opportunity for such experience, it is a dubious investment of the student's time.

If suitable field work placements in community organization are not available, the teacher is under obligation to devise substitutes. Two types of substitutes merit consideration. One is the formulating of assignments that give the student a hypothetical experience. The student is provided with the description of a committee or a board and with the statement of a problem the group is facing. He is then asked to formulate a plan of procedure and to prepare over a period of weeks the documents required to implement his plan, such as agenda for meetings, sub-committee reports, minutes,

staff memoranda and the like. The plan and the documents are discussed and criticized either by the teacher or in small seminar groups. Because this approach is not organically related to a reality situation, it should be supplemented, if possible, by observation in local agencies. There is some basis for believing that observation is educationally more productive when it is associated in this way with an ongoing classroom experience in methodology.

SKILLS

Among the skills useful in community organization none is of greater importance than the capacity to formulate. Characteristically the practitioner of community organization works with a group that is struggling with a problem. Opinions are expressed, some of which may not be germane to the subject at hand. Diverse views are presented. Facts are cited. Some modifications of opposing views begin to emerge. If at this point a clear and succinct formulation is introduced, it is often the catalyst that crystallizes opinion and provides the basis for agreement, forward movement and unified action. Thus the ability to formulate may be the major professional contribution to the process. This ability involves two components: (1) aptitude in discerning, among the relevant and irrelevant comments of members of a group, a core principle or proposition to which a considerable number of the comments can be related; (2) skill in stating the core principle or proposition clearly and, above all, succinctly.

To be successful, a formulation must stem from the antecedent consideration of a problem that needs to be resolved. Hence the student is asked to consider a document in which a problem is disclosed. If the document reveals only one point of view as is sometimes the case, he may first be obliged to reconstruct alternative views that could have been advanced. He is not ready to formulate until he has clearly discerned the issue and has considered variant solutions. When this point is reached, his task is to state, preferably

either in a single declarative sentence or in the form of a single question, a general principle or a broad proposition. In actual professional practice this formulation, if accepted, will enable the group to add the details and to move toward a solution. In the classroom the formulation can only be subjected to the scrutiny and criticism of fellow students and teacher. But experience suggests that the criticisms offered by the students tend to become increasingly astute; as a result, loose formulations and illogical propositions are quickly ruled out. This encourages belief that some increase in ability to formulate results from this approach. Observation indicates that most of the successful practitioners of community organization have more than average skill in the art of formulating. It is the obligation of the teacher to emphasize the importance of this skill and to do what he can to develop it in his students.

Other skills highly useful in community organization are already familiar to the student from antecedent courses in casework and group work. Among these are the capacity to relate to individuals and groups, to evaluate the behavior of individuals and of groups, to identify and cultivate leadership, to effect group formation, to generate group feeling, to promote unity of purpose within a group. It is the responsibility of the teacher of community organization to help the student to see how these skills he has already learned in these other courses are utilized in the community organization process.

Some of the devices needed in community organization may have been mastered in a course in administration. If not, they should be included in the community organization course. They are the mechanisms and procedures that facilitate orderly development of group affairs, such as the preparation of agenda, the writing of minutes, the drafting of resolutions, memoranda and the like. Perceptiveness in human relations is at the heart of the professional contribution to community organization, but this contribution should not fail for want of knowledge and skill in handling the ordinary mechanisms required in group operations.

THE COMMUNITY ORGANIZATION SEQUENCE

A proliferation of courses is no guaranty of scholarship. Content adequate for one course can be spread over three courses without great effort. The good student quickly discerns the thinness of the resulting sequence and his respect for the subject matter declines correspondingly.

What are the distinctive features of a course in "advanced community organization?" Is there in community organization, as in casework, one situation in which the problem is primarily environmental and another in which the problem is primarily behavioral? Or is there some other kind of valid distinction that makes one type of situation more difficult to grasp than another? By its very nature the community organization process is never restricted to preoccupation with the environment; always the central concern is with psychological reactions. "Advanced community organization" may therefore be a misnomer. Courses beyond the basic course are undoubtedly different from the basic course in content or in method or in both, but is this difference of a character that warrants use of the term "advanced?"

A basic course in community organization is commonly required of all candidates for a professional degree regardless of their area of specialization. Those who wish to specialize in community organization are entitled to additional opportunities. These opportunities can be provided in four ways: (1) field work placements; (2) additional classroom courses; (3) independent supervised reading; and (4) independent supervised research.

It is obvious that the student specializing in community organization should have the benefit of good field work placements in community organization, preferably in more than one setting. In addition to the basic required classroom course in community organization, he is entitled to additional academic education in his field of specialization. If a group of students specializing in community organization is available, a seminar, flexible in content, can be profitable. This would not be an "advanced" course in the

sense that it encompassed material of an order of difficulty different from that of the basic course. The seminar enables students to examine certain methods and principles in greater detail and to view them in relation to a broader range of settings than is attempted in the basic course. It would also provide some students with an opportunity to investigate certain instrumentalities, concepts, methods or principles, in which they have a special interest, such, for example, as the Charities Endorsement Bureau, or representativeness as reflected in the composition of local boards of trustees, or the policy of presenting alternatives in preparing memoranda for boards or committees. An individual reading course is a good substitute for a seminar or may be provided for students who, having completed the seminar, are desirous of further work in community organization. The reading program is planned jointly by the student and the teacher and is accompanied by periodic conferences. Some students may also be interested in undertaking a piece of research in community organization under faculty guidance. If a problem of suitable scope and character can be found, this experience should have prime educational significance.

It should be mentioned parenthetically that some students desire highly specialized classroom courses, as, for example, "the techniques of fund-raising" or "methods in public relations," and such courses are sometimes listed as part of a community organization sequence. Where such courses are not offered, students sometimes cover similar material in preparing reports for seminars or in a focused reading course. It is misleading to consider these highly specialized courses an integral part of what must be included in basic education for community organization. Actually they are specialized applications and adaptations of the basic community organization principles and methods.

One purpose of the preceding two paragraphs is to question the desirability of a proliferation of classroom courses in community organization. Graduate students should be able to master what is actually known about community organization in a single substantial course. After that the emphasis should be upon individual-

ized education that allows the student to explore more intensively those subject areas presented in the basic course that challenged his imagination or aroused his desire to specialize. The great risks in offering a series of several classroom courses are:

1. The content of successive courses designed for a group may fail to meet the needs of the students as adequately as they could be met by a more individualized approach.

2. Repetitiousness and "drill" tend to creep into a consecutive series of courses if the known subject matter is circumscribed in scope.

3. The effort to avoid repetitiousness may lead to the introduction into the courses of material which, though in some way related, is not an integral part of the subject matter.

4. The need to divide material among several courses produces watered-down content that does not make adequate demands upon the student.

From the outset leaders in social work education were aware of the need to teach community organization. With no pattern to follow, they had to start as best they could. In 1910 a course offered by Jane Addams and Graham Taylor was described in the announcements of the Chicago School as follows: ". . . those more or less organized agencies will be studied through which the people of a neighborhood or larger community cooperate with each other and with the officials and departments of their local government. Among the agencies thus to be studied—are public school, library, museum, and recreational centers, settlements, local improvement societies and social work under church and religious auspices. In connection with this course conferences will be held with boys' and girls' club leaders on educational and recreational work with children."

Under such gifted leadership this was undoubtedly a great course, but it obviously lacked focus. The experience of the intervening years has helped to correct this defect. Gradually agreements have developed as to what the content of community organization is. Principles of community organization have been formulated and methods have been identified. As recently as 1930

the courses in community organization were very dissimilar in content from one school to another. The more grotesque of these differences have now disappeared. No matter where he takes his work in community organization, the social work student of today will cover material, a very considerable proportion of which would be much the same in any other school.

The differences that persist are predominantly in organization and division of material among courses and, more especially, in the objectives and the methods of teaching. It is important in a professional curriculum to achieve agreement on objectives. Some teachers would wish to expand the list of objectives enumerated at the beginning of this paper; perhaps others would wish to curtail or modify the list. Some latitude in this area may be defensible, but, in a subject designed to fit students for professional practice, there should be a core set of objectives recognized by everyone as essential to the attainment of professional competence.

Differences in methods of teaching will be with us always. Gifted teachers develop unique means of attaining their objectives. Much can be learned, however, by comparing and evaluating methods—particularly in a subject area that is scarcely out of its infancy. Evidence suggests that some teaching methods now in use are wasteful of time and ineffective and that others may lend to the material the unwarranted caste of dogma. An earlier decade did much to establish the solid core of content in community organization. Perhaps the contribution of the present decade will consist of weeding out the ineffectual methods of teaching the subject.

A Point of View About Community Organization for Social Welfare

C. F. MCNEIL AND ROBERT B. LEFFERTS

BASIC CONCEPTS IN SOCIAL WORK

All social work has, until very recently, been considered to be divided into at least three parts. These are social casework, social group work and community organization. Only within the decade has there been serious study of the basic premises upon which these areas of practice have been founded to reveal that there is much in common to all.

The following lists the most obvious:

1. The social worker strives to understand the client with whom he works, to accept him and to work with him toward the development of his maximum capacities. Respect for the individual human personality and his right to determine his destinies are part of this concept—universal to all social work. As a social caseworker, he deals with the individual or family; as a social group worker, the group and the individual in his relationship to the group; as a community organization worker, the "community" becomes the primary client—but it becomes increasingly evident that the individual and his development, groups and their particular roles in the dynamics of community life must be seen in proper perspective in any enlightened approach to community organization. While it is recognized that the sets of relationships within which the social worker operates in these areas of practice vary substantially, the objectives are, or should be, the same in all instances.

2. The social worker, in whatever area of practice or setting, is principally an "enabler." The extent to which he is a "doer" will vary with the area of practice, the setting and the particular job he

occupies. For example, a social worker administering a large department of public welfare is leading a life quite different from that of a social worker who is a community worker in a settlement house.

3. Understanding about and contributing to growth and development of the individual are objectives common to all social work practice. In social casework this is, in its simplest form, helping an individual who wants help to solve his problems and to reach his fullest potential as a person, a parent, a family member or a worker. While social group work places considerable importance upon development of the group itself, the focus is inevitably upon the individual and meeting his needs through group experience.

While community, the primary client in community organization, might be defined in terms of a collection of individuals, there are obviously aspects of community which transcend this limited definition. Community is a complex of individuals, of groups, or organizations, of religious, cultural, industrial, professional and other forces that frequently defy characterization in any single term or definition. Yet the process of growth and development that takes place in community does so largely in direct relation to the growth and development of the individuals who make the community "tick." While we are certain that participation of citizens in social welfare organizations and activities contributes to individual growth and development, we need to know more about the effects of various kinds of experience.

It seems clear that our concepts of growth and development have universal application.

4. Individualization is another universal. While "personality" in the community is hard to define, there exists, nevertheless, a uniqueness in the particular hamlet, town or city making it different from all others; in a sense comparable to differences in individuals. Failure of the community organization worker to understand this community "personality," to work with "it," and help "it," will result in failure as surely as for the caseworker who fails to understand his client.

5. It is generally agreed that in the area of human relations, so-

cial work's knowledge about and concern for the whole person has represented a major contribution. This concept of "totality" pervades all of social work practice. In community organization, it is articulated as "total need," "total services," "all the people," "balanced program," and so on.

6. Use of relationship is another universal. This may run from simple to very complex. It is agreed by many that the sets of relationships in community organization are among the most diverse and difficult. The community organization worker must work with the aggressive, the hostile, the introvert, the extrovert; with groups and organizations representing a wide range of community interest.

7. One of the unique characteristics of any profession is in the way in which the professional person consciously, deliberately and in a disciplined manner, carries out the obligation of his position. "Conscious use of self" is another familiar term which in this viewpoint is applicable universally in the professional social work job. In all of the complex relationships established and maintained by the professional worker in community organization, this "conscious use of self" will emerge in some form. Most frequent examples cited are in his relationship to the committee. This is certainly valid but should not cause one to overlook the same factor in interviewing, consultation, group conferences and other situations.

The above is spelled out in brief to establish the first premise of this paper, and to make simple, and we hope more meaningful, the remainder.

GENERIC TRAINING

This premise is simply that throughout all social work practice run common threads as to process, similar characteristics of method, and especially a body of knowledge, a quality of understanding needed by the social worker in any area of practice and in any setting.

What then should be the foundation for practice from which

specialization should stem? The suggestions herein lay weight on an understanding of community which reaches considerably beyond that now available in most schools for the casework and group work trainee—and the community organization student as well. Certain assumptions are made; first, that the student has or will secure a good liberal arts preparation probably with social science emphasis. While it cannot be developed here, the hope is expressed that the Curriculum Study will resolve some of the uncertainties that exist now as to undergraduate preparation.

A second assumption is that the school of social work has screened the student for readiness for graduate education for professional practice and is assured of intellectual, emotional, physical and social preparedness for this field of work.

Third is the obvious assumption that, given the above, the school faculty will have the proper educational "know how" to help the student learn, understand and perform effectively.

DESIRABLE QUALITIES

We submit the following four qualities as the minimum desirable for our new worker:

    I. A personal commitment to a set of common values.
    II. A composite of knowledge that will make it possible for the worker to use his skill intelligently and efficiently.
    III. A variety of technical skills.
    IV. An ability to establish and maintain relationships that will be personally satisfying and professionally productive.

GENERIC CONTENT

It is clear that these qualities are desirable in any new worker, whether he is headed for casework, group work or community organization. It follows then that we might consider the focus of content of social work education in the light of these four qualities.

I. A commitment to a set of common values
(Items listed are the focus of course content—not necessarily suggested courses)

Focus A. Historical perspective of social problems and the development of the social services—voluntary and governmental.

Focus B. Basic concepts of social work—such as given as examples in the first section of this paper.

Focus C. The development of social work as a profession: ethical concepts; developments in relation to other professions.

Focus D. Social and economic theories, principles and laws, and their relationship to social welfare needs and services.

II. A composite body of knowledge

Focus A. Related to individual behavior.
(1) Growth and development of the individual
(2) Psychopathology
(3) Cultural component in human relations
(4) Basic concepts and methods in social work practice—common and distinctive elements
(5) Social casework

Focus B. Related to group behavior and group process
(1) (See "basic concepts and methods," IIA, 4, above)
(2) Theories and principles in group behavior
(3) Social group work

Focus C. Related to community
(1) (See "basic concepts and methods," IIA, 4, above)
(2) Social structure of communities
    (a) Kinds of communities
    (b) Class, caste, power structure
    (c) Industrial, educational, political organization
    (d) Cultural, religious institutions
    (e) Community planning
(3) Community pathology (dependency, ill health, maladjustment and recreational need)

(4) The organization of community health, welfare and recreation services

(5) Community organization for social welfare

(6) Financing health, welfare and recreation services (voluntary and governmental)

III. A variety of technical skills
Focus A. Interviewing and individual consultation
Focus B. Recording
Focus C. Elements of research method essential to use and interpretation of social data

IV. Ability to establish and maintain relationships
It is assumed that this quality will be assessed in terms of potential of the admitted student and will be developed in both the classroom and the field. Knowledge, understanding and skill must be blended with particular emphasis upon:

Focus A. The nature of relationships in social work
Focus B. Use of professional self
Focus C. Role of the professional worker
Focus D. The place and role of the service, committee and board volunteer

To this point we have dealt entirely with content considered to be generic—to be needed by all students of social work. The various categories are recognized to be interrelated and interdependent. No differentiation as between classroom and field instruction has been attempted. Our four "qualities" can—must—we believe, be developed at both points. Further comment will be made as to the content and setting for field instruction.

SPECIALIZED COMMUNITY ORGANIZATION TRAINING

The above outline includes areas of knowledge, understanding and skill required of all social work students. What then are the

special requirements "for the preparation of students for beginning positions in agencies whose major function is organizing community social work?"

The simplest way to answer this question is to add to our four categories (qualities) those additions which are considered to be necessary.

I. A commitment to a set of common values
—no additions

II. A composite body of knowledge
Focus A. Related to individual behavior
—no additions
Focus B. Related to group behavior and group process
—no additions
Focus C. Related to community
add
(7) Community processes—institutionalization, specialization, interdependence, social change, development of leadership, cooperation, metropolitanism, regionalism, suburbanism, and so on.
(8) Community organization
(a) Background and development
(b) Theories and practice
(c) Analysis of cooperative processes, *e.g.*, joint budgeting, joint financing, joint planning
(9) Agency structure and administration
(a) Advantages and limitations of structure
(b) Special problems of administration
(10) Local, state and national services and their interrelationships

III. A variety of technical skills
add
Focus D. Committee organization and administration

Focus E. Statistical and research method

Focus F. Administrative problems and processes

Focus G. Methods of communication, including public relations and publicity

Focus H. Recording in community organization

Focus I. Methods in joint budgeting, joint financing and joint planning

IV. Ability to establish and maintain relationships
add

Focus E. Understanding of variety and complexity of relationships confronting the community organization worker

Focus F. The role of the professional worker in community organization

FIELD INSTRUCTION—GENERIC

Field instruction is considered an essential and integral part of graduate social work education. As such, it should serve to assist in the refinement of the student's values, skills, knowledge, and particularly his ability to establish and use relationship in order to achieve professional goals.

It has been implicit throughout the previous material that, dependent upon the student's ability, maturity and life experiences, it is possible—perhaps preferable—to prepare students for practice in community organization who have not had experience in social casework and social group work. At the same time, it is recognized that certain highly specialized positions may require substantial orientation to a field or experience in it. The emphasis in the above approach to course content has been in terms of generic social work education. It would be logical, therefore, to suggest the first-year field work placement in a generic setting, but there are few, if any, such agency settings. Thus it would appear that the first-year placement should include experience under supervision

in an agency or agencies where social casework as well as social group work services are provided. Such placements should be related to administration and to the agency involvement in community organization process. One purpose should be to help the student gain first-hand understanding of the total agency operation, and by this exposure, to increase his understanding of social casework and group work practice. Opportunities for involvement in specific problems of administration, public relations and community relations should be assured, and special emphasis in the assignment would be the agency's participation in community organization processes. This assumes that the agency and its supervisory staff are conscious of their roles in community organization and can assist the field work student in understanding community organization "from the agency point of view." It also assumes a generic orientation on the part of agency staff so that the common elements of group work, casework and community organization can be called to the student's attention.

SPECIALIZATION

The second-year placement should be in an agency whose primary function makes it necessary to employ staff trained and experienced in community organization. Furthermore, such staff should be primarily engaged in community organization practice. This placement should include assignment of the student, under supervision, to an appropriate and "regular" responsibility in the agency. Thus, such an assignment should not be something "created" just for the student. If field work is to represent the integration of theory with community reality, then the student's responsibilities and assignments must be "real ones." To place responsibility for such a piece of work with the field work student assumes that proper supervision is available. This presents a major problem since there is so little in the way of systematic knowledge regarding supervisory processes and methods in community organization. The lack of

process recording even by field work students makes it difficult for supervision to focus, as we believe it should, on the matter of relationships; the role of the worker and the "professional use of self." To a considerable degree the supervisory process in community organization has been focused on administrative matters and development of technical skills. The importance of these should not be underrated while we search for ways to improve the supervisory process. To be fully effective, field work should bring about a balanced integration of the student's total performance in terms of his skills, knowledge, values, and ability to make use of relationship.

This does not mean to suggest field work in community organization is a highly protected experience. On the contrary, the greatest value of field work as a part of the preparation of the community organization practitioner is that it assures that the student is aware of the reality in community organization practice and is able to deal with this reality professionally and successfully. In general, we would see field instruction as a process of "progressively unprotected reality."

In addition to assignment of a particular set of responsibilities in the agency, a considerable amount of "planned observation" will assist in the student's preparation. Through proper supervision, such observation can be meaningful because the student can be "involved" in activities even though he does not carry work responsibility. The complexity and diversity inherent in community organization processes and methods make it most helpful for the student to have a wide range of exposure to practice.

The preparation of a thesis or original research project by the student should be closely related to advanced field instruction. Such a "community organization" project, if it is carried on in the agency setting can contribute greatly to integration of classroom theory with practice. At the same time, such a piece of research is frequently tangible compensation to the agency which assumes a part of its responsibility for training professional personnel through making available field work placements.

THE THIRD YEAR

Throughout this paper, we have emphasized the complexity of relationships in the community organization job. At the same time we have held that practice in a "functional" area of social work need not precede admission to practice in community organization. It would be difficult to make a "case" for "maturity" in one area of practice as against another. Certainly the caseworker who may hold in his hand the destiny of an individual or a family needs to draw upon all of the resources at his command to meet the perplexities of many situations that face him. It can be said or argued, however, that the community organization worker holds within his grasp the potentiality of great good for the many or, in error, consequences that may affect scores or hundreds.

The true professional never reaches the point of having learned enough. When the community organization worker believes he has "all the answers" retrogression has already set in. The two-year graduate program is a minimum.

For the younger, inexperienced student of community organization a kind of "internship" arrangement for one year following completion of master's work may have merit. The selection of the agency would involve some of the same criteria as for the second year of field work. These would be agencies "whose major function is organizing community social work." The student would be paid an annual stipend approximating the usual beginning salaries for practice. It would differ from a regular job in that:

1. Selection of the agency would be related to its capacity to further "teach" the student. Quality of its program and professional competence of its personnel would determine its "eligibility."

2. Supervision by a capable person would be assured.

3. The student would approach the "job" as a concentrated period of "learning through practice"—and as that final step up the ladder toward "unprotected reality."

This third year could be a rounding out of experiences and add to the student's perspective as well as skills.

Inevitably it would be the larger agency that would be called upon for such service. This in itself might well add to the student's total experience. Getting commitments for such "internships," while not impossible, may well be difficult. It is our hope that some experimentation with this and other methods of preparing the community organization practitioner can occur in the near future.

Basic Course in Community Organization for Social Welfare for all Students

WILBUR I. NEWSTETTER AND MEYER SCHWARTZ

INTRODUCTION

Since the publication in 1947 of the papers by Pray [1] and New-stetter, [2] which attempted to describe the nature of social work practice in the field of social welfare organization, there has been a growing body of general agreement with the central ideas posited in these papers; as witness the papers and publications of Barry, [3] Carter, [4] Murphy, [5] Ross, [6] and Sieder. [7]

The agreement on the common characteristics of social work practice in all areas is not disputable, judging from these publications and papers. The differences of opinion appear to center around what specific activities in the field of social welfare organ-

---

[1] Kenneth Pray, "When Is Community Organization Social Practice?" in *Social Work in a Revolutionary Age* (Philadelphia: University of Pennsylvania Press, 1949).

[2] Wilber I. Newstetter, "The Social Intergroup Work Process" in *Proceedings National Conference of Social Work* (New York: Columbia University Press, 1947).

[3] Mildred C. Barry, "Community Organization Process: An Approach to Better Understanding," *Social Work Journal,* October, 1950. "Assessment of Progress Made By Community Organization in Identifying Basic Concepts and Methods for Utilization in Social Work Education" (New York: Council on Social Work Education, 1956).

[4] Genevieve Carter, "Practice Theory in Community Organization," Mimeographed, 1957.

[5] Campbell Murphy, *Community Organization Practice* (New York: Houghton Mifflin Co., 1954).

[6] Murray G. Ross, *Community Organization Theory and Principles,* New York: Harper & Brothers, N.Y., 1955. "Conceptual Problems in Community Organization," Mimeographed. Prepared for Community Organization Workshop, Council on Social Work Education, Buffalo, January, 1956.

[7] Violet M. Sieder, "The Tasks of the Community Organization Workers—the Professional Method Related to the Community Organization Process," Mimeographed, 1957.

ization can be considered as outside the limits of social work as a professional practice. Ross appears to rule out certain activities of the social agency such as "community service" projects and "community relations" projects as embodying a social work process in social welfare organization. Ross also questions the obligation of the profession to work for welfare objectives in the community through the use of a social work process.[8] Unlike Ross, Newstetter sees that social welfare objectives or goals are part of the *raison d'etre* of social work process, and must be worked out. Newstetter [9] would not regard administration on the interagency level, nor promotion as professional social work processes. His position is predicated on the difference between the *relationships* of those who are parties to administrative and promotional processes, and those who are parties to social work practice processes, stemming from quite different philosophies. Dunham [10] would disregard such distinctions.

Nevertheless, the recent spate of papers and publications, amplifying by and large, on the common characteristics of social work as professional practice in all areas, and some of the specifics in social welfare organization does allow us to proceed to construct a course in community organization for social welfare which should be offered in all schools of social work for all students, and would recognize that the activities with respect to all three processes, namely (1) social intergroup work process (2) administrative process on the intergroup or interagency level; and (3) the promotional process are pertinent for learning experiences.

SOME OBSERVATIONS ABOUT CURRENT ACTIVITIES

Before suggesting the objectives of such a course, it would be well to weigh certain significant observations about the current activi-

[8] Murray G. Ross, *Op. cit.*
[9] Wilber I. Newstetter, *Op. cit.* Footnote no. 2.
[10] Arthur Dunham, See exchange of correspondence between Dunham and Newstetter, *Social Work Journal,* October, 1949, and April, 1950.

ties of social workers which should influence the objectives of this
course.

1. *The average social worker in casework and in group work has
   become separated from the whole area of involvement in social
   policy formulation and implementation.*

We are witnessing a "triumph of technique over purpose" in
our culture and in our profession. Much of it may be a reflection of
the necessity to catch up with the increase in knowledge about
human growth and development, and an increasing awareness of
the sophisticated methods of analysis of the behavioral sciences
which beckon us to make their application in the field of social
work practice. The very vastness of the subject matter to be mastered leads to a preoccupation with techniques.

This divorcement of social work practice from social policy involvement is abetted by the fact that (a) the major political parties
have assumed responsibility for social welfare legislation, and
(b) social policy formulation and implementation tends to be
identified with legislation and separated from the area of private
voluntary association activities in community betterment which
are non-legislative, non-political and non-governmental.

On top of all this there is a fear of "sticking your neck out" on
social policies which has permeated not only the attitudes of educators, doctors, lawyers, and so on, but social work practitioners as
well. Even more striking, parenthetically, is the observation made
by Whyte [11] that many persons are not even aware that there are
issues to "stick one's neck out" about. Such is the current pervasive
atmosphere of conformity.

2. *The average social worker in casework and in group work tends
   to separate himself from the distinctive community organization
   agencies, workers and programs.*

He tends to question whether social work is really practiced in
these agencies by the workers. He knows that the programs of these
agencies effect social welfare services, but there is little under-

11 William H. Whyte, Jr., *The Organization Man* (New York: Simon and Schuster,
1956).

standing that a growing body of social welfare organization workers operates at times with the same ethical or philosophical basis that social work practitioners do, use similar methods and techniques of study diagnosis and treatment (plan of action) in a problem-solving context, and call upon the same body of knowledge about human growth and development and dynamics of social process. (To be sure, there are many workers in this broad field who are not social workers; but there are some who are professionally trained in social work who do not identify themselves as being in a social work role, nor do their boards identify them as such. Hopefully, this will be overcome as we clarify our ideas about professional social work practice and its role in social welfare organization, and enable the schools to train students in larger numbers for social work practice as well as other appropriate activities in this kind of setting.)

3. *The average social worker in casework and group work tends to look upon the social welfare organization worker as having the sole responsibility for a better articulation of community resources and human needs.*

When the average casework and group work agency participates in social welfare activities, it is regarded as a secondary matter. There is, in too many instances, a sloughing off of responsibility on the part of these agencies for undertaking appropriate social welfare activities in conjunction with other groups. There are circumstances in which these agencies can and must undertake such activities, utilizing the practice appropriate to the specific circumstance and problem. If they cannot do so, they should make use of social welfare organization agency consultation.

4. *On the other hand, the average social worker in casework and group work does not recognize the responsibility for and the opportunities to bring to social welfare organization agencies and workers their identifications of unmet community needs, whether with respect to total or partial gap or inadequate coordination of existing services.*

There appears to be an inability or even inhibition to generalize from specific needs which he readily identifies, to a whole class of needs shared by a community and needing community study, diagnosis and treatment (plan of action as it is termed in social work practice in social welfare organization).

5. *The average social worker in casework and group work does not know his differential role in conducting himself as an agency representative, as a professional practitioner and as a citizen when participating in social welfare organization activities.*

It is a common observation that he is either silent and passive, or goes to the opposite extreme with little regard to his appropriate role or roles.

The inherent nature of the social welfare organization field—its involvement with correlating social objectives, social resources and human needs—offers a context in which the teaching of the responsibility of the profession for ". . . an obligation to foster the social changes necessary to attain social welfare objectives" is most natural.[12] Likewise, there is opportunity to bring into sharp focus the unity of social work as professional practice in all settings, and to identify the nature of social work practice specifically in any social welfare organization setting. There is also educational opportunity to overcome the gap (*sic!*) between activities in the casework and group work agency programs and the activities of workers in other social welfare organization agencies.

OBJECTIVES

The objectives for a basic course in community organization for social welfare for all students are conceived as follows:

1. To initiate and develop in the student an obligation to give appropriate support to citizens and to participate as a professional,

12 Harry L. Lurie, "The Responsibilities of a Socially Oriented Profession," in *New Directions in Social Work*, ed. Cora Kasius. New York: Harper & Brothers, 1954, p. 31.

in social processes necessary to define and attain social welfare objectives.

2. For the student to have knowledge and understanding of the basic unity of the social casework process, social group work process and social intergroup work process.

3. For the student to have knowledge and understanding of, and beginning skill in the distinctive social work practice process in the field of social welfare organization—social intergroup work.

4. For the student to have knowledge and understanding of other activities and processes in social welfare organization—promotion and administration on the interagency or intergroup level, research, and to recognize the use of these ancillary activities.

5. For the student to have knowledge and understanding of the responsibility of all social agencies, public and private, and other professional practitioners operating in the field of social welfare organizations, to have skill in initiating and maintaining such activities by these agencies where fitting, and of making apt use of social welfare agencies programs and workers.

6. For the student to have knowledge and understanding of community needs and problems and the application of useful concepts in analysis of such community needs and problems.

7. For the student to acquire knowledge and understanding of his differential role as representative of his agency, as representative of his profession, and as a citizen.

IMPLICATION FOR FIELD INSTRUCTION

To achieve these objectives, it is obvious that the field experience and learning must be correlated with this basic course in social welfare organization. At present the field placement of caseworker and group worker is, by and large, limited to service to individuals and groups in the context of social casework and social group work. Very seldom is provision made for these students to observe and/or to participate in social welfare organization activities, whether under the sponsorship of their agency or another social welfare

organization agency. Such activities are usually carried on by the executive, assistant director, or supervisor.[13] The basic course in social welfare organization for all students [14] should be offered in the second year, third semester—after the students have secured some mastery of their so-called specialization—casework and group work knowledge, understanding and skill; this is advocated not because such knowledge, understanding and skill is a prerequisite for social welfare organization but because the students having secured some mastery of their primary social work process will be more free to look upon and engage in other appropriate activities. Moreover, the students will have been, by the time of the third semester, exposed to the knowledge and understanding of basic concepts of social work theory and practice and will be more readily prepared to see their application in other settings.

CONCEPTS

The concepts which should be presented in a basic course for social welfare organization should reflect the objectives of the course. Moreover, these concepts should reflect the basic agreements on what constitutes the characteristics of social work practice in any setting. While this last consideration means some repetition of the concepts taught in other parts of the curriculum, it should be, in a sense refracted in the particular setting of social welfare organization. In short, there is a beam of unifying concepts which is shaded and colored in different ways by the social welfare organization setting.

[13] In the field placements in casework and in group work during the third semester, concurrent with this course, appropriate time should be provided for observation and/or participation in social welfare organization activities.

[14] For all students only in those schools where there is no specialization in social welfare organization. In those schools in which there is a social welfare organization sequence starting in the second year, the basic course outlined in this paper would apply.

In Pittsburgh, we are thinking of a sequence in social welfare organization which would start in the first year. Hence, the students specializing in social welfare organization would be taught the content of this basic course in their first year.

The concepts set forth below are numbered in relation to the objectives as previously noted.

1. *Regarding Social Policy:*
   (a) Social workers and social work must be concerned with people and things as they "ought to be," *i.e.,* the socially desired norms. The possession of socially desired norms by the professional practitioner is inevitable and desirable.[15]
   (b) In working toward what "ought to be" it is mandatory that the professional social worker pose the alternative courses of action to clients and clientele and in helping them to evaluate the probable cause and effect relationship of the various choices of action open to them—while still, above all, maintaining and developing the kind of relationship which leaves people free as possible to choose and therefore to really learn.[15]
   (c) This decision-making by the client or clientele is effective as a learning experience only if the client or clientele participates appropriately in the process, and the same is true for the professional person involved. The professional person has a responsibility for helping to provide an adequate basis for decision-making. Hence there is a responsibility for professionals engaging in social welfare organization activities to make provisions of appropriate processes for citizen participation. More often than not, the "right" decision will, in a sense pre-exist, to some extent, in the means for making the decision.[15]

2. *Regarding Basic Unity of Social Work Practice in Any Setting:*
   (a) That social process is essentially the psychic interaction that takes place between people in connection with adjustive efforts in group and communal living. These efforts include man's attempt to satisfy his basic biological and

15 Wilber I. Newstetter, "The Concept of the Community and Other Related Concepts," in Social Work Practice in Field of Tuberculosis—*Symposium Proceedings.* July, August, 1953. Edited by Eleanor E. Cockerill, pp. 70–75.

personal needs in relation to the cultural atmosphere in which he breathes the breath of social life. They include also man's attempt as an individual to rise above the biological level, to live harmoniously in relation to the culture of which he is a dynamic part, and his attempt to modify this culture from time to time so as to create a more suitable climate in which he may live a personally satisfying life.

These adjustive efforts likewise include collective man's attempt—such as a community's and society's attempt—to meet corporate needs through such essentials as a reliable system of law, order, protection, health, housing, division of labor, education, transportation, recreation, welfare, and religious expression. The democratic community also needs provision for the learning of cooperation, participation, delegation of responsibility and authority, and, finally, accountability. These are all needs which have to be satisfied or the community and society will collapse, leaving a condition in which individual man would find it difficult if not impossible to satisfy his personal needs.

Just as an individual cannot exist apart from the reasonable satisfaction of basic biological and personal needs, so also a community and a society cannot exist unless collective and corporate needs are adequately met. These two aspects of social adjustive effort, namely individual need and community need, provide the two foci about which the mutual seeking and mutual becoming of the social process revolve.

(b) That the nature and quality of any specific instance of social process is affected by the objectives, knowledge, methods, techniques, and philosophies of those who are parties to that process. In a sense, the process may be viewed as the result of the application of methods and techniques as well as of other factors such as the component parts of the immediate situation and, particularly, the relationships of the parties to the process.

(c) That there is a core of indispensable and communicable knowledge which, when directed toward the specifically defined purposes of social work and when translated into action through consistent methods and techniques applied in a defined role, constitutes the professional practice of social work.

(d) That a social process such as some specific effort in community organization and planning, becomes a social *work* process in the technical sense when:

(1) The objectives are social work objectives, and

(2) The process is being consciously effected by a person, selected or accepted by the groups involved, whose professional capacity and role in the process is primarily that of bringing the disciplines of appropriate knowledge and method and skills to bear on the problem-solving process within the limits of social sanction compatible with the philosophy of the profession in the particular setting.[16]

3. *Regarding the Distinctive Social Work Practice in the Field of Social Welfare Organization—Social Intergroup Work:*

(a) The primary need to be met is not that of particular individuals who require adjusting to other individuals, but rather the need of groups in a given community of groups to maintain mutually satisfying relations with other groups.

(b) The second focus of intergroup work is again related to meeting community and societal needs, but may be defined as specific social goals selected and accepted by the groups involved, as for example, such specific social goals as child welfare service, family welfare service, recreation, housing, tuberculosis control, fair employment practices, and the like. In other words, the quality of the adjustmental relations between the groups in terms of some specific social goal is the over-all objective of the intergroup work process.

16 Newstetter, *Op. cit.,* pp. 90–91.

Accomplishment in this process is incomplete, no matter how well adjusted and related the individual representatives may become with respect to each other, unless the adjustmental relations between groups are furthered in terms of the selected social goal. Conversely, no matter how well adjusted or related to each other the representative individuals become through the social process in the intergroup (this is conceived of as the group of group representatives), such results, although important, are to be judged unfruitful from the intergroup work point of view unless and until the adjustmental relations between the members of the groups represented in their routine and customary or calculated contacts are actually improved in terms of the specific selected and accepted social goals. For example, representatives from groups such as unions, management, racial and religious groups, participating in an intergroup work process in which fair employment practices are the selected social goal, are not effective in accomplishing this goal unless they are instrumental in bringing about the actual employment by management of members of the racial and religious groups involved.

(c) This points to two of the crucial aspects of the social intergroup work process:

    (1) There must be mutually satisfactory relations between the members of the groups (not merely between one or two of their representatives in the intergroup) involved in attaining the selected social goal; and

    (2) What may be termed the 'from and to' relationship between the groups responsibly represented, and their representatives.[17]

(d) The functions of the social intergroup worker are:

    (1) To enable the intergroup to develop suitable structure and operating practices to attain the achievement of the social goals selected.

---

[17] Newstetter, *Op. cit.*, pp. 96–97.

(2) To enable individuals in the intergroup to function adequately both with respect to the activities of the intergroup and with respect to the groups they are representing or are representative of; and

(3) To enable the groups represented to participate appropriately in the process.[18]

(e) By and large, there are at least three discernible types of intergroups, classified according to representation:

Type I: the members are official delegates of their groups and are instructed, thus restricting voting action.

Type II: the members are official representatives of their groups but are more or less free to take responsible action for their groups within limitations which the representatives themselves impose.

Type III: the members are merely representatives of certain groups—are usually not designated or selected by the groups they are adjudged to be representative of, but rather are selected by some person or some group for a given intergroup purpose.[18]

(f) These types vary with respect to potentialities for maintaining the life line of the intergroup work process—the "from and to" relationship between the intergroups and the groups involved. Type I is an intergroup with a partially insured "from and to;" Type II is a group with a nominal "from and to," while Type III is a group with only a potential "from and to" . . . many intergroups are combinations of types.[18]

(g) Different community problems may call for different types of intergroups. The worker has to differentiate between what type of intergroup is most suitable to the solution of the problem at hand.

(N.B. A social intergroup record is used in class to illustrate.)

[18] Newstetter, See footnote no. 2.

4. *Regarding Other Activities in Community Organization—Administration and Promotion:*

    (a) Other practices such as promotion and administration must be appropriately used.

    (b) These activities are not conceived as social work practices because they have in common the element of a plan of action *already* made, to be sold or implemented or delegated to a body to carry out in a salesmanlike, or a controlling, authoritative manner. The primary focus is not on enabling, self-determination, or self-growth of groups in their ability to cope with community problems in their interactions with other social groups.

    (c) The promotional process is used to sell a program using the gamut of public relations methods (use of various mass media) and educational methods (e.g., institutes, seminar, conferences, forums).[19]

    (d) The administrative process on the interagency level is the carrying out of policies which have been agreed upon by two or more groups and which have been delegated to a body to exercise, using such administrative methods as allocation and budgeting of funds, control of expenditures, operation of common services, and so on.[19]

5. *Regarding the Casework and Group Work Agency in the Field of Social Welfare Organization Making Germane Use of Social Welfare Organization Agencies and Workers:*

    (a) Industrialization and Urbanization was made possible in part by specialization, and specialization has increased the tempo of Industrialization and Urbanization.[20]

    (b) Casework and Group Work agencies are specialized, dealing with certain facets of human problems for which treatment

19 Helen D. Green, *Social Work Practice in Community Organization* (New York: Whiteside-Morrow, 1954), pp. 50–68.
20 Harold L. Wilensky and Charles N. Lebeaux, *Industrialization and Social Welfare* (New York: Russell Sage Foundation, 1955), pp. 38–43; pp. 63–68; pp. 163–166.

they possess specific knowledge, understanding and skill.[18]

(c) On the other hand, we have the concept of the whole human organism—the indivisibility of the whole being—a concept the professional in any agency professes to deal with.

(d) The segmentation of social welfare services in specialized agencies inevitably calls for an intense degree of joint effort by citizens and professionals in coordinating services, in planning for unmet needs, and in general making for a healthy, integrated community. Hence, social agencies, if they are to discharge their segmented functions adequately, must assume responsibility for participation in social welfare organization activities.

(e) The nature of this responsibility not only embraces adequate referral systems and use of community resources, but, above and beyond these aspects, there is a responsibility for communicating insights to the community about what needs to be met and how, so that effective social welfare organization practices can be brought to bear on these problems. These social agencies can communicate these objectives to the Community, thus contributing to the making of social change necessary to attain social welfare objectives.

(f) Frequently the appropriate channels exist in the large urban community through which these agencies can participate in social welfare organization activities. These are social welfare organization agencies. They have the characteristics of being sponsored by public or private voluntary bodies; of being financed by tax or voluntary contributions, of embracing in their constituency representatives of different kinds from varied social groups; of having as their common denominator working within the area of matching community resources to community needs; of involving citizens in democratic participation to carry on the functions of financing, coordinating, planning, fact-finding, interpreting and to make policy on an intergroup (including agencies) level.

(g) There are certain types of social welfare organization agencies which are found in most urban communities. These types on the local, state and national level are identified as:

(1) Federated fund-raising agencies (united funds and community chests)

(2) Health and welfare planning agencies (council of social agencies and sub-divisions)

(3) Neighborhood or area planning agencies (community councils, urban removal and urban redevelopment authorities)

(4) Interracial and intercultural betterment agencies (Urban League, community relations councils, local and state governmental commissions)

(5) Citizens associations for social action on health and welfare measures (PCA, state charities association)

(6) State governmental commissions and bureaus (commissions on aging, mental health, and so on)

(7) National welfare planning bodies (National Social Welfare Assembly; Department of Health, Education and Welfare, U.S. Government)

(N.B. These social welfare agencies are presented in class from the viewpoint of their functions, structure and operating practices.)

(h) There are instances in which social agencies in a large urban or rural community undertake social welfare organization activities under their own sponsorship because of the nature of the function it is mandated to carry out, e.g., a settlement house charged with changing its interracial policy engages many citizens' groups to help develop the objectives, timing, procedures, and so on, or a child guidance clinic agency undertaking the sponsorship of an educational institute, drawing upon citizen groups for participation in the planning and implementation—all done to discharge its "preventative" function in mental health. Consultation is available for these agencies from appropriate social welfare

organization agencies; a "social work process" (social inter-group work) or a "promotional process" or an "administra-tive process" can be utilized by the direct service agency—and consultation will be, probably, necessary.

(N.B. It has been found helpful to give students an assign-ment in which they report in class on this type of experience of the agency in which they are currently placed for field instruction. Naturally, close contact with the field instructor by the class instructor is necessary, if the experiences re-ported upon are to be useful for analytical discussion.)

6. *Regarding Community Needs and Problems:*
   (a) Community defined as structure—the relatively fixed way or channels through which intergroup relations flow within the walls of geography and legal boundaries.[21]
   (b) Community defined as functional—process, psychological in nature, of psychic interaction between groups, a reciprocal give and take affecting others and being affected, of chang-ing others and being changed.[22]
   (c) The functional definition of community lends itself to a social work practice since it is focused on social relation-ships between social groups.[22]
   (d) The kind of communities and sub-communities we are con-cerned with are multiple and infinite.
   (e) In defining a need and problem in the field of social wel-fare organization, it is necessary to relate it to a specific community, functional in nature.[23]
   (f) Hence study of community needs and problems and their resolution must be a problem-solving approach in terms of different functional communities, i.e., identification of the particular social group interrelationships at a given time and place.[23]
   (g) The problem-solving approach in social welfare organiza-

21 Eduard Lindeman, "Community" Encyclopedia of the Social Sciences.
22 Newstetter, *Op. cit.* See footnote no. 15.
23 Carter, *Op. cit.* See footnote no. 4.

tion to varying functional communities is analogous to the study-diagnosis-treatment-concept in casework.[24]

It embraces the elements of:

(1) The worker is simultaneously involved in acquiring and interpreting information.

(2) The client (community) is "productively related to the study process."

(3) The worker "seeks to engage the conscious participation of the client in the treatment process." [24]

(h) In applying the study, diagnosis, action sequence to community organization, it is helpful to think of study as answering the question "what," diagnosis as answering "why," and treatment as answering "how." What factors influence the functioning of a community? Why did these factors produce this set of problems? How could a community be helped to help itself? What plan of action could be developed to fit the situation? How could a plan of action be developed? [24]

(i) Within the "problem-solving" context several useful analytical concepts can be brought to bear for the understanding of any functional community and its particular needs, problems, and probable solutions: The concepts of social stratification, status, role, norm and power.[25]

(N.B. In class, examples are cited of the use of these concepts within the problem-solving context orientated to a study-diagnosis and action.)

---

[24] Hope McDermott and Gela Fehr, "Study, Diagnosis and Treatment Sequence as an Aid to Initiating Community Organization Service" in *Proceedings, Sixth Biennial Alumni-Faculty Conference*, April, 1954. Graduate School of Social Work, University of Pittsburgh. Pp. 80–100. There is a striking convergence of ideas in the papers of Carter (footnote no. 4) and Barry (footnote no. 3—"Assessment of Progress . . .") with the ideas of McDermott and Fehr. The "cause and effect" relationship in "study, diagnosis and treatment" of human behavior is not so nearly well known as in the physical sciences. Some would argue that purposive behavior of man makes it imposible to predict. Nevertheless, we must think and act on the assumption that Man is knowable, cause and effect relationships exist, causation in human affairs is multiple, etc. (See Conceptual Framework in Social Casework, University of Pittsburgh Press, 1952.)

[25] Newstetter, See footnote no. 15.

7. *Regarding Participation of Casework and Group Work Agency Professionals in Social Welfare Organization Activities:*

   (a) The professional as a representative of his agency needs to delimit his role in line with the mandate given to him by his agency.

   (b) The professional as a representative of his profession, rather than the agency which employs him, needs to delimit his role in line with his professional competence relating to the matter under consideration.

   (c) The professional acting as a citizen without being ascribed the role of agency representative or profession representative needs to delimit his role in line with his citizen responsibilities, noting explicitly that he does not represent anyone else but himself.

SUBJECT MATTER OF ADDITIONAL COURSES

If what has been delineated as the objectives and concepts to be taught in a basic course in social welfare organization for all students, then what should be taught to those students who will go on from this basic course to major in social welfare organization or who will have started the social welfare organization sequence in the first year?

It is not within the scope of this paper to attempt to detail such a course sequence (i.e., to specify the objectives and concepts for other social welfare organization course content) nor to deal with such matters as a two-year concentration in social welfare organization, the nature and extent of field placement for social welfare organization, and the relationship in a course sequence for social welfare organization majors to the basic curriculum. Hopefully, the Curriculum Study will shed light on these matters.

However, we can point up, *tentatively*, subject matters which should be covered for students majoring in social welfare organization, as follows:

1. *Functions of the Social Worker in Intergroup Work:*
   Course would cover the specific identifiable functions such as those "in dealing with the groups to be represented; in dealing with each representative in regard to his functioning in the intergroup; in dealing with each representative in relation to his functioning in his group or groups; in dealing with the intergroup as a whole, or its constituted parts, such as committees; in dealing with groups not represented in the intergroup, but related to its activities and purpose; in dealing with the agency that makes his services available, if not the intergroup itself.[26]

2. *Promotional Processes in the Feld of Social Welfare Organization:*
   Analysis of the circumstances which makes appropriate the development of such a process; knowledgeability and skill in the use of promotional methods such as mass publicity media (press, magazine, brochures, radio, T.V., institutes, forums, conferences, conventions) and involvement of citizen groups and public and private agencies in promotion.

3. *Communication Processes in the Field of Social Welfare Organization:*
   A course which is based on the development of skills in verbal and written expression via writing of notices, agendas, minutes, memoranda, reports, presentation of studies; skill in group discussion method in interviewing, in consulting and in negotiating. Study of formal and informal networks of communication in the community.

4. *Administrative Processes in the Field of Social Welfare Organization:*
   Analysis of circumstances which make appropriate the development of such a process on the intergroup level; knowledge-

26 Newstetter, See footnote no. 2.

ability and skill in the use of administrative methods, such as goal setting, budgeting (including priorities), control of expenditures, joint rendering of services and development of administrative and organizational process and structure.

5. *Operating Practices, Structure and Functions of Selected Social Welfare Organization Agencies and Programs:*
This would be a survey course which would seek to make the student knowledgeable and understanding of the most prevalent sub-settings in social welfare organizations, in which they are, at present, most likely to be employed, and of which the profession has the most contact and understanding. The significant operating practices, structure, and functions of these agencies and programs are examined in such detail as to prepare the student to orientate himself more speedily in these sub-settings. The agencies and programs are specified on pages 223 and 226 of this paper.

Subject areas, such as the historical development of social welfare structure and function including the community chest, united fund and council movement, national social work agencies and their local, state and national programs, should be included in the sequence on "Social Services" (it is named, sometimes, "Social Work Organization and Problems").

Use of and interpretation of welfare service statistics can be included in the sequence in Social Work Research; likewise the methods of doing community surveys and studies of needs and problems.

The social welfare organization major needs to know and understand the administrative practices within the wide range of social welfare agencies, their basic functions, structures, and operating practices. Whether this requires a separate course and a new kind of field placement concept for social welfare organization majors has to be explored. It may well be that a careful examination of the total curriculum will reveal that certain courses in casework and group work lend themselves to the purpose of making social wel-

fare organization majors knowledgeable and empathetic to the casework and group work agency.[27]

CONCLUDING NOTE

The core of the problem in the education and training of social welfare organization majors revolves around seeking to inculcate a "generalist" understanding of "basic" matters and of preparing students technically equipped to grapple with distinctive sub-settings in social welfare organization. Both extremes should be avoided with this qualification: At this stage of the development of social welfare organization as a field for the professional practice of social work, we have a general agreement on the "universal" characteristics of social work practice, and a limited agreement on the specific social work practice in social welfare organizations. Hence, we must of necessity introduce in the training of majors in social welfare organizations a stiff dose of "universals" and coverage of what appears to be the demands of the field regardless of disagreement as to what aspects should be considered social work practice. It would be foolhardy to train students to function as professional practitioners without some reference to job demands. The curriculum of social welfare organization majors, therefore, should and must embrace some knowledge of specific job demands which it is most likely they will be asked to meet. The problem here, is to find the most common job demands in social welfare organization, and prepare our students to meet them skillfully. However, the field of social welfare organization has so many varied sub-

[27] Just as with caseworkers and group workers there is a tendency to separation from social welfare organization agencies, staff and program, so there is also with social welfare organization workers in relationship to other agencies. Some of this tendency can be attributed to the fact that in the hierarchy of the social work profession, the social welfare organization worker is the best paid, consorts with "power" figures in the community, and occupies positions which carry a measure of control and authority regarding the distribution of health and welfare services and funds in the community. Hence, the reasoning that in the training of social welfare organization workers there should be a conscious effort to develop an attitude of respect for other type agencies and staffs, based on an understanding of the unity of the social work practice.

settings that the acquisition of knowledge, understanding and skill distinctive to every sub-setting, is an unrealistic goal. But we can single out in the curriculum those sub-settings which are most prevalent, which practitioners at this stage of the game are most likely to work in, and of which we have the most understanding of the specific job demands. And we can teach it, along with the "universals," with the perspective that the intelligent, trained social welfare organization student will find speedy ways of acquiring distinctive knowledge, understanding and skills of other sub-settings.

It is our view that the most prevalent kind of social welfare organization agencies and programs are those which are specified on pages 223 and 226 of this paper. It is these agencies and programs which social welfare organization students are most likely to be employed in and of which we have the most understanding of the specific job demands. Hence, we include in the basic course in social welfare organization, reference to the operating practices, structure and functions of these agencies and their programs. For social welfare organization majors more detailed knowledge and understanding is necessary.

The Case for a Curriculum in Community Organization for Social Welfare

EVERETT C. SHIMP

INTRODUCTION

The development of any specialized curriculum in a university is predicated on several factors, such as: (1) the need for such specialized education, (2) the existence of a body of knowledge applicable to the specialization, (3) opportunities for professional practice in identifiable settings, and (4) adequate numbers of people desirous of availing themselves of such professional preparation.

Each of these factors needs to be examined before discussing the nature, objectives, method and content of a curriculum designed to provide professional preparation for community organization practice in social welfare.

THE NEED FOR SPECIALIZED EDUCATION

The increasing complexity of society, the interdependence of people, the conflicting forces evident in every community, however defined, and the desire of significant numbers of individuals to improve community life demand a quality of leadership not currently available in many locations. Certain personal qualities appear essential for community leadership roles but these personal qualities alone are no longer sufficient for the task. The ability to use one's self knowingly in a situation, to assist others to work together more effectively, to diagnose a community situation through knowledge of appropriate factual data and stimulate both professional and lay citizens of a community to reach a satisfactory

solution, indicates a need for specialized education, even specialized within the field of social work itself.

THE EXISTENCE OF A BODY OF KNOWLEDGE APPLICABLE TO THE SPECIALIZATION

Twenty-five years ago few books or articles were written which delineated, in any concrete fashion, a philosophy, a set of principles, objectives, or even agreed upon methods by which practitioners, working on a community-wide basis, might effect solutions to social welfare problems. The trial and error process was very much in evidence. The development of a body of knowledge in community organization for social welfare has progressed but in no sense can it be thought adequate for thoroughly satisfying professional preparation or practice.

Much of the literature, with some excellent exceptions, deals with methods and procedures rather than with significant philosophy or conceptual theory. There is a place for both types of literature, but at this stage of development we need more critical examination and research relating to our philosophy and objectives. The field of practice has not contributed a great deal to fundamental knowledge and to basic literature. Much of what can be said to be known and thus available for more formal educational purposes has been slow to emerge. Within the field of practice and in academic settings there is a tendency to overemphasize social welfare organization or structure. Efforts of people in areas of practice, where substantial numbers of people find employment, have been directed toward the solution of immediate problems rather than toward a broad concept of community organization as an ongoing process. Both efforts are necessary. The latter needs emphasis. The literature currently available is exceedingly helpful, though inadequate in quantity and quality for some needs in an academic setting.

OPPORTUNITIES FOR PROFESSIONAL PRACTICE IN IDENTIFIABLE SETTINGS

A discussion of this factor necessitates a clarification of definition of community organization for social welfare. There are those who

see it as heavily weighted on the side of structure versus those who see it as a process employing the skills of other areas of social work proper.

We see community organization for social welfare as a process rather than a type of agency or a program. As a process—an orderly way of working—it is utilized, in varying degrees, in every type of social agency. With certain types of agencies it becomes their primary responsibility. The principal objective of the community organization process in the field of social welfare is to help people to find ways to use their interest and talents to improve the quality of living of all people within the area of influence of con- sciously directed effort. It seeks to help people work cooperatively toward solutions of community problems and to develop and coordinate appropriate resources which may be brought to bear upon the problems.

Just as social work borrows from other disciplines for much knowledge, and perhaps has its own uniqueness in the way in which such knowledge is put together and used, so is community organization within social work a special way of working with the community as client, different from working with the group or the individual with need. We shall, therefore, also define community organization for social welfare as a process which demands a philosophy, a set of principles, with definable objectives and goals. Its practice, therefore, is both idealistic and practical. It operates in a philosophical framework as well as within an organizational structure. Organizational structures may be quite different but yet not affect the philosophical framework.

In the United States, professional practice in community organ- ization is most readily found: (1) in agencies concerned with federated financing and community-wide social welfare planning; (2) in agencies functioning on a state-wide basis, such as state planning councils, departments of health or welfare, and individ- ual special purpose agencies which employ staff to work with local communities; (3) on a broadly defined base, in agencies func- tioning on a national basis who have relations with one another, with state and local branches or affiliated units; and (4) in a wide

variety of settings, such as the United Nations in its various programs, the United States State Department, international agencies and community development projects in foreign areas, either sponsored by individual foreign countries or in cooperation with an appropriate agency of the United States.

The level of skill, experience and maturity required differs in each of the settings indicated above. The Personnel Department of United Community Funds and Councils of America, Inc. indicates a need for at least thirty young people each year who have been trained in community organization for social welfare. Such people are immediately placeable in assistant level positions in federated financing agencies and social planning councils, where appropriate supervision is available for continued growth and development of the individual. With the increased development in these areas of service, it is reasonable to assume that larger numbers of people must be trained in community organization and not recruited directly from other areas of social work practice without a more extended professional preparation in community organization.

As the degree of responsibility for self-direction and decision increases, in settings for community organization practice, recruitment from within the body of those trained and experienced in community organization must take place. The opportunities for newly trained people and those with experience in practice are constantly far in excess of the number of persons available and properly prepared for such responsibilities.

PEOPLE DESIROUS OF AVAILING THEMSELVES OF PROFESSIONAL PREPARATION

There are able young people directly out of undergraduate colleges and those with non-professional agency experience who seek professional education. A substantial number of potentially good student prospects are unable to enroll in schools of social work, which offer specialized training in community organization, because of their inability to finance a two-year graduate education program. Agencies employing personnel with specialized training in community organization have, in general, lagged far behind

other areas of specialization in providing scholarship assistance. This need is emphasized because many of these applicants for admission to schools of social work have more maturity, which is desirable, and frequently more family responsibilities. There is now a sufficient number of persons seeking professional education in community organization to warrant the conclusion that there is a need for such a specialized curriculum.

PRESENT STATUS OF CURRICULA IN COMMUNITY ORGANIZATION

The origin of graduate training in community organization, to the best of our knowledge, dates back to the Summer of 1921 when special courses were offered for credit in the School of Social Administration of The Ohio State University. A formal program of study leading to a degree for graduate students in the School was inaugurated in 1929. The first Master of Arts in Social Administration (now Master of Social Work) degree for community organization majors was granted in 1931.

Some other schools of social work have developed a curriculum in community organization in subsequent years. A number of schools are giving study to this need at the present time. There is considerable variation in the thinking concerning objectives and content of such a curriculum. There are undoubtedly some common concerns facing the administrators and faculty of schools desiring to offer a sound professional training program in community organization for social welfare. An objective study of the problem is indicated.

There is evidence that schools of social work have moved from the concept of training people for positions in special agencies to a broader preparation for practice in community organization. The soundness of this position would not appear to be debatable in an academic institution. Hence, the curriculum for a community organization student would include a base which is generic to all social work specializations, plus advanced knowledge and

content designed to develop skill in the community organization process.

Workshops at annual meetings of the Council on Social Work Education and its predecessor organization, efforts of the Association for the Study of Community Organization (now a part of the National Association of Social Workers), and other groups, have given considerable thought to the bases of advanced education for community organization practice. There is still a lack of agreement on philosophy, objectives, and content of courses offered and the nature of the field instruction program.

A CURRICULUM IN COMMUNITY ORGANIZATION

There is little disagreement over the advisability of including an introductory course in community organization in the basic curriculum for all social work students. The content of this course, however, differs somewhat in various schools. Our concept of this course is that it should provide all social work students with an understanding of the objectives, philosophy, principles and structure of primary agencies in which community organization is practiced. It should enable all social workers to work through appropriate channels and use proper methods in helping to effect solutions to community-wide problems.

The curriculum for community organization majors will be discussed in the light of one school's extensive experience with such a curriculum, its relation to basic educational concepts and the needs of the field of practice. It is our thesis that these elements are compatible and must be in any sound social work curriculum. It is our judgment that the two-year curriculum must encompass the following:

(1) philosophy of social work;
(2) both broad and specific knowledge of the social services;
(3) dynamics of human behavior—individual, group and community;
(4) methods and skills;

(5) administration;

(6) research.

These are normally organized into specific courses and agency instruction with a proper integration of the two. It does not seem necessary to list any series of courses for a community organization curriculum. They will be integrated into the total curricula in different ways in different schools. We do wish to comment upon three areas of concern which appear to have special significance in preparing people for community organization practice. They are unlike the areas of concern in social casework and social group work by virtue of the differences in the clientele of each of the three processes. These areas of concern are:

(1) philosophy and attitudes;

(2) methods and skills;

(3) knowledge and understanding.

The discussion here presupposes an acceptance of the basic concepts of relationship, the dynamics of individual, group and community behavior, a knowledge of social welfare organization structure, and the development of one's self in relation to his professional responsibilities. The community organization specialist must have knowledge of the scientific method, the purpose and use of research data and a keen awareness of the administrative process, workable structure, and the operation of administrative skills to accomplish service objectives. These concepts and elements we see as a part of every social worker's educational program and, therefore, an integral part of the generic curriculum. However, we are convinced that special effort must be devoted to developing skills in research, administration and knowledge of community relationship on a more extensive and intensive basis than for people preparing for practice in other areas of social work. (More attention will be given to these special needs at a later point in the analysis and discussion.)

The *philosophy and attitudes* of a community organization specialist encompass the same basic beliefs held in other areas of social work, with emphasis in some special areas. These beliefs are:

(1) the worth and dignity of the individual and faith in democratic processes;

(2) the desirability of improving relationships among individuals, groups, organizations of people, neighborhoods and communities;

(3) the right of individuals, groups and communities to differ but still retain a responsibility for the well being of others;

(4) the ability of individuals, groups and communities to change;

(5) the process of interaction as an instrument to effect change;

(6) the right of self-determination;

(7) that the end result cannot be divorced from the means;

(8) that in a democracy, participation of people from all walks of life is essential in reaching appropriate decisions;

(9) that a worker's self-awareness is an integral part of his performance and accomplishment;

(10) that an orderly process is essential and compatible with desirable change in value systems and social institutions.

These beliefs taken as a whole, we are convinced, extend beyond those held or practiced currently by many professional caseworkers and group workers but still embrace the basic beliefs of the two groups. We recognize the role of casework and group work, but believe it demands a larger perspective on the part of the community organization specialist. The community, while made up of individuals and groups, is something different from the individuals and the various groups when they are viewed as parts of the community, which is the client of the community organization specialist.

If community organization is a process, and we contend that it is, then skill in numerous areas is imperative for successful practice and accomplishment. Community organization is not a field of social work practice. The fields may, for example, be cooperative planning for social welfare or federated fund-raising or other such activities. Neither is community organization a structure or a state of development of a specialized service at any given time.

As a process, it is a way of working on an orderly, conscious basis to effect defined and desired objectives and goals. As such, the

process, therefore, needs direction of skilled professional people to assist citizens of the community to:

(1) identify, diagnose and define community problems or needs;

(2) ascertain appropriate factual data regarding the problem or need;

(3) analyze the data, determine their significance;

(4) consider possible solutions and decide upon the most appropriate or acceptable course of action; and

(5) set in motion actions determined by the community to be most likely to achieve the goal sought.

Certain *identifiable skills* must be a part of the equipment of the community organization specialist. Specific knowledge and understanding are necessary for practice of the community organization process. The principal areas are:

(1) relationships;

(2) participation and representation;

(3) leadership and its development;

(4) authority and how it is derived in a democratic process;

(5) use of one's self as an enabling or helping person;

(6) the fusing of the above into an acceptable way of working in moving from problem to solution.

The community organization specialist must have knowledge of and facility in the use of administration, committees, conferences, interviewing, recording, community relationships, research methods, consultation, financing, budgeting, promotion and educational methods. He must likewise know how to develop adequate and efficient financing of community services.

We have indicated that there is an increasing *body of knowledge* available to teacher, student and practitioner of community organization. While the body of knowledge is far from adequate today, it is ample for a sound curriculum. Research in community organization must take on new methods and new approaches guided by intellectually vigorous and disciplined teachers and practitioners. The recording of community organization practice must be stimulated. Objectivity of analysis and evaluation must be extended. Research specialists outside the field of social work are

available and need to be used to a much greater extent. The community organization process is in need of more facts. Factual data are essential in promoting any worthwhile idea or endeavor. A way must be found to extend knowledge and validate the many methods used in community organization practice.

Numerous books, monographs, special studies and other materials are available. As yet, all too few good community organization teaching records are available. Episode and situation reports objectively reported by skilled practitioners could add much to teaching materials currently. These must be used while more basic and fundamental knowledge is developed through carefully planned research and made available.

Another, but most important part of the curriculum for a student in community organization, is the agency instruction program. It must be an integrated part of the total learning process. It is our conviction that a social worker must be knowledgeable in the casework, group work and community organization processes. It is too much to expect equal skills in all three areas. However, it is essential that a student develop awareness of self and the appropriate use of one's self in a professional situation and learn the effect one has upon others in a first-year concurrent agency placement in either a social casework or social group work setting. Prior experience in a social agency does not appear to be an adequate substitute for the learning which takes place when academic instruction and field instruction are carried on simultaneously.

The second-year agency placement in our judgment must be in a community organization agency, and preferably on a full-time or block basis. A wide range of experience for the student is essential to the proper grasp of the complexity and interrelated nature of many activities, skills and methods employed in community organization. Opportunity must be given for observation, participation and limited staff responsibility in the day to day program and services. This, again, can best be understood and learned over a period of time and through seeing the total agency program in operation.

The agency selected for the community organization placement

ideally will be in a medium-sized community. Such a community offers training experience which has variety but is still not too large or too complex to prevent the student from gaining some perspective of the total job to be done.

SUBJECT MATTER AND CONTENT OF ADVANCED COURSES FOR COMMUNITY ORGANIZATION MAJORS PREPARING FOR POSITIONS IN COMMUNITY ORGANIZATION AGENCIES

Advanced courses for community organization majors are of two types. The first deals with a deepening and refining of concepts and methods employed by the practitioner in the day to day job and general content courses in administration, research, public relations, and financing of welfare services.

The introductory course, as we have indicated previously, must provide all social work students with understanding of the objectives, philosophy, principles and structure of agencies in which community organization is the primary function. It is necessary for the major student to achieve a deepened level of understanding and an extension of knowledge of the same content. The method of teaching may be different and the use of more involved problem situations and case episodes are expected. A knowledge of structure of community organization agencies is essential to orderly functioning of staff and laymen. Structure is important only insofar as it provides effective channels for accomplishing objectives. A knowledge of structure and how it is used in a community organization agency is just one aspect of this area of understanding. Knowledge of the fields of service, of public and voluntary agencies, of community welfare agencies, of different geographical settings of these agencies, and of the purposes and functions of each is essential in relating activity of individuals, groups and agencies to the cooperative solution of community problems. The community organization specialist must develop ability to work within existing community structure and realize that its change is a slow process. He must recognize that people are more important than institutions or organizations and that, when a choice must be made, the needs of people have priority.

While all social workers are committed to the preservation and extension of the rights of individuals and groups, the community organization specialist must extend the same philosophy and skill to his client—the community. He must recognize and accept the right of people to differ. He has, however, a very special responsibility to see that any identified need or problem is clearly understood in its proper relationship to a host of other problems and concerns a community has for its people. The development of this understanding may require simple fact finding or intensive research, the results being presented in such a way as to make their implications in the solution of a problem clear to all concerned. We, therefore, believe that the advanced courses for community organization majors must contain more content in, and develop greater skill in, the use of research and satistics. This must also include skill in interpreting the findings so as to be most useful.

It is recognized that the committee is one of the most important tools in the process of finding solutions to problems in a community. The committee in community organization is different from the committee, for example, in social group work. The committee in community organization has for its objective not so much the development of the participants as the contribution each member can make to the solution of the problem confronting the committee. This does not imply that committee members may not grow in their knowledge of problems, relationships and how to move from one step to another in solving problems on a democratic basis. Indeed, such growth is a part of the community organization specialist's function in assisting citizens to assume larger responsibilities in their communities. What we must emphasize is that the objective in community organization is to move from problem to solution for the benefit of the community as a whole. It is, therefore, imperative that the community organization major develop real skill in how to select, organize and assist committees to function with fact, objectivity, knowledge of desirable goals and reasonable speed in their operations. This skill comes from both course and field experience. The role of the community organization specialist in relation to other professional social work-

ers, to the intelligent, informed and concerned laymen, is an area in which the curriculum can give some insight, give direction through sound philosophical concepts, but this role must mature through professional experience.

More than the usual skills in public relations, community education, the stimulation of community concern and understanding of social problems, or however it may be described, is required of the community organization specialist. All that is done, not done, said or not said, has public relations significance. The extension of public concern about problems confronting people is a major responsibility of the social worker in any area of social work practice. The community organization specialist must be able to help interpret social data, analyze problems and stimulate people to action. His knowledge of appropriate methods, media, community resources and timing is of utmost value. The community organization major must, therefore, have an opportunity to develop skill in this aspect of his future professional responsibility.

It is our contention that the fields of social planning and federated financing can no more be separated than mind and body if an integrated whole is to function. The objective of community organization in social work is to create and maintain a progressively more effective adjustment between community resources and community needs. In this effort no major community improvement is likely to be accomplished without involving a plan to modify or extend financial support to put a proposed plan or solution into operation. Likewise, the expenditure of funds, from voluntary or governmental sources, without a well conceived and executed plan of service, is unwise and wasteful of resources. There is conviction on the part of many community leaders that participation of citizens in social planning and federated fund-raising develops a community spirit of cooperation that is beneficial to the community in other than social welfare activities and programs. The process of involving citizens in community-wide endeavors to meet the financial resource needs of health and welfare services is a community organization job. The degree of understanding of the philosophy of social work's service and objectives is sometimes

obscured in the mechanical and administrative phases of a federated fund-raising effort. The executive is in a unique position to
give leadership to this annual cooperative endeavor and will, if he
has conviction about the validity of social work, extend this conviction to many people with immeasurable results in achieving
deepened concern for community social welfare. The extent to
which financial resources, both voluntary and governmental, are
provided to meet community needs is an important index of a
community's concern for its citizens. It is the pulse rate of the
community's heart. The community organization major must
therefore know, not only from where financial resources are obtained, but how to secure, maintain and extend them for expanding effort to more effectively meet human needs.

Of no less importance to the securing of funds to finance social
services is the wise allocation and expenditure of funds available
for any given period. Every decision by any agency, fund raising,
planning, executive, legislative or budgeting body is in reality a
planning decision. Wisdom in allocating funds to any function or
service is predicated on knowledge of needs, values and efficiency
of operation. The community organization major must have the
opportunity to study financing, campaigning, budgeting and public accounting of expenditures as a part of his preparation for practice.

Any program of professional education, whatever the field, falls
far short of what the perfectionist sees as desirable. Within the two-
year graduate curriculum in social work it is our conviction, from
experience in watching advanced educational work develop in
community organization for social work in schools of social work,
and observing the needs of the field of practice and the accomplish-
ments of graduates, that a reasonably adequate curriculum is an
attainable goal. Unless high quality professional leadership in
community organization is developed through schools of social
work, service to individuals and groups will expand at a slower
rate and at a quality level inconsistent with present day knowledge
and capacity. Professional leadership for practice in community
organization for social work cannot continue to be recruited from

non-professional sources without serious damage to social welfare services. Community organization for social work has an educational and experience content based on the same general beliefs, concepts and values as social casework and social group work, but in addition an extension of these concepts to the community as client. It has a body of knowledge of its own, broader objectives than other areas of social work practice and specific and necessary skills which can be learned by able students through schools of social work.

The Tasks
of the Community Organization Worker

VIOLET M. SIEDER

The Professional Method Related to the Community
Organization Process

Community organization has been rather generally accepted as one of the three basic methods of social work practice, along with casework and group work. It is also usually conceded that of the three methods, community organization has the least well-formulated concepts of process, knowledge and skills required for professional practice. Although these concepts have not been enunciated in such a way as to gain formal or general acceptance, I believe that there is a common body of knowledge and skills both in the literature and in general use by social workers which only awaits documentation and systematic testing.

Inasmuch as community organization, as social work practice, has a rich background of experience to draw upon; and since in my capacity as practitioner, consultant, and teacher, it has fallen to my lot to observe widely and analyze this experience, I herewith attempt to present a systematized statement of the tasks performed in community organization practice. This paper makes no claim to setting forth original ideas; rather it is a descriptive statement of current practice and herein lies its strength.

Because of the limitations of time, no attempt will be made here to define community, or to expound philosophy, or to trace the relationship of other social work methods to that used by the community organization practitioner. I will presume to take as

my point of departure the paper I gave at the 1956 National Conference of Social Work.[1]

The social worker engaged in the practice of community organization draws upon the basic philosophy, principles and ethics of his profession, and both uses and contributes to the methodology which forms the generic core of social work. Fundamental to all social work practice is the concept of helping or enabling the client —whether individual, group or community—to identify problems and needs, to formulate a plan for meeting these needs, to accept the plan and to implement it through appropriate action. This activity is premised on a respect for the inherent rights and responsibilities of people, in a democracy, to determine their own course of action and to share in directing their own destiny. These decisions are reached through the interaction of individuals and autonomous groups and their wisdom will depend upon knowledge, mutual understanding and respect for difference, and a statesmanlike willingness to relinquish personal or group gains on behalf of the larger community.

In community organization programs, this activity depends upon both the quality of indigenous leadership of the autonomous groups within the community and the skill of professional community organization leadership which is free to work objectively with all groups. Aside from the idealism reflected in this approach to helping people, there is abundant evidence to show that it is also realistic in terms of pragmatic tests. Change and progress is achieved and maintained best when people affected are involved in the decision-making process.

The concept of change in order to achieve growth and development is fundamental to all methods of social work practice. Community organization in social work is concerned: (1) with solving problems of or involving intergroup and interorganizational relationships which affect the welfare of the community; and (2) with providing a network of interrelated and integrated services for the

1 Violet M. Sieder, "What Is Community Organization Practice in Social Work?" in *Proceedings of the National Conference of Social Work*. New York: Columbia University Press, 1956.

prevention and treatment of social ills. The practice of community organization involves the use of methods which will effect change in the behavior of organizations and institutions of the community through which problems are created and/or services are rendered or determined. Institutions, by their very nature, have vested interests in their own programs, structures, and attitudes and change in one organization may start a chain reaction of acceptance or resistance in other interrelated bodies. It follows that bringing about an improved, new, combined, or eliminated service is often an extremely painful and difficult task. To work with organizations in the community organization process is essentially to work with people who are their leaders and representatives. These leaders in turn influence the members who ultimately control policies and program. People fundamentally resist change unless strongly motivated by an awareness of gains to themselves, the organizations with which they are identified, or the larger community within which they, their families and their organizations exist. It follows that the broad task of the community organization worker is to work with the community through its constituent parts, individually and collectively, so as to help it identify its problems, and motivate it toward change. This is done through professional knowledge, skills and the art of practice, of which timing is a major factor.

The literature of community organization for the most part, defines it as a "process" in which the community is engaged, but, unlike casework and group work, there is no accepted definition of community organization as a social work method. Since the "process" of organizational interaction resulting in modification of institutional behavior takes place as a natural dynamic reaction of community life, such definitions do not clarify the role of the professional community organization worker. This is comparable to defining the process of interpersonal interaction within the family or the group as natural phenomenon without indicating the social worker's role in the use of methods which facilitate a healthy development in these relationships.

For example, a family in difficulty can resolve its problems of

tense relationships by breaking up the home; or a group can find harmony by excluding members or gain satisfaction by engaging in antisocial behavior. By the same token, a community may attempt to resolve its problem of juvenile delinquency by establishing a playground or by passing a curfew law. When a social worker undertakes to help these clients with these same problems, the result can be expected to be a more socially desirable and effective solution. In each instance the social worker plays the role of assisting the client to understand the realities and nature of the problem, and on the basis of professional diagnosis and use of knowledge and skills, to help movement from problem situation to appropriate and desirable goals.

Recognizing then, that a "process" of community organization takes place in a community under any circumstance, let me attempt to define community organization as a method of social work practice which affects that process consciously and positively as a professional service.

DEFINITION OF COMMUNITY ORGANIZATION AS METHOD

Community organization is a method of social work practice which helps a community determine and achieve continuously more desirable program goals which meet constantly changing social welfare needs by facilitating the interaction of its constituent parts (organizations, institutions, individual leaders, and geographic subdivisions) in such a way as to make maximum use of its internal and external resources while at the same time strengthening its potential ability to undertake the solution of new and more difficult problems. Its focus is upon helping individuals and groups increase their capacity and motivation to work together to bring about progressive change and better integration in the social services of the community. This is achieved by helping the community to identify needs, rank these needs, formulate a plan to meet them, implement the plan of action, and assess this action in

terms of its adequacy and consequences. This method is based in social work philosophy, principles and ethics, and depends upon knowledge of the social structure and dynamics of a community social welfare program content, the science of human relations, and the art of professional practice. This definition is close to the point of view of Murray Ross, University of Toronto.

In using the community organization method the worker makes conscious and disciplined use of himself in interpersonal, group and intergroup relations, through the appropriate choice and use of such skills as the interview, consultation, conference, committee delegate groups, and with the support of such administrative tools as fact finding, interpretation and public relations, budgeting, financing, and administration.

To take a meaningful look at the tasks performed by the community organization worker, we must view them against a conception of the totality of the community organization process within which the tasks operate and to which they relate. This conception, by the very nature of community organization practice, must be multi-dimensional and therefore complex. First it will be outlined in steps; and then presented through a chart which concludes this article.

I. AN ASSESSMENT OF THE REALITY FACTORS IN THE COMMUNITY SITUATION

This involves two approaches: first an awareness of what elements in the situation have been identified, recognized and understood by which leaders or representatives of what organized community interests. This implies an assessment of community knowledge, degree of interest, and negative or positive attitudes for the purpose of establishing a base line of problem definition from which the community organization is prepared to move toward some solution. Evidence of community concern with problems may be ascertained through intergroup situations such as delegate assemblies, forums, or committees or through relationships to specific organizations or leaders.

The second approach is a professional assessment of the situation made in the light of the worker's knowledge about socio-economic,

cultural, organizational, political, religious and other factors affecting potential group interaction and integration; and his knowledge about social work programs and goals appropriate to the problems uncovered. The results of the community assessment and the professional assessment may be quite different. The first may control the immediate goal; the second help in developing steps to a long-range goal.

II. DIAGNOSIS OF THE COMMUNITY SITUATION

Before moving into an action program, a careful diagnosis of the reality factors must be undertaken. This involves problem-identification, interorganizational relationships analysis, and an evaluation of individual leadership potential.

In classifying problems it is important to identify them both in terms of relative urgency, and probable length of time required to achieve a solution. A tentative outline of steps from problem to goal should be developed as a test of the feasibility of solution and the measure of community readiness. This is especially important in determining the project or committee load which can be effectively handled by the community organization worker, and hence affects the intake policies of the organization for which he works.

An interorganizational relationship analysis is dependent upon: (1) ascertaining the service functions of public and voluntary welfare organizations which have a bearing upon the problem situation; (2) assessing the positive or negative interests of various citizen organizations—civic, religious, fraternal, professional, business, labor, political, and so on; (3) determining any special interests or biases within geographic subdivisions of the community; (4) understanding the function of various coordinating structures to which these organizations relate, both vertically and horizontally; and (5) evaluating these various programs and interests in relation to the community power structure.

In addition to problem-identification and organizational analysis, there is need for an evaluation of individual leadership potential. This includes: (1) identification of persons (professional and lay) with special knowledge and skills in the problem or program areas

under consideration; (2) identifying the direct and indirect leaders in the community and assessing their influence and power in relation to prestige, economic, social, political and other factors, and (3) evaluating the potential of these leaders as participants or leaders in the democratic process of community interaction.

III. FORMULATION OF THE COMMUNITY'S SOCIAL GOALS OR OBJECTIVES

There is need to develop a suitable organizational structure or structures through which representatives of community interests may work together with the help of the community organization worker. This involves a plan to provide for legislative and policy-making bodies, staff, budget and other administrative considerations. A major purpose of this structure is to facilitate intergroup communication and interaction in formulating and carrying out commonly agreed upon goals and objectives. It also provides organizational authority and controls to the role of the community organization worker.

At the stage of formulation of goals, the community organization worker (1) facilitates the bringing together of representatives of appropriate groups and individuals for study, evaluation, and formulation of a plan; (2) stimulates and helps maintain communication between organizational representatives and the groups they represent during the process of developing a plan; and (3) broadens the circle of communication for information and reaction to such developing plans, to other interested groups and individuals (a) in various related planes of activity (national, state, metropolitan area, neighborhood, international) and (b) in related functions (city planning, board of education, public officials, and so on).

In this crucial stage of community organization process, the community organization worker brings to bear on the formulation of community goals his special expertness in professional skills. A primary skill is work with committees. He assists in their formation and operation not only in terms of selection of members and such administrative procedures as: developing an appropriate charge, clarifying lines of authority; arranging for minutes and reports,

making appropriate physical arrangements for meetings; but also by facilitating the group process through the professional use of himself in his relationship to the chairman and the individual members of the committee. His role as professional secretary to a committee includes not only facilitating productive interaction during meetings through assisting the chairman in clarification of questions or issues, supplying information, relieving tension, and so on, but also through activities outside of and between meetings. These would include: gathering essential facts and helping the committee develop appropriate methods of study and research; securing consultant advice and help from appropriate resource people both within and outside of the community on substantive content areas; and helping to delineate the problem and plan for solution through sensitivity to the need for *timely interpersonal relationships* with individuals of influence because of their particular knowledge, skills, prestige or power, and their potential affect upon the development or retardation of plans. These interpersonal relationships may take the form of:

An interview—to ascertain the point of view, substantive facts, or other pertinent information necessary to committee deliberation.

Getting consultation from an expert in an area of special skill (research or public relations) or on substantive matters, or on organizational problems.

Giving consultation to a chairman, leader or participant who seeks advice or guidance on procedural matters, professional content, or relationship problems.

A conference, formal or informal, with groups in a position to give or use special help with a community organization problem, including their own interrelationships.

A negotiation to resolve a conflict between persons or groups holding opposing points of view which impede progress within the community organization process.

It should be noted that the community organization worker may use the skills of interview, consultation, conference, or negotiation alone or in combination to assess the problem before a committee is appointed. In some situations involving a limited number of

organizations, a problem may be resolved on short contact through a conference or two; or an organization may only seek and need consultation in regard to its handling of a community or agency problem. Although much of a community organization worker's time is given to work with committees, undoubtedly a greater percentage of staff time is spent in other activities.

The implementation of a plan usually involves policy decisions. The formulation of any social policy needs to be reported for purposes of reaction, modification or endorsement to the representatives of the organizations engaged in the community organization process. The delegate assembly which serves as a forum and/or action and legislative body is the usual community organization device for this intergroup activity. The community organization worker has some special tasks to carry out in this connection which include: (1) preparation of informational materials for advance deliberation by the delegates and their organizations; (2) definition of issues or questions to be discussed; (3) preparation of a report of the meeting and its actions; (4) follow-up with organization representatives on their reporting back to their groups and from these groups to the intergroup; (5) development of next steps toward a plan for implementation of the action in cooperation with responsible administrative leaders and organizational subdivisions; and (6) publicity before and after the delegate meeting. In short, the community organization worker uses his professional skills to assure open, active and meaningful channels of communication between the central planning body and its related organizations.

IV. IMPLEMENTATION OF THE PLAN TO ACHIEVE THE GOAL

Although by intent this is designated as a separate step, the implementation of the plan is in large part inherent within the process engaged in by the community representatives and the community organization worker in defining the action objective.

As has been noted, the best guarantee to securing change is to assure genuine involvement of those whom it will affect in the process of problem-identification and formulation of the plan.

There are, however, some specific tasks to be undertaken by the community organization worker to implement the goal.

A bridge between formulation of plan and implementation is the use of public relations and interpretation skills. This involves preparing reports, releases, speeches, and using appropriate media to dramatize the situation and to sell the plan. Strategic timing of special meetings, conferences, or institutes and getting a spot on the program of other organizations holding conferences or meetings is an important device.

If the program objective requires legislative action, the community organization worker has responsibility for assuring that specialized legal and other necessary expert skill is mobilized to prepare, analyze, and submit drafts of bills through appropriate channels. The art of timing combined with detailed and thoughtful advanced planning on strategy is essential to this task. A concomitant community organization function is the mobilization of community forces back of the desired action. This usually involves operating toward time limited targets and coordinating the separate activities of many groups so as to achieve the greatest impact. The choice of the specific skills used by the community organization worker will depend upon the degree of unanimity and the emergent nature of the situation.

Whether the plan to be implemented affects public or voluntary agencies, there is bound to be a problem of financing. Presentation of the facts to budget hearings and appropriating bodies requires special skill in preparation of materials and selection of spokesmen.

It is important for the community organization worker to understand the community tax structure and its relationship to federal, state and local tax supported programs. Knowledge of federated financing under sectarian and nonsectarian auspices, and the relationship of these financing structures to each other and the community planning organizations is essential. This requires establishing a good working relationship with all related appropriating bodies through their staff and lay leadership.

The establishment of a new service inevitably calls for an evaluation of its worth in relation to other existing programs. The

budgeting and financing functions call for skill in ranking services on a priority basis in relation to resources and needs. The task of the worker is to help the community develop policy and criteria which they can apply to specific programs in relation to the substantive facts and their own value judgments.

In the actual implementation of a plan, there may be need to modify it in order to gain necessary support. The community organization worker must be skillful in negotiation and compromise so as to protect essential features of the proposed program and not jeopardize long-range goals.

V. REASSESSMENT OF COMMUNITY SITUATION AND SETTING NEW GOALS

In community organization process, no achieved objective may be considered a final goal. In tackling one problem others are frequently uncovered; and new knowledge of treatment methods or changing community values call for a constant reassessment of existing services. The community organization worker must establish such devices as central reporting of services and unmet needs to assure community awareness and sensitivity to developing trends. Here he brings to bear special knowledge and skill in fact finding and statistics. He must be sensitive to the interrelatedness of services both within and outside of the welfare organizations. This he achieves through formal and informal relationships to these organizations.

At this point the process in community organization has come full circle, and the worker is back at the task of "assessing the reality factors in the situation" as a first step toward developing new goals. Actually the situation for the community organization worker is not that neat. He will be involved in a number of projects, each in different stages of development at any given time. To complicate matters still further, they will involve a number of separate fields of service and content areas. Obviously the worker needs skill in moving each of these plans toward its goal and at the same time keeping them related and integrated within the broad framework of the welfare planning organization.

PERSONAL APTITUDES

It follows that the community organization worker must bring to his task not only learned knowledge and skills, but special personal aptitudes which briefly may be characterized as: imagination and social vision; initiative and resourcefulness; an ability to work with all kinds of people without regard to economic, social, racial, religious or status factors; organizational ability including capacity to carry a variety of simultaneous assignments and meeting commitments promptly; intellectual alertness necessary to identify the core of an issue, to analyze data and facts, and to anticipate conflict situations; intellectual and professional integrity which permits compromise on substantive matters without compromising on basic principles, and an ability to maintain confidences in organizational and individual relationships; leadership qualities which are constructive in developing leadership in others as well as in exerting active influence in community deliberations; and the personality to attract the liking, respect and confidence of lay leaders and professional social workers.

SOME SPECIAL FACTORS

A unique aspect of community organization practice in social work is the role of the volunteer who is at once the client, the service volunteer, and the final administrative authority. This calls for a clear understanding of the role of the professional in relation to the volunteer, and a clear conception of the different relationships called for on the part of the social worker as he works with volunteers carrying these different roles. The use of supervisory, consultant, direct and indirect leadership techniques are involved here. A basic skill in working with laymen is an ability to interpret professional concepts in understandable, usable language and at all times to avoid professional jargon.

Another unique condition of community organization work is the possibility of building upon a continuity of relationships over a long period of years with organizations within the com-

munity. Unlike casework and group work, where there is shifting in the cases or groups served, in community organization the community as a unit remains the same focus of attention over the years. To be sure the problems and goals change, and the character and variety of organizations may change, but there remains a core of identity built upon history, tradition, and experience which may either limit or strengthen the ability of the worker to help effect necessary change. It is for this same reason that the maximum effectiveness of a community organization worker in a given community is reached only after a two- or three-year experience, the time depending upon its size and complexity. This time might be shortened if community organization workers developed adequate systems of recording which would serve to inform and initiate incoming staff.

A third factor is the multi-dimensional character of the relationship of the worker to people who participate in the community organization process. Not only must he understand and relate to them as individuals in terms of his knowledge about personality, cultural background and other factors affecting their behavior, and so on, but also in their role as representatives of groups. This latter requires knowledge about the organizational policy, program and biases as well as characteristics of the behavior of the group in its relationship to other groups; and the extent to which the organization is being fairly represented by the individual. Although the focus of the relationship is not a therapeutic one, it does frequently require handling of personality problems and helping the individual or the group to grow and develop in the process of working on community objectives. The importance of providing people with a satisfying experience as effective members of the community is more and more recognized as basic to mental health both for the individual and the community.

CONCLUSION

A review of the tasks required of the worker in the community organization process seem to indicate clearly that they call for a

high degree of professional knowledge, skill, maturity, energy, and ability. Although based in the generic concepts of social work, I believe that community organization is a separate and unique method of social work practice.

There are some who will question the validity of this statement. Their doubts may be traced in part to confusions resulting from the historical development and emphasis in recent years in which social work practice has become equated with casework in the minds of many people. More recently group work has come to achieve professional status as an accepted method of practice. Both of these methods have the advantage of engaging in face to face contacts with individuals who are identifiable as the direct beneficiaries of the service. On the other hand, there has been an unforunate tendency for some social workers to think of community organization as an action technique through which the worker does things to the community such as neating-up the community service pattern by clarifying agency functions and relationships. This is sometimes conceived as primarily an administrative operation which implies a scientific analysis of the community by the professional expert who then skillfully manipulates the situation to bring about the ends he determines as good for the community. This confusion is heightened when the practitioner is referred to as the "community organizer" instead of the "community organization worker" or "community worker."

Clearly this is not the task or method of the professional community organization practitioner. He neither sees the intergroup process as an end in itself or goals as desirable regardless of the means to the end. Rather he uses his methods to forward the process of community organization by consciously using himself to help the community determine, achieve and extend services toward those social goals which it finds desirable. Community organization as a method of social work practice is a direct and necessary service to the community.

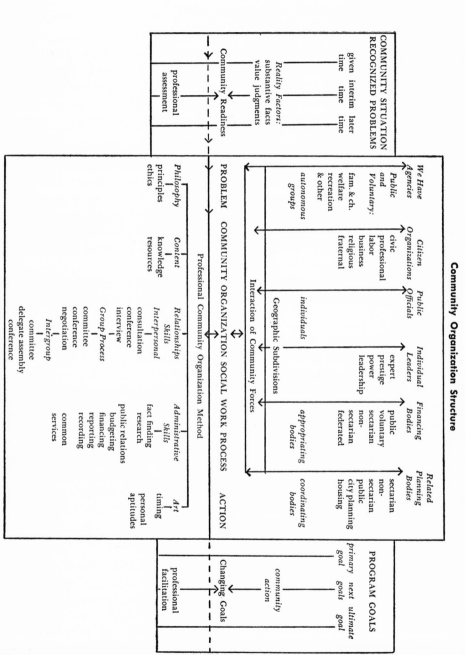

Community Organization Structure

Selected Bibliography

American Association for Adult Education. Committee on Community Organization. *Community Education in Action: A Report on Community Organization and Adult Education.* Cleveland: The Association, 1948.

American Association of Schools of Social Work. *Community Organization in Schools of Social Work.* New York: The Association, 1943.

American Public Health Association. Committee on Community Organization for Health Education. *Community Organization for Health Education.* New York: The Association, 1941.

Association for the Study of Community Organization. *Recording in Community Organization in Social Welfare Work.* (Community Organization Materials, no. 2.) New York: The Association, 1951.

Atwater, Pierce. *Problems of Administration in Social Work.* Minneapolis: University of Minnesota Press, 1940.

Barry, Mildred C. "Assessment of Progress Made by Community Organization in Identifying Basic Concepts and Methods for Utilization in Social Work Education," in *Community Organization in Social Work.* New York: Council on Social Work Education, 1956.

———. "Current Concepts in Community Organization," in *Group Work and Community Organization, 1956.* Papers presented at the 83d Annual Forum of the National Conference of Social Work. New York: Columbia University Press, 1956.

———. "Community Organization Process—an Approach to Better Understanding." *Social Work Journal,* XXI (October, 1950), 157–163.

Batten, Thomas R. *Communities and their Development: an Introductory Study with Special Reference to the Tropics.* London: Oxford University Press, 1957.

Blackwell, Gordon W. "A Theoretical Framework for Sociological Research in Community Organization." *Social Forces,* XXXIII (October, 1954), 57–64.

Bouterse, A. David. "Marshalling Public Support for Social Legislation," in *Proceedings of the National Conference of Social Work, 1948.* New York: Columbia University Press, 1949.

Blanchard, Ralph H. *The Future of Federation.* New York: Community Chests and Councils of America, 1949.

Bright, Sallie E. *Public Relations Programs—How to Plan Them.* New York: National Publicity Council for Health and Welfare, 1950.

Buell, Bradley, *et al. Community Planning for Human Services.* New York: Columbia University Press, 1952.

Carter, Genevieve W. "Practice Theory in Community Organization," *Social Work,* III (April, 1958).

Chase, Stuart, and Chase, Marian T. *Roads to Agreement; Successful Methods in the Science of Human Relations.* New York: Harper & Brothers, 1951.

Cincinnati Council of Social Agencies. *Cincinnati Report:* an Appraisal by 600 Citizens of Governmental and Voluntary Social Services in Cincinnati and Hamilton County, Ohio, 1950–1952. Cincinnati: Cincinnati Council of Social Agencies, 1952.

Colcord, Joanna C. *Your Community: Its Provision for Health, Education, Safety, and Welfare.* 3d ed. Revised by Donald S. Howard. New York: Russell Sage Foundation, 1947.

Class, Norris E. "Child Welfare Services and Community Organization," *Social Service Review,* XVI (June, 1942),247–255.

Community Chests and Councils of America. *Neighbors United for Better Communities.* New York: Community Chests and Councils of America, 1956.

———. *Toward Improved Chest Council Agency Relations.* New York: Association Press, 1951.

———. *Community Planning for Social Welfare: A Policy Statement.* New York: Community Chests and Councils of America, 1950.

Council of Jewish Federations and Welfare Funds. *Building the Successful Campaign.* New York: Council of Jewish Federations and Welfare Funds, 1948.

———. *Social Surveys:* A Guide for Use in Local Planning. New York: Council of Jewish Federations and Welfare Funds, 1949.

Council on Social Work Education. *Community Organization in Social Work: Its Practice in Old and New Settings.* New York: CSWE, 1956.

Dahl, Robert A., and Lindblom, Charles E. *Politics, Economics, and Welfare.* New York: Harper & Brothers, 1953.

Danstedt, Rudolph T. "Current Conflicts in the Approach to Community Organization." *Social Service Review,* XXIV (March, 1950) 67–73.

Dillick, Sidney. *Community Organization for Neighborhood Development—Past and Present.* New York: Woman's Press, 1953.

Dunham, Arthur. *Community Welfare Organization; Principles and Practice.* New York: Thomas Y. Crowell Co., 1958.

———. "What Is the Job of the Community Organization Worker?" in *Proceedings of the National Conference of Social Work, 1948.* New York: Columbia University Press, 1949.

———. *Pennsylvania's Ten Year Program for Child Welfare.* (Association for the Study of Community Organization. Monograph, No. 3.) New York: Association Press, 1949.

Fasteau, Irving Jack. "International Social Welfare," in *Social Work Year Book, 1957.* New York: National Association of Social Workers, 1957.

Friedlander, Walter A. *Introduction to Social Welfare.* New York: Prentice-Hall, 1955.

Goodall, Frances. *A Narrative of Process in Social Welfare Organization.* St. Louis: George Warren Brown School of Social Work, Washington University Press, 1948.

Gordon, Spencer R. *The Reorganization of the Winston County Unemployment Relief Board.* (Association for the Study of Community Organization. Monograph, no. 2.) New York: Association Press, 1949.

Green, Helen. *Social Work Practice in Community Organization.* New York: Whiteside, 1954.

Greenwood, Ernest. "Social Science and Social Work: a Theory of their Relationship." *Social Service Review,* XXIX (March, 1955), 20–33.

Gunn, Selskar M., and Platt, Philip S. *Voluntary Health Agencies: An Interpretative Study.* New York: Ronald Press, 1945. (Under the auspices of The National Health Council.)

Hawley, Amos H. *Human Ecology: A Theory of Community Structure.* New York: Ronald Press, 1950.

Hertzler, Joyce O. *Society in Action: A Study of Basic Social Processes.* New York: Dryden Press, 1954. (Available from Henry Holt & Co.)

Hiller, Robert I. *The Education and Work Experience of Community Organization Practitioners:* A Study of the Education and Work Experience of 266 members of the Association for the Study of Community Organization Engaged Primarily in the Practice of Community Organization for Social Welfare in the Year 1947. New York: Association for the Study of Community Organization, 1949.

Hillman, Arthur. *Community Organization and Planning.* New York: Macmillan Co., 1950.

Holberg, Otto, G. *Exploring the Small Community.* Lincoln, Nebraska: University of Nebraska Press, 1955.

Hollis, Ernest V., and Taylor, Alice L. *Social Work Education in the United States; the Report of a Study Made for the National Council on Social Work Education.* New York: Columbia University Press, 1951.

Howard, Donald S. "Social Work and Social Reform," in *New Directions in Social Work,* ed. Cora Kasius. New York: Harper & Brothers, 1954.

————. "New Horizons for Social Work." *Compass,* XXVIII (November, 1947), 9–13.

Hunter, Floyd, Schaffer, Ruth C., and Sheps, Cecil G. *Community Organization: Action and Inaction.* Chapel Hill: University of North Carolina Press, 1956.

Hunter, Floyd. *Community Power Structures; a Study of Decision Makers.* Chapel Hill: University of North Carolina Press, 1953.

Johns, Ray. *The Cooperative Process Among National Social Agencies.* New York: Association Press, 1946.

————. "Critical Issues of Council-Agency Relationships," in *The Social Welfare Forum, 1951 Proceedings of the National Conference of Social Work.* New York: Columbia University Press, 1951.

Johns, Ray, and DeMarche, David F. *Community Organization and Agency Responsibility.* New York: Association Press, 1951.

Johnson, Arlien. "Community Organization in Social Work," in *Social Work Year Book, 1945.* New York: Russell Sage Foundation, 1945.

————. "The Respective Roles of Governmental and Voluntary Agencies." *Social Service Review,* XXII (September, 1948), 298–311.

Jackson, Nelson C. "Community Improvement and Social Work," in *A Program for Improving Your Community. Proceedings of the Regional Institute of the National Conference of Social Work*

and the Colorado Conference of Social Welfare. Denver: Colorado Social Welfare Journal, 1954.

Kaufman, Manuel. "Relating Community Services to Community Needs." *Social Casework*, XXXII (April, 1951), 149–155.

King, Clarence. *Organizing for Community Action.* New York: Harper & Brothers, 1948.

———. *Your Committee in Community Action.* New York: Harper & Brothers, 1952.

King, Edith Shatto. *The Social Service Exchange:* A Device for Facilitating the Exchange of Confidential Information among Welfare and Health Agencies. (U. S. Bureau of Public Assistance. Bureau Circular, no. 16.) Washington: U. S. Government Printing Office, 1943.

Kraus, Hertha. "Community Planning for the Aged: Outline of a Working Hypothesis." *Journal of Gerontology,* III (April, 1948), 129–149.

Kurtz, Russell H. "The Range of Community Organization," in *Proceedings of the National Conference of Social Work, 1940.* New York: Columbia University Press, 1940.

Lane, Robert P. "The Field of Community Organization," in *Proceedings of the National Conference of Social Work, 1939.* New York: Columbia University Press, 1939.

———. "Reports of Groups Studying the Community Organization Process," in *Proceedings of the National Conference of Social Work, 1940.* New York: Columbia University Press, 1940.

Lasker, Bruno. *Democracy through Discussion.* New York: H. W. Wilson Co., 1949.

Lee, Porter R. "Social Work as Cause and Function," in *Social Work as Cause and Function and Other Papers.* New York: Columbia University Press, 1937. (Published for the New York School of Social Work.)

Lewin, Kurt. *Resolving Social Conflicts; Selected Papers on Group Dynamics, 1935–1946.* Edited by Gertrud Weiss Lewin. Harper & Brothers, 1948.

Lindeman, Eduard C. "Democracy and Social Work," in *Proceedings of the National Conference of Social Work, 1948.* New York: Columbia University Press, 1949.

———. *The Community: An Introduction to the Study of Community Leadership and Organization.* New York: Association Press, 1921.

Lippincott, Earle. *Our Home Town.* New York: Association Press, 1949.

Lippitt, Gordon L. and Schmidt, Warren H. *My Group and I.* New London, Connecticut: Educator's Washington Dispatch, 1952.

Lippitt, Ronald. *Training in Community Relations: A Research Exploration Toward New Group Skills.* New York: Harper & Brothers, 1949.

Loring, William C., Jr., Sweetser, Frank L., and Ernst, Charles F. *Community Organization for Citizen Participation in Urban Renewal.* Boston: Massachusetts Dept. of Commerce, 1957. (Prepared by Housing Association of Metropolitan Boston.)

Lurie, Harry L. "Social Action: A Motive Force in Democracy," in *Proceedings of the National Conference of Social Work, 1941.* New York: Columbia University Press, 1941.

Lurie, Walter A. "Intergroup Relations," in *Social Work Year Book, 1957.* New York: National Association of Social Workers, 1957.

Lynde, Edward D. "The Role of the Community Organization Practitioner," in *Selected Papers in Group Work and Community Organization, 1952.* Presented at the Annual Meeting of the National Conference of Social Work, 1952. Raleigh, N.C.: Health Publications Institute.

———. "Two-Pronged Approach to Community Planning," in *Selected Papers in Group Work and Community Organization, 1951.* Presented at the Annual Meeting of the National Conference of Social Work, 1951. Raleigh, N.C.: Health Publications Institute, 1951.

MacIver, Robert M. *Community: A Sociological Study,* 3rd ed. London: Macmillan Co., 1924.

MacRae, Robert H. "Community Welfare Councils," in *Social Work Year Book, 1957.* New York: National Association of Social Workers, 1957.

———. "Social Action," in *A Program for Improving Your Community. Proceedings of the Regional Institute of the National Conference of Social Work and the Colorado Conference of Social Welfare.* Denver: *Colorado Social Welfare Journal,* 1954.

Mayo, Leonard W. "Community Organization in 1946," in *Proceedings of the National Conference of Social Work, 1946.* New York: Columbia University Press, 1947.

———. "Community Planning for Health and Welfare," in *The Social*

Welfare Forum, 1952 Proceedings of the National Conference of Social Work. New York: Columbia University Press, 1952.

McLean, Francis H. *The Central Council of Social Agencies.* 2nd ed. rev. New York: American Association for Organizing Family Social Work, 1921.

McMillen, Wayne. "A Base Line for Community Welfare Agencies." *Social Service Review,* XXIV (September, 1950), 285–295.

———. "Community Organization in Social Work," in *Social Work Year Book, 1947.* New York: Russell Sage Foundation.

———. *Community Organization for Social Welfare.* Chicago: University of Chicago Press, 1945.

———. "The Content of Professional Courses in Community Organization." *Social Service Review,* IX (March, 1935), 68–82.

———. "Financing Social Work," in *Social Work Year Book, 1954.* New York: American Association of Social Workers, 1954.

McNeil, C. F. "Community Organization in Social Work," in *Social Work Year Book, 1954.* New York: American Association of Social Workers, 1954.

Murphy, Campbell G. "Community Organization for Social Welfare," in *Social Work Year Book, 1957.* New York: National Association of Social Workers, 1957.

———. *Community Organization Practice.* Boston: Houghton Mifflin Co., 1954.

National Social Welfare Assembly. *Shall We Make a Survey?* New York: NSWA, 1949.

New York (State). University. *Problems Confronting Boards of Education: A Manual for Community Participation in Educational Planning.* Albany, 1944.

Newstetter, Wilbur I. "The Social Inter-Group Process: How Does It Differ from Social Group Work Process?" in (1) *Proceedings of the National Conference of Social Work, 1947.* New York: Columbia University Press, 1948. (2) Howard, Donald S. (ed.), *Community Organization: Its Nature and Setting.* New York: American Association of Social Workers, 1947.

Norton, William J. *The Cooperative Movement in Social Work.* New York: Macmillan Co., 1927.

Ogden, Jean, and Ogden, Jess. *Small Communities in Action: Stories of Citizen Programs at Work.* New York: Harper & Brothers, 1946.

Persons, William F. *The Welfare Council of New York City.* New York: The Welfare Council of New York City, 1925.

Pettit, Walter W. *Case Studies in Community Organization.* New York: Century Co., 1928.

Platt, Clarice C. and Dunham, Arthur. *Community Organization for Child Welfare in Carver County.* (Association for the Study of Community Organization. Monograph, no. 1.) New York: Association Press, 1949.

Portner, Faye. *Training for Community Organization:* A Summary of a Study of the Curricula in Community Organization in Thirty-Four Member Schools of the American Association of Schools of Social Work for 1946–47. New York: Association for the Study of Community Organization, 1952. (Mimeo.)

Pray, Kenneth L. "When is Community Organization Social Work Practice?" in (1) *Proceedings of the National Conference of Social Work, 1947.* New York: Columbia University Press, 1948. (2) His *Social Work in a Revolutionary Age and Other Papers.* Philadelphia: University of Pennsylvania Press, 1949. (3) Howard, Donald S. (ed.), *Community Organization: Its Nature and Setting.* New York: American Association of Social Workers, 1947.

———. "Social Work and Social Action," in *Proceedings of the National Conference of Social Work, 1945.* New York: Columbia University Press, 1945.

Rogers, Maria. "Chester I. Barnard's New Conception of Social Organization." *Autonomous Groups Bulletin,* V (Spring–Summer, 1950), 4–29.

Ross, Murray G. *Case Histories in Community Organization.* New York: Harper & Brothers, 1958.

———. *Community Organization: Theory and Principles.* New York: Harper & Brothers, 1955.

———. "Conceptual Problems in Community Organization." *Social Service Review,* XXX (June, 1956), 174–181.

Sanderson, Ezra D., and Polson, Robert A. *Rural Community Organization.* New York: John Wiley & Sons, 1939.

Seifert, Harvey. *The Church in Community Action.* New York: Abingdon Press, 1952.

Sieder, Violet M. "The Community Welfare Council and Social Action," in *Social Work in the Current Scene, 1950 Proceedings of*

the National Conference of Social Work. New York: Columbia University Press, 1950.

Sieder, Violet M. "The Relation of Agency and Community Welfare Council Structure to Community Organization," Howard, Donald S. (ed.) in *Community Organization: Its Nature and Setting.* New York: American Association of Social Workers, 1947.

———. "Solving Health and Welfare Problems Through Neighborhood Participation," in *The Social Welfare Forum, 1951 Proceedings of the National Conference of Social Work.* New York: Columbia University Press, 1951.

———. "What Is Community Organization in Social Work?" in *Community Organization in Social Work.* New York: Council on Social Work Education, 1956.

Sorenson, Roy. *The Art of Board Membership.* New York: Association Press, 1950.

Steiner, Jesse. *Community Organization: A Study of Its Theory and Current Practice.* Rev. ed. New York: Century Co., 1930.

Stone, Walter L. *Community Welfare Planning and Organization.* Hanover, Indiana: Informal Education Services, 1949.

Stroup, Herbert H. *Community Welfare Organization.* New York: Harper & Brothers, 1952.

Tead, Ordway. *Art of Leadership.* New York: McGraw-Hill Book Co., 1935.

Thompson, Guy. "Community Chests and United Funds," in *Social Work Year Book, 1957.* New York: National Association of Social Workers, 1957.

Trecker, Harleigh B. *Group Process in Administration,* 2d ed. New York: Woman's Press, 1950.

United Nations. Economic and Social Council, Social Commission. *Principles of Community Development: Social Progress through Local Action.* Report by the Secretary-General. New York: United Nations, 1955.

———. *Report on Concepts and Principles of Community Development and Recommendations on Further Practical Measures to Be Taken by International Organization* Report by the Secretary-General. New York: United Nations, 1957.

U. S. Children's Bureau. *Controlling Juvenile Delinquency: A Community Program.* (Children's Bureau Publication, 301) Washington: U. S. Government Printing Office, 1943.

U. S. Children's Bureau. *State and Community Planning for Children and Youth*. (Children's Bureau Publication, 312) Washington: U.S. Government Printing Office, 1945.

U. S. Interdepartmental Committee on International Social Welfare Policy. *An Approach to Community Development*. Washington: U. S. Social Security Administration, International Service, 1952. (Mimeo.)

———. *Teamwork in Community Services, 1941–1946*. Washington, 1946. Found in NYSSW collection.

U. S. Women's Bureau. *The Outlook for Women in Community Organization in Social Work*. (Bulletin no. 235–5, Social Work Series) Washington: U.S. Government Printing Office, 1951. Prepared and written by Grace E. Ostrander.

Van Valen, Donald. "Community Organization: Manipulation or Group Process?" in *Social Work in the Current Scene, 1949 Proceedings of the National Conference of Social Work*. New York: Columbia University Press, 1949.

Warren, Roland L. *Studying Your Community*. New York: Russell Sage Foundation, 1955.

Wilensky, Harold L., and Lebeaux, Charles N. *Industrial Society and Social Welfare: the Impact of Industrialization on the Supply and Organization of Social Welfare Services in the United States*. New York: Russell Sage Foundation, 1958.

Witte, Ernest F. "Community Development in India, Iran, Egypt, and the Gold Coast," in *Community Organization in Social Work*. New York: Council on Social Work Education, 1956.

Wolff, Max. "Community Organization: Education for Democracy." *Journal of Educational Sociology*, XXIII (November, 1949), 141–149.

Youngdahl, Benjamin E. "The Role of Social Agencies in Social Action." *Social Work Journal*, XXXI (July, 1952), 146–151.